Demographic Change and the Family in Japan's Aging Society

SUNY series in Japan in Transition
Jerry Eades and Takeo Funabiki, Editors
and
SUNY series in Aging and Culture
John W. Traphagan, Editor

Demographic Change and the Family in Japan's Aging Society

EDITED BY

John W. Traphagan
and
John Knight

State University of New York Press

Published by
State University of New York Press, Albany

© 2003 State University of New York

For information, address State University of New York Press,
90 State Street, Suite 700, Albany, NY 12207

Cover photo courtesy of John Traphagan

Production by Diane Ganeles
Marketing by Jennifer Giovani

Library of Congress Cataloging-in-Publication Data

Demographic change and the family in Japan's aging society / edited by John
Traphagan and John Knight.
        p. cm. — (SUNY series in Japan in transition) (SUNY series in aging and
    culture)
    Inlcudes index.
    ISBN 0-7914-5649-8 (alk. paper) — ISBN 0-7914-5650-1 (pbk. : alk. paper).
        1. Japan—Population. 2. Family policy—Japan. 3. Aging—Japan. I. Traphagan,
    John W.
    II. Knight, John, 1960– III. Series. IV. Series: SUNY series in aging and culture

    HB3651 .D438 2003
    304.6'0952—dc21   2002066784

10 9 8 7 6 5 4 3 2 1

Contents

Acknowledgments

This volume developed out of two panels organized by the editors. The first panel, organized by John Knight and John Traphagan, examined "Demographic Change and the Family in Contemporary Japan" at the annual meeting of the American Anthropological Association in Philadelphia in 1998. The second, organized by Traphagan, was entitled "Health and Living Arrangements among Older Japanese: Integrating Demographic and Anthropological Approaches to the Study of Aging in Japan" and took place at the annual meeting of the Association for Asian Studies in Boston in 1999. We are grateful to both associations for providing excellent opportunities for exploring the ideas presented here. We also wish to thank the four anonymous readers at SUNY Press for their helpful comments on the initial draft of the volume. Many of the chapters, and the volume as a whole, have benefited from their insights. James Raymo raised several important points in the process of preparing the introduction and the interludes between chapters, and we are grateful for his comments. In addition, we also appreciate the work of Lori Jennex and Jennifer McDowell, who provided formatting and other administrative assistance in the production of the manuscript, Blaine Connor, who provided editorial assistance, Michelle Acuña, who helped with the index, and Tomoko Watanabe Traphagan, who assisted with proofreading Japanese terms.

Introduction

1

The Study of the Family in Japan: Integrating Anthropological and Demographic Approaches

John Knight and John W. Traphagan

Anthropology and Demography

As Kertzer and Fricke note in their introduction to *Anthropological Demography: Toward a New Synthesis*, the relationship between sociocultural anthropology and demography has been less than harmonious—spanning a spectrum ranging from ambivalence to mutual distaste and distrust (Kertzer and Fricke 1997, 1). The emphasis in anthropology on small samples, long-term fieldwork, and qualitative analysis of ethnographic data often seems at odds with the aggregate data and quantitative approach commonly used by demographers. However, the two disciplines are, in many ways, two sides of the same coin. Demographers and anthropologists are concerned with similar themes and research problems, although their approaches may differ considerably. The institution of the family is a prime illustration of this. For both demographers and anthropologists, family organization and behavior has been a central research topic that has shaped the historical development of the disciplines.

In this book, we are interested in examining the relationship between the Japanese family and one of the most problematic demographic trends in contemporary Japanese society—population aging. Bringing together anthropologists and demographers working on Japan, we present the respective contributions of the two disciplines to the analysis of the Japanese family, with an emphasis on issues relating to aged individuals. The chapters in this book illustrate the potential for synthesizing the approaches of the two disciplines, at the same time raising questions related to the limits of such a synthesis. Different disciplines begin and develop research methods and ideas from different sets of assumptions about the aims of research and the nature of empirical data, and this is obvious from the chapters of this book. In general, demography is more comfortable with the assumptions of the positivistic tradition than is contemporary anthropology. Anthropologists have called into question the idea of the detached observer distanced from those being studied, and have reflected at length on the relationship between knowledge and power in their discipline, especially in relation to the control over data and its interpretation. No such debate over the role and power of the researcher has arisen in demography (Rosenau 1992, 27). Nonetheless, both demography and anthropology are empirical traditions, grounded in the assumption that detailed data collection (even if the natures of the data are different) is the basis of intelligent and accurate interpretation.

It is important to recognize that the two fields have, on occasion, overlapped. Local level community studies, in the form of extensive fieldwork, have been introduced into demography in recent years. Some demographers have employed long-term fieldwork in an attempt to move demography away from an exclusive focus on the "measurable [quantitative] features of individuals (age at marriage, desired family size, etc.)", instead focusing on the relationships that link people together and affect the demographic features of the groups to which they belong (Jeffery and Jeffery 1997, 35). This trend has been viewed as part of "a new era in demographic research" that "will allow demographers to incorporate cultural meanings into their explanations of demographic processes" (Fricke 1997b, 825). There is a growing recognition among demographers of the need for a greater sensitivity to cultural variation in order to interpret the meanings of demographic data. Micro-approaches to collecting and analyzing demographic data in locales such as India, have brought anthropological or anthropologically informed research into the realm of demography (Caldwell, Hill, and Hull 1988; Caldwell, Reddy, and Caldwell 1988). However, as Fricke notes, even amidst considerable "methodological and conceptual borrowing" from anthropology, the conceptualization of culture in demography has largely ignored the importance of micro-variation in relation to cultural meanings (Fricke 1997a, 251). Demography has tended to make use of ideas of culture from an earlier era that essentialize others by placing them into broad categories, and neglected more recent theories of culture that emphasize human agency—that is, the improvisation, contestation, and negotiation through which culture is generated and constantly changing.

Conversely, anthropologists have been considerably less interested in the ways in which demographic data and methods can inform their own analyses. "Hard," quantitative demographic data have tended to be at odds with the so-called interpretive turn in cultural anthropology of the 1960s and 1970s—spearheaded by Clifford Geertz—according to which the discipline switched its focus from social structure and behavior to meanings and symbols. The statistical exploration and manipulation of quantitative data that characterizes much of demography has at times been viewed with suspicion due to its inability to answer questions about why particular social trends exist and occur. Yet, prior to the rise of interpretive or symbolic anthropology, demographic data were routinely used in anthropology. Anthropologists have had a longstanding interest in population, in relation to variables such as household size, village population, and population movement. From a methodological perspective, anthropologists have historically employed census taking as an initial means of data collection within the communities they study, and the study of population was important in the ethnographic research associated with the cultural ecology that was in vogue during the 1960s and 1970s—Rappaport's (1968) classic ethnography of the balance maintained among "people, pigs, and natural resources" through a Melanesian ritual is but one example (Kertzer and Fricke 1997, 9). From the perspective of cultural ecology, culturally ordered population limitation or regulation represents a key aspect of human adaptation to a given natural environment. These studies did not involve a direct borrowing from the works of demographers, but instead incorporated population as an aspect of the ethnographic study. Although an interest in population has been part of anthropology throughout much of its history, unlike demographers, anthropologists have generally not shown much interest in borrowing methods and concepts from the other side.

This is in part related to perceptions of need. Much of the borrowing of anthropological methods and ideas in demography stems from concerns among demographers about the inadequacies of purely quantitative research and the imperative of incorporating qualitative research in order to explain and interpret the results of quantitative data analysis. Some demographers view qualitative techniques, such as focus group interviews, as a solution to this problem, although this sort of approach is often far removed from the detailed qualitative data collection characteristic of ethnographic fieldwork (Fricke 1997a, 251). Although anthropologists have not been without their own paradigm crises, the rise of postmodern critiques of anthropology has not suggested a need to adopt quantitative techniques from other social sciences that purport to provide objective data. Instead, the crisis in anthropology (if it, indeed, can be viewed as a "crisis") is largely centered around a challenge to Enlightenment notions of reason and objectivity, a theoretical trend that is inherently at odds with the kind of social science that characterizes much of demography (Harris 1999; Marcus and Fischer 1986). The contributors to this book share the view that qualitative/quantitative or micro/macro approaches to data collection and analysis can be complementary rather than necessarily at odds, and used to mutually inform interpretation and explanation.

Demography in the Japanese Context

Anthropologists have been particularly critical of demography on account of the "lingering influence [on it] of the Eurocentric theory of modernization" (Greenhalgh 1995, 8). Modernization assumptions are especially evident in demographic transition theory, according to which societies are held to move from "traditional" states of high fertility and high mortality to "modern" states of low fertility and low mortality. Anthropology offers an alternative approach to making sense of demographic behavior: by placing such behavior in its social, cultural and political contexts, the full range of its variation is revealed. An obvious parallel to such a demographic anthropology would be the sub-field of economic anthropology in which economic behavior, by being viewed in its social and cultural context, is shown to be more diverse than the tradition of neoclassical economic theory based on the idea of *Homo Economicus* allowed. A demographic anthropology would similarly aim to explore the cultural denominations of demographic behavior, and consider how these denominations vary and overlap.

Much of the study of modern Japan has taken place in the shadow of modernization theory—what is known as the "convergence thesis" or Westernization, according to which Japanese society is seen to be socially, economically, and culturally "converging" with Western societies, while losing much that is perceived as traditionally Japanese. It has been against this background that the anthropology of Japan has tended to emphasize Japanese difference—Japan is modern but retains distinctive characteristics. However, this emphasis has laid Japan specialists open to the charge of exceptionalism—of exaggerating the distinctive or unique character of Japanese culture and society. In this connection, demographic theory offers a challenge to the anthropology of Japan. In a remarkably short period of time Japan has undergone (to use the language of transition theory) a demographic transition from high fertility and high mortality to low fertility and low mortality. In this respect, Japan would appear to show a demographic "convergence" with other urban-industrial societies, as well as indicating the direction in which developing societies (including those in southeast Asia, such as Thailand) are moving (Knodel, Chamratrithirong, Debavalya 1987). One of the tasks of this book is to show that this degree of formal demographic "convergence" does not necessarily result in a corresponding social and cultural convergence. These new conditions of low fertility or of extended elderly lifespans can have varied and unpredictable effects on the Japanese family and on society more generally.

In order to set the stage for the chapters that follow, in the remainder of this introduction we will focus in turn on three overlapping areas that bring together demography and anthropology in the Japanese context: the Japanese family, population trends (national and regional), and aging. These areas are important not only from the scholarly (or "etic") perspective of Japan studies, but also as aspects of culture and society that have been problematized by the Japanese government and the mass media. As will become evident throughout this book, family, population, and aging each form part of a public discourse that presents demographic behavior and trends as a central concern and a source of social problems within Japanese society.

The Family in Japan

The family system has been one of the key areas of debate in the sociology and anthropology of Japan. One question concerns the extent to which the *ie* or stem family has survived in post-war Japan, despite its legal disestablishment in the Occupation period and the impact on it of the forces of urbanization and modernization (e.g., Kawabe and Shimizu 1994). Although this debate remains open, there are reasons to believe that, at the beginning of the twenty-first century, the stem family remains relevant to Japanese self-understandings (Traphagan 2000). Intergenerational ties in Japan remain strong, and compared to other industrial societies, a large percentage of elderly people reside with or near their

children. As recently as 1995, around half of Japan's elderly population were coresiding with their children (see chapter 2). In this
key respect, Japanese modernity appears different from modernity
elsewhere, and raises important questions, such as the degree to
which the extended family persists in post-industrial Japan (Kurosu
1994, 180) and the implications that this might have for elderly
welfare provision in what is an increasingly aged society.

The stem family also appears to be undergoing change in
contemporary Japan. A critical aspect of the stem family is marriage, and, typically, in a marriage involving the male heir the
bride moves into the husband's family. The Japanese term for bride
is *yome* and is used in conjunction with the verb "enter" or "receive," indicating a view of marriage in which the bride "enters" the
family to become the "family wife" (*ie no yome*), and as such recog-
nizes the authority structure of the husband's family. Although
this notion of marriage is found, to some extent, in the marriages
of other, non-succeeding sons who form new (branch) families, it is
most pronounced with the wife of the succeeding son because succession often involves coresidence with the husband's parents and
direct submission to their authority. But, as Traphagan points out
in chapter 10, the *yome* role is being renegotiated by Japanese
women who either refuse to accept the traditional responsibilities
of the *yome* or set new conditions for fulfilling this role.

Several chapters in this book examine intergenerational
conflict, especially with regard to elderly welfare. One response to
this problem of friction between the generations is, of course, for
the younger couple to opt for a wholly separate residence upon
marriage and live physically apart from the parental couple. There
has been a major trend towards such separate residence in recent
decades, to the point where many Japanese brides insist on it as
a condition of marriage. But in recent years there has emerged
another alternative to old-style joint residence. Enterprising housing companies have established what is known as *nisetai jūtaku* or
"three generation housing" (literally, "two-household housing")—
specially designed housing units that permit joint residence with a
degree of separation of actual living quarters, allowing families to
live under one roof but retaining a high degree of domestic independence. In chapter 3, Naomi Brown examines this new form of
housing by describing the initial idea of the housing companies
and the reality of the new housing arrangements in terms of
intergenerational relations. She presents case studies that show
how, in practice, daily life in the new housing units can fall far
short of the ideal of intergenerational harmony promised by the

housing companies. The phenomenon of "two-household housing" is a striking expression of the continued relevance of the stem family in contemporary Japan.

Another indication of the resilience of the stem family in Japan is the persistence of the practice of adopting adults to ensure patrilineal succession and the continuation of the family line. In this form of marriage arrangement the husband, known as the *mukoyōshi*, marries into the wife's natal family and takes on her family name. The practice of husband adoption tends to be seen as a vestige of premodern times which is disappearing in the present day. But, as Keith Brown has noted, *mukoyōshi* marriages have actually increased among rural populations in recent years (Brown 1998). The percentages of husband adoption in the northern city of Mizusawa have actually surpassed levels found nationally in the 1920s. Although husband adoptions dropped for several years following World War II, they have recently begun climbing again as family size has decreased (Ochiai 1997, 153–54; Traphagan 2000, 54). Adoption of adults has historically been one way in which the Japanese family responds to infertility or infant mortality. Family succession is not dependent on giving birth to a male heir, but on having a male available, either through birth or adoption, to succeed. In times like the present, when, due to low fertility there are more "son-less" families, or families in which a son is unwilling or unable to take on the responsibility of succession that existed in the past, the practice of adopting male heirs may be one means by which families adjust to demographic realities.

The stem family is an institution that includes not only the living members of the family, but also those who have died. This is clearly evident in the practice of ancestor veneration, according to which families routinely memorialize deceased family members (including those from the distant past) at the domestic altar and at the family grave. According to the Japanese notion of *jōbutsu*, the posthumous repose of the dead depends on the living family members regularly carrying out their memorial duties. However, in a society that no longer neatly fits into so many different *ie* family units, memorialism of the dead becomes problematic. In chapter 7, Satsuki Kawano examines the growing problem of "getting buried" in contemporary Japan. She focuses on those people (such as childless couples or the unmarried) who, by leaving no descendants behind, find themselves condemned to the prospective status of *muenbotoke* or restless ghosts. She shows how such people attempt to redress this problem, and ensure their posthumous well-being, by collectivizing memorialism in conjunction with Buddhist temples

and therefore, in effect, establishing alternative relations of memorialism to those of the *ie*. Kawano's chapter illustrates a more general
theme that runs through the following chapters: the way in which
Japanese people, rather than simply adopt a Westernized model of
the family, reinterpret, adapt, and extend the sentiments and responsibilities associated with the traditional stem family in response
to contemporary demographic, economic, and social conditions.

Population in Japan

Population growth has been a central feature of modern Japan. At
the start of the modern period in 1868, Japan had approximately
30 million people; in 1945, the year of Japan's wartime defeat, it
had 72 million people; by the end of 1990 the population had reached
123 million, and by about 2010 it is projected to peak at 130 million. Thereafter, the population of Japan is expected to fall, with a
projected decline that may fall below 80 million by 2050. Although
such population trends are dramatic, it is important to recognize
that both population growth and decline in Japan, as elsewhere,
take place in a political context through which people interpret and
ascribe meanings to demographic change. Population size and rate
of growth have been the object of political concern throughout
modern Japanese history. Japan has long seen itself as having too
many people and too little land, a sentiment that is manifested in
a wide variety of ways. Japanese people readily contrast their country unfavourably with the expanses of North America or Australia.
The shortage of land is an abiding preoccupation in Japan (e.g.,
small farm size, limited cemetery space, the creation of artificial
islands). Every Japanese knows of the reference to Japanese dwell-
ings as "rabbit hutches" made in a European Common Market
report in the late 1970s, a remark which only reinforced the Japanese self-perception of land scarcity and overpopulation.

In particular, Japan's mountainous archipelago has long raised
concerns with the shortage of arable land and doubts about the
ability to grow enough food for the population. In pre-war Japan,
especially in the 1920s and 1930s, there was a national fixation
with excessive fertility. Rural poverty was attributed to population
surplus and insufficient land. In 1927, the Minister of Finance
declared that "[t]he fundamental solution of the Food versus Population Problem is the one grand aim of the present government's
economic policy" (in Crocker 1931, 53). But with the rise of milita-
rism, the concern shifted from controlling population to boosting it.

In 1941, the pronatalist wartime state issued a mandate in which a target was set for increasing the national population over the next twenty years from 73 million to 100 million people (Miyake 1991, 278–79). In the post-war period the preoccupation of the Japanese government was again with overpopulation—and the problem of excess population growth. This has been avoided primarily through the use of induced abortion rather than contraception, although increased contraceptive use has also contributed (Hardacre 1997, 60). Between 1947 and 1957, Japan more than halved its birth rate: the total fertility rate fell from 4.5 in 1947 to 2.0 ten years later, where it remained relatively stable at replacement level until the early 1970s (Coleman 1983, 34). Since the 1970s total fertility has continued to decline. In 1980 it fell to 1.75 and in 1990 it declined to 1.54. By 2000, the total fertility rate in Japan stood at approximately 1.35 children per woman over the lifecourse, a drop from 2.14 in 1973 and well below the 2.10 required to maintain a stable population when transnational migration does not account for significant population increases (Raymo 1998; Sōmuchō 2000, 37).

As a result of this decline, late twentieth and early twenty-first century Japan is again preoccupied with boosting fertility. In the 1980s and 1990s the declining national birth rate became problematized as a significant social issue both by the government and in the media. There is particular concern over the changing role of women in society, whereby women become less and less likely to follow the traditional paths of marriage and childrearing; indeed, this has been elevated to the level of a moral discourse in which women are criticized for not carrying out their roles in society properly (Traphagan 2000, 34). The falling birth rate is the object of nationalistic fears, and the trend is even seen as threatening the future existence of the nation. In 1990, the director-general of the Economic Planning Agency expressed the fear that the increase in the number of women taking up careers and postponing marriage could eventually lead to the disappearance of the Japanese people: "if this excellent Japanese tribe is on its way to becoming extinct, then I cannot die easily" (Uno 1993, 321).

Rural Depopulation

Population decline is a particular concern in rural Japan. Japanese urbanization in the pre-war period has long been seen as a smooth and harmonious process in which the large-scale displacement of population was relatively free of the anomic disruptions that marked Western urbanization (Vogel 1971; De Vos 1973, 204–8). In the post-war period, this image of harmonious, orderly urbanization gave way to one of imbalance and distortion. The large-scale transfer of population to urban areas brought about a situation of simultaneous urban overpopulation and rural depopulation—or *kamitsu* and *kaso*, in Japanese (Yūki 1970). The effect of depopulation has been to deplete villages of their fertile age-band, thus causing a secondary effect on the next generation. Depopulated villages have seen a collapse of their birth rates, to the extent that some remote villages have virtually no residents of normal childbearing age.

Many of the chapters in this book deal with rural Japan. The municipalities of Tōwa-chō (chapter 5), Hongū-chō (chapter 6), and Kanegasaki-chō (chapter 10) have all undergone large scale depopulation in the postwar decades. One of the features of depopulated areas in Japan is the way that population maintenance has become problematized as the central, overriding task of local governments. The chapters by Chris Thompson and John Knight both examine the efforts of municipal governments to tackle the depopulation problem. On the one hand, these efforts are directed to encouraging local people to live and work locally rather than to outmigrate for work in the large cities. On the other hand, a variety of pronatalist policies are evident, albeit with seemingly little effect. In response to depopulation and its debilitating effect on local communities, municipal governments attempt to promote fertility in a variety of ways. They encourage births by providing one-time payments to cover the costs of pre-natal care, childbirth itself, as well as post-natal payments to contribute to the costs of infant care. Marriage has become a major concern in rural areas of Japan. Rural bachelorhood, in particular, is a serious problem; it is not at all unusual to find villages where half of all men in their thirties are unmarried. What the Japanese mass media calls the rural "bride drought" (*yomehideri*) or "bride famine" (*yome kikin*) is commonly characterized as the "farm successors' marriage problem," but extends to upland forestry villages and coastal fishing villages as well. The difficulty that rural men have in finding brides can become yet another reason for leaving the village in search of better prospects elsewhere. In response, many municipal governments have become directly involved in marriage brokerage (Knight 1995).

The preoccupation with depopulation is not confined to the rural town hall but is evident at a popular level as well. Depopulation or *kaso* has even become a kind of stock popular explanation of decline, one that is invoked in local communities to account for all manner of specific problems. Examples include:

> 'Because of *kaso* lone-dwelling old people die without any-body noticing.' 'Because of *kaso* work is not going well.' 'Because of *kaso* I can't find a bride,' and so on. . . . [T]he problems of S village are not examined one-by-one, but are treated as all caused by *kaso*. (Yasui 1997, 67–68)

The diffusion of this "depopulation consciousness" can be under-stood as an example of a "folk demography" or "demographic consciousness," to use Ardener's terms (Ardener 1989, 110, 117). Evidence of this demographic consciousness is visible in the entryway of almost any town hall in rural Japan, where the current population total, including losses and gains, is presented on a large sign for all to see and contemplate. In short, demo-graphic behavior—both actual behavior to date and prospective behavior in the future—becomes a major subjective theme in rural Japanese society, as well as an objective characteristic of rural populations.

The chapters in this book illustrate the way in which demo-graphic trends in contemporary Japan are unevenly spatially dis-tributed. In the later decades of the twentieth century Japan's youth migrated en masse to the cities, leaving behind them eld-erly regions, unable to reproduce themselves. Migration trends appear to have brought about a fundamental transformation of the social character of rural space in Japan—to the point where, at the beginning of the twenty-first century, the very idea of a discrete "rural society" hardly seems to apply. In other words, as Knight puts it in his chapter, Japan's rural regions have increas-ingly ceased to be *lifecourse* spaces, in which people live out their lives following established local occupations, and have become instead *lifephase* spaces, in which only one or two parts of the lifecourse are lived locally, the rest being spent in the city that becomes the site of their working lives.

Aging in Japan

Population aging has become a major problem to societies through-out the world. One of the major challenges it poses is in the area of welfare provision. Up until the 1970s much of the Japanese political establishment took the welfare states of Western Europe as its welfare model. But since the 1970s this has been largely replaced by an alternative welfare model, known as the "Japanese-style welfare society" (*Nihongata fukushi shakai*), that ostensibly draws on traditional Confucian values such as filial piety, obligation, and respect for seniority, and that posits the family as the basic provider of elder care (Goodman 1998, 150). A key element of this claim is Japan's persistently high level of intergenerationl coresidence, something that the government proclaims to be a "unique asset that can be tapped to offset the adverse consequences of population aging" (Ogawa and Retherford 1997, 76). In addition to its claimed compatibility with Japanese cultural values, the "Japanese-style welfare society" model also promised economic benefits to the state in the form of lower welfare spending, and therefore lower taxation, than would be the case with the Western welfare state model. Despite the above emphasis on its social and cultural specificity, this Japanese welfare model has acquired a wider appeal in recent years. In the area of welfare for the elderly, as in the area of economic performance, Japan has become something of a model, with both Japanese and Western commentators lauding its family-based system of welfare provision. Japan has come to exemplify an East Asian "welfare model" that offers one way of dealing with the problem of population aging faced in many advanced industrial societies (White and Goodman 1998, 10–13).

These discussions of Confucian-based welfare models are apt to give the impression of a traditional intergenerational solidarity and harmony in Japan and other East Asian societies. Yet in Japan this supposed solidarity between the generations should not necessarily be taken at face value. At times the elderly have been viewed as a potential burden on the family. One recalls the well-known *obasuteyama* legend in which the elderly grandmother, whom the family can no longer feed, is abandoned in the mountains by her son.[1] Many anthropologists and folklorists who have worked in remote areas of Japan will be familiar with tales of local spots in the mountains—often referred to as "Hell Valley" or *Jigokudani*—where in earlier times the old (and the sick) are said to have been discarded and which today are considered inauspicious, haunted places to be avoided. Whether this kind of "geronticide" ever existed on any appreciable scale is open to question, but every Japanese person knows of the tale and it looms over many a discussion of elderly welfare in Japan. More generally, the motif finds expression in the expectation, still widely found in rural Japan, that the old should, as much as they are able to, continue to contribute to the household, whether this be through babysitting grandchildren, house-minding, or cultivating vegetables for the kitchen table.

This problem of social disconnection among the elderly is set to become all the more pronounced under the demographic conditions of twenty-first century Japan. Japan presents one of the most striking examples of societal aging in the world, having the longest life expectancy in the world—76.4 years for men and 82.9 years for women in 1995 (see chapter 2). This increase in longevity, combined with the decrease in fertility, has meant that the Japanese population as a whole has aged at a remarkably rapid pace. In 1950 people over 65 accounted for less than 5 percent of the national population, but in 2000 they made up 17 percent, and by 2025 they are projected to exceed 27 percent (Sōmuchō 2000, 41). In conjunction with the decline in national birth rates, this trend has profound implications for the Japanese family in the future. The rapid increase in the elderly population also poses a major challenge to municipal and national government agencies in developing social services and facilities that can effectively address the medical and other needs of an aged population.

Growth in the number of elderly people is invariably accompanied by growth in the number of people in need of some form of health care. In the case of Japan, within the over-65 population there has been a dramatic increase in the number of people aged 75 and over—what are sometimes referred to as the "old old." "The ratio of the population aged 75-plus to the population aged 65-plus is projected to increase from 40 to 57 percent between 1995 and 2025 . . . higher than projected for any other country" (Ogawa and Retherford 1997, 62–63). This creates a welfare burden both for the elderly themselves, who must find ways to cope with their declining physical and mental condition, and for their children (in many cases themselves advanced in years), who are often the ones to provide financial assistance and/or assistance in the activities of daily living (ADL). In Japan the burden of care primarily falls upon women—either a daughter-in-law or, increasingly, a daughter. In chapter 9 Brenda Robb Jenike presents ethnographic examples of just such a situation that focus the spotlight on the continued salience of an "intergenerational contract" in present-day Japan and the pressures to which it is subject. In particular, she shows how daughters-in-law, who find themselves obligated to care for elderly parents with advanced dementia, attempt to cope in the face of social tensions with husband and in-laws and bureaucratic obstacles to the provision of care services.

Japan's "aging society" or *kōreika shakai* has been the object of much governmental, academic, and media concern since the 1970s (see Campbell 1992). There has been a wide range of plans and programs developed or supported by the government via subsidies since the 1950s. One major initiative was the Gold Plan (proposed in 1989), a ten-year plan that set a range of targets, including dramatic increases in home helpers and nursing home beds, and called for an increase in senior centers for less populated areas, more short stay beds, and centers to coordinate in-home care of the frail elderly (Campbell 1992, 246). Throughout most of the history of government elder care programs in Japan the emphasis has been placed on those without traditional, family-centered forms of support (including single-dwellers, childless people, and older couples without nearby family). Facilities such as nursing homes were largely viewed as welfare for the needy and tended to carry a stigma in the eyes of many Japanese. But, as Campbell argues, the Gold Plan initiated a shift in attitudes about government-provided care. The Gold Plan reduced or eliminated means-tests for using services and facilities, greatly expanded the types of services and facilities available, and contributed to a growing demand that the government should provide some degree of care to older people even when there are family caregivers at home (Campbell 2000, 90). Nonetheless, the services and facilities provided by the Gold Plan were largely a supplement to in-home, family-provided care rather than an institutionalized system that met the needs of the frail elderly and their family members. It lacked the scale needed to actually affect a shift in responsibility from families to government in terms of providing care for the frail elderly and was insufficient to meet the demands of a rapidly expanding elderly population.

Rather than simply expanding the Gold Plan, an approach that faced financial and administrative problems due to its limited infrastructure, the Japanese government proposed and initiated, beginning in 2000, a long-term care insurance program (LTCI) (*kaigo hoken*) as a means of coping with the rise in bedridden elders and others in need of assistance with ADL. LTCI is a social insurance program that has been designed along lines similar to the German program, which was enacted in 1994 and is the only other LTCI program to have been initiated in an industrial or post-industrial nation. This program requires the participation of those over the age of 40 and involves mandatory premiums for the purpose of supporting long-term care for those in need. In addition to the premiums, recipients of long-term care are required to pay 10 percent of the cost of care. Services that the insurance program supports include in-home care, home-visiting by healthcare professionals such as nurses, home-helpers, and physical therapists, as well as in-home counseling by public health workers, doctors, dentists, and others. The program also supports in-home bathing services for the elderly, day-care service at elder day-care centers, short-stay programs at nursing homes, subsidies for the purchase or rental of equipment and for home renovations to help with ADL (e.g., handrails or Western-style toilets rather than the squat-toilets typical of older Japanese houses), and long-term institutional care (Mizu sōgō kikaku 1999).

It remains to be seen what consequences the LTCI program will have for the provision of care in Japan, or for the Japanese economy. Official estimates of the costs for LTCI expect more than $50 billion in spending by 2010—an estimate that appears to be rather optimistic (Campbell 2000, 96). Given the size of the program, underestimating the costs involved with LTCI may mean that serious problems loom for Japanese fiscal policy and the health care system. It is interesting that, undoubtedly cognizant of this potential for serious problems, along with the advent of the long-term care insurance program, a rhetoric of non-use has emerged in which government officials talk of new and pre-existing senior centers, elder day-care facilities, and other institutional settings as being aimed at providing a context in which elders can sustain good health and so avoid using the long-term care insurance. It will also be interesting to see how the advent of the LTCI era affects population movement among the elderly. In recent years, a trend seems to be emerging whereby the nation's elderly are moving to rural regions—something permitted by the recent phenomenon of *kaigo ijūsha* or "care migrants" in which older people migrate to rural localities on account of their superior welfare provision (see chapter 6). Across Japan, rural municipalities have established what are variously known as "Silver Areas" and "Welfare Villages"—special zones consisting of advanced welfare provision (including home helpers, visiting nurses, special housing, customized medical facilities, and integrated shopping facilities) aimed at attracting elderly migrants to their areas. It is distinctly possible that in the future places like Hongū-chō, Tōwa-chō, Kanegasaki-chō, and Mizusawa-shi could become primary sites of welfare provision for the nation's elderly.

In this way, elderly welfare provision in Japan has been focused on the family as the principal source of care. As Akiko Hashimoto notes, the system of social support for the elderly in Japan is based upon a notion of security structured around the idea of protection. There is a strong emphasis among older Japanese on a support system that protects and guarantees care, rather than one that promotes independence and autonomy. Hashimoto argues that the comparatively "high rate of filial co-residence in Japan is one obvious example that attests to this fundamental ideal of long-term security" (Hashimoto 2000, 20). The family, rather than social institutions such as nursing homes, is viewed as the primary locus of a secure old age. However, many old people end up living (and dying) in old people's homes (*rōjin hōmu*) or other institutional settings such as hospitals for the elderly. In Japan the old people's home has long been tainted with *obasuteyama* imagery and viewed as a site for the disposal of the elderly (Bethel 1992, 130–31). One of the issues this raises is that of giving institutional care in Japan a more human face. In chapter 4, Leng Leng Thang offers a case study of an age-integrated facility, Kotoen, which consists of both an old people's home (and a day-care center) and a nursery for children. Kotoen explicitly promotes "intergenerational contact" with the children in an attempt to counter the sense of social estrangement associated with institutions for the elderly. The existence of an ancestral altar in Kotoen, recalling the ancestral altars found in Japanese homes, suggests that the institution strives to recreate a family atmosphere for its residents. Kotoen represents a fascinating example of the way in which the trappings of the Japanese *ie* are extended to institutions beyond it.

Anthropology and Demography in the Future

Population aging is one of the most pressing problems facing policy makers in advanced industrial societies and a problem that many developing societies will face in the future. It poses a major challenge to those who study such societies. Population aging represents a transformation in the demographic shape of a society, along with a new set of conditions in which the relationship between the family (in its varied forms) and the wider population develops and changes. Both the process of population aging (along with its social ramifications) and, more generally, the relationship between demographic and cultural change, are areas that need more social science research. Population aging should be studied in ways that cross disciplinary boundaries, because insights from one discipline can inform and influence the formulation of research questions in other disciplines. Yet only recently has population aging begun to be addressed in a truly cross-disciplinary way. Susan O. Long's

(2000) edited volume is one notable example of an attempt to bring together researchers from a variety of fields—sociology, anthropology, economics, medicine, political science, and social work—to consider the practical implications of cultural variation in relation to provision of elder care. There remains considerable room for further collaboration among researchers from different disciplines.

However, combining disciplines as methodologically and epistemologically distinct as anthropology and demography within the confines of a single edited volume can present difficulties, particularly in relation to the technical terminology and jargon associated with each discipline. Throughout the meetings and other exchanges that led to this volume, difficulties in translating discipline-specific terminology frequently arose. Terms such as "decomposition" on the part of the demographers or "liminality" on the part of anthropologists are routinely used in the respective disciplines, without being specifically defined or problematized. This tendency often inhibits scholars from reading extensively outside of their own disciplines, particularly in areas that approach research from perspectives that seem fundamentally at odds with their own.

As will become clear in the pages that follow, there is much to be gained from persisting with the language and the methods of other disciplines, whether it is narrative-rich ethnographic interpretation or number-rich demographic analysis, to get at underlying insights that challenge our own assumptions and ideas. In many respects, this volume represents a first step. Although the chapters here clearly inform and connect to each other, they remain distinctly anthropological and demographic entries into the literature on the family and aging in Japan. The next step is to begin research projects that, from the inception of grant-writing through the process of data collection and publication, involve anthropologists and demographers in collaborative research teams. A true synthesis will involve scholars from both disciplines working together on specific projects that direct their respective approaches to the study of common research questions.

The policies that are developed over the coming years to cope with population aging should be informed both by the macro-level quantitative data and analysis that demographers can provide and by the micro-level ethnographic data and analysis in which anthropologists specialize. Conclusions developed through processes of social scientific inquiry are inherently limited because human vocabularies reflect particular perspectives on the world. Ethnography, demography, positivism, and subjectivism are all cultural products of human beings. Although social scientists may begin at different epistemological starting points, they are inevitably faced with the limitations of their own science. In this volume, we offer a tether between two disciplines.

Notes

1. The *obasuteyama* tale is ubiquitous in Japanese folklore, and is the subject of *noh* plays, literature, and films.

References

Ardener, Edwin. 1989. *The voice of prophecy and other essays.* Edited by Malcolm Chapman. Oxford: Basil Blackwell.

Bethel, Diana. 1992. Alienation and reconnection in a home for the elderly. In *Re-made in Japan: Everyday life and consumer taste in a changing society,* edited by Joseph J. Tobin. New Haven, Conn.: Yale University Press.

Brown, L. Keith. 1998. Family history and the ancestors. Paper presented at annual meeting of the American Anthropological Association, Philadelphia.

Caldwell, John C., Allan G. Hill, and Valerie J. Hull, eds. 1988. *Microapproaches to demographic research.* London: Kegan Paul.

Caldwell, John C., P. H. Reddy, and Pat Caldwell. 1988. *The causes of demographic change: Experimental research in South India.* Madison: University of Wisconsin Press.

Campbell, John Creighton. 1992. *How policies change: The Japanese government and the aging society.* Princeton, N.J.: Princeton University Press.

———. 2000. Changing meanings of frail old people and the Japanese welfare state. In *Caring for the elderly in Japan and the U.S.: Practice and policies,* edited by Susan O. Long. New York: Routledge, 82–97.

Coleman, Samuel. 1983. *Family planning in Japanese society: Traditional birth control in a modern urban culture.* Princeton, N.J.: Princeton University Press.

Crocker, W. R. 1931. *The Japanese population problem: The coming crisis.* New York: Macmillan.

De Vos, G. A. 1973. *Socialization for achievement: Essays on the cultural psychology of the Japanese.* Berkeley: University of California Press.

Fricke, Tom. 1997a. Culture theory and demographic process: Toward a thicker demography. In *Anthropological demography: Toward a new synthesis,* edited by D. I. Kertzer and T. Fricke. Chicago: University of Chicago Press.

———. 1997b. The uses of culture in demographic research: A continuing place for community studies. *Population and Development Review* 23(4): 825–32.

Goodman, Roger. 1998. The "Japanese-style welfare state" and the delivery of personal social services. In *The East Asian welfare model: Welfare orientalism and the state,* edited by Roger Goodman, Gordon White and Huck-ju Kwon. New York: Routledge.

Greenhalgh, Susan. 1995. Anthropology theorizes reproduction: Integrating practice, political economic, and feminist perspectives. In *Situating fertility: Anthropology and demographic inquiry,* edited by Susan Greenhalgh. Cambridge: Cambridge University Press.

Hardacre, Helen. 1997. *Marketing the menacing fetus in Japan.* Berkeley: University of California Press.

Harris, Marvin. 1999. *Theories of culture in postmodern times.* Walnut Creek, Calif.: Alta Mira Press.

Hashimoto, Akiko. 2000. Cultural meanings of "security" in aging policies. In *Caring for the elderly in Japan and the U.S.: Practices and policies,* edited by Susan O. Long. New York: Routledge.

Jeffery, Roger, and Patricia Jeffery. 1997. *Population, gender and politics: Demographic change in rural North India.* Cambridge: Cambridge University Press.

Kawabe, Hiroshi, and Hiroaki Shimizu. 1994. Japanese perceptions of the family and living arragements: The trend toward nuclearization. In *Tradition and change in the Asian family,* edited by Lee-Jay Cho and Moto Yada. Honolulu, Hawaii: East-West Center.

Kertzer, David I., and Tom Fricke. 1997. Toward an anthropological demography. In *Anthropological Demography: Toward a New Synthesis,* edited by David I. Kertzer and Tom Fricke. Chicago: University of Chicago Press.

Knight, John. 1995. Municipal matchmaking in rural Japan. *Anthropology Today* 11(2): 9–17.

Knodel, John, Apichat Chamratrithirong, and Nibhon Debavalya. 1987. *Thailand"s reproduction revolution: Rapid fertility decline in a third-world setting.* Madison: University of Wisconsin Press.

Kurosu, Satomi. 1994. Who lives in the extended family and why? The case of Japan. In *Tradition and change in the asian family,* edited by Lee-Jay Cho and Moto Yada. Honolulu, Hawaii: East-West Center.

Long, Susan O., ed. 2000. *Caring for the elderly in Japan and the U.S.: Practices and policies.* New York: Routledge.

Marcus, George, and Michael Fischer. 1986. *Anthropology as cultural critique: An experimental moment in the human sciences.* Chicago: Chicago University Press.

Miyake, Yoshiko. 1991. Doubling expectations: Motherhood and women's factory work under state management in Japan in the 1930s and 1940s. In *Recreating Japanese Women, 1600–1945,* edited by Gail Bernstein. Berkeley: University of California Press.

Mizu sōgō kikaku. 1999. *Yoku wakaru! Kaigo Hoken* [Understand well! Long-term care insurance]. Tokyo: Takahashi Shoten.

Ochiai, Emiko. 1997. *The Japanese family system in transition: A sociological analysis of family change in postwar Japan.* Tokyo: LTCB International Library Foundatin.

Ogawa, Naohiro, and Robert D. Retherford. 1997. Shifting the cost of caring for the elderly back to families in Japan: Will it work? *Population and Development Review* 23(1): 59–94.

Rappaport, Roy A. 1968. *Pigs for the ancestors.* New Haven, Conn.: Yale University Press.

Raymo, James M. 1998. Later marriages or fewer? Changes in the marital behavior of Japanese women. *Journal of Marriage and the Family* 60(November): 1023–34.

Rosenau, Pauline Marie. 1992. *Post-modernism and the social sciences: Insights, inroads, and intrusions.* Princeton, N.J.: Princeton University Press.

Sōmuchō [Japanese Office of General Affairs]. 2000. *Kōreishakai Hakusho* [Aging society white paper]. Tokyo: Ōkurashō insatsu kyoku.

Traphagan, John W. 2000. *Taming oblivion: Aging bodies and the fear of senility in Japan.* Albany: State University of New York Press.

Uno, Kathleen S. 1993. The death of "good wife, wise mother." In *Postwar Japan as history,* edited by Andrew Gordon. Berkeley: University of California Press.

Vogel, Ezra F. 1971. *Japan's new middle class: The salary man and his family in a Tokyo suburb.* 2nd ed. Berkeley: University of California Press.

White, Gordon, and Roger Goodman. 1998. Welfare orientalism and the search for an East Asian welfare model. In *The East Asian welfare model: Welfare orientalism and the state,* edited by Roger Goodman, Gordon White and Huck-ju Kwon. New York: Routledge.

Yasui, Manami. 1997. "Furusato" kenkyū no bunseki shikaku. (The analytical vision of furusato research). *Nihon Minzokugaku* 209: 66–88.

Yūki, Seigo. 1970. Kamitsu kaso: Yugamerareta nihonrettō (Overcrowding and depopulation: The distorted Japanese archipelago). Tokyo: Sanichi Shinsho.

Family and Living Arrangements

Changes in expectations and patterns of residence are among the most pressing issues facing the Japanese elderly. Historically, Japanese society has placed great emphasis on filial coresidence as not only preferable, but as the normative pattern of family living arrangements. Older people who are unable to live with their children have often been pitied, even stigmatized, for their inability to adhere to the expected pattern of residence in later life. In Japan one of the most commonly heard refrains on the subject of old age is that the older person living alone is *sabishii* or "lonely." Although this perception remains common, it is also true that many elderly do not wish to coreside with their children, preferring to retain independence and privacy. Some women, in particular, comment that following the death of their husbands, they are enjoying the first period of true freedom in their lives and want to delay or altogether avoid coresidence with their children. Younger generations, too, appear to be less willing, and sometimes even completely opposed, to coreside with parents. Hesitation on the part of spouses (particularly wives) to coreside with in-laws is thought to play an increasingly important role in decisions about coresidence and the often associated expectation (for women) about provision of elder care should the need arise. These attitudes limit the degree to which older generations feel they can or wish to depend upon their children for coresidential social support as they grow older. What is clear in the current cultural milieu is that conflict over ideas about the proper residential arrangements for older family members is a regular feature of Japanese family life.

As James Raymo and Toshiko Kaneda show in their contribution to this section, traditional filial coresidence—where parents reside with a child and his or her family—has declined markedly during the past twenty years. The authors look into various factors, economic and social, that have contributed to the decline in coresidence and show that despite the decline, the rates are perhaps higher than one might expect given what is found in other industrial and post-industrial societies, even though the trend towards a decrease is likely to continue in the future. The life table analyses Raymo and Kaneda provide help in understanding how changes in mortality and nuptiality have contributed to changing patterns of coresidence in late life. They also point to some of the important reasons, such as fewer children and increased education, that may contribute to these changes. Where the approach taken by Raymo and Kaneda reaches its limits is in determining the attitudinal changes that have accompanied changes in demographic behavior related to coresidence.

Naomi Brown picks up on this theme, raising the question of why coresidence has declined by considering changing attitudes about living patterns. She considers how the discourse of traditional filial coresidence has changed and looks at the ways in which the Japanese have improvised alternatives to filial coresidence in order to address the tensions that tend to arise from it. The emergence of the two-generation house, in which the older couple lives on the first floor and the younger family lives on the second floor (each with their own, private, living areas accessible only through an outside door), is a good example of how people use existing cultural frameworks to recast and reinterpret living patterns. In this case, the basic ideal of filial coresidence is maintained while also ensuring a degree of privacy for the younger generation.

These chapters point out both the extent of demographic and attitudinal changes related to filial coresidence in Japan and the manner in which people adjust and address the needs that arise as those changes occur. The simple fact that the Japanese system of institutional support for the frail elderly is designed to augment in-home, woman-provided care to the elderly is important for understanding the manner in which Japanese people respond to and experience the changes in demographic behavior that have emerged in contemporary Japanese society.

2

Changes in the Living Arrangements of Japanese Elderly: The Role of Demographic Factors

James M. Raymo and Toshiko Kaneda

In recent years, changes in living arrangements and the future of the extended family have become the subject of considerable policy interest in Japan (Ogawa 1982; Campbell 1992; Ogawa and Retherford 1997; Yashiro 1997). This interest is stimulated by the implications of rapid population aging in Japan. Projections suggesting that the speed and the magnitude of changes in Japan's population age structure will be without historical precedent (e.g., Ogawa 1989; Kōno 1996; National Institute of Population and Social Security Research 1997) have created a sense of urgency concerning the provision of adequate care for the rapidly growing elderly population. One policy response has been to focus on the extended family as a valuable resource for limiting the fiscal burden of rapid population aging and to direct policy efforts at strengthening the family and facilitating family-provided care for dependent elderly (Campbell 1992, chapter 7; Ogawa 1997; Ogawa and Retherford 1997). In addition to establishing the long-term care insurance program, government initiatives have promoted increased capacity for institutional care, leave to care for sick family members, increased numbers of home helpers and visiting nurses, more day-care centers for elderly, and provision of technical aids and professional advice to facilitate home care (Ministry of Health and Welfare 1987; Maeda 1996; Ogawa and Retherford 1997).

However, some scholars have suggested that the willingness and the ability of families to continue providing elder care may be declining (Ogawa 1997; Ogawa and Retherford 1997; Yashiro 1997). Although older Japanese have long relied on coresident family members (particularly married children and their spouses) for the provision of economic, physical, and emotional support, the proportion of the population aged 65 and over coresiding with children has declined steadily over the past twenty years. This can be seen in Table 2.1, which presents household type distributions by age and sex calculated from 1975 and 1995 census data. The upper panel (both sexes) shows that, between 1975 and 1995, the proportion of the population aged 65 and over coresiding with children fell from 72 percent to 49 percent and that there has been a corresponding increase in the proportion of older Japanese living alone (from 7% to 12%) and in couple-only households (from 15% to 28%). The middle and lower panels show corresponding figures for men and women, respectively. Further declines in coresidential living arrangements are projected in the coming decades (Hirosima 1997). Although the proportion of Japanese elderly coresiding with children remains quite high by international standards (Management and Coordination Agency 1982, 1987), and despite the fact that spouses and noncoresident children are often capable of providing the necessary support for frail or ill elderly persons, the decline in intergenerational coresidence may have important implications for the provision of care to Japan's growing elderly population.

Explanations for Declining Coresidence

Explanations for the shift away from extended family living have focused on several factors. To facilitate a concise summary of the existing literature, we categorize explanations of declining coresidence into those which focus primarily on economic, social, and demographic factors.

Economic factors include:

1. *Structural changes in the economy.* The declining prevalence of self-employment, particularly in agriculture, has reduced the economic advantage of coresidence. It is no longer necessary that children, especially older sons, remain at home to provide labor or to continue the family business (Ogawa and Retherford 1993). It is also possible that the attractiveness or feasibility of coresidence has been reduced by the urbanization and suburbanization that have accompanied structural changes in the economy. For example, the ability to coreside may be restricted by the smaller houses and apartments of urban and suburban residents.

Table 2.1: Distribution of Household Type by Sex and Age, 1975 and 1995

Household Type and Year

Age	Single Person		Couple		Coresident		Other		Institutional	
	1975	1995	1975	1995	1975	1995	1975	1995	1975	1995
Both Sexes										
65+	0.07	0.12	0.15	0.28	0.72	0.49	0.03	0.07	0.03	0.04
65–69	0.07	0.11	0.20	0.37	0.68	0.46	0.03	0.06	0.02	0.01
75+	0.07	0.13	0.09	0.17	0.77	0.55	0.03	0.08	0.05	0.08
Men										
65+	0.04	0.06	0.23	0.39	0.68	0.50	0.02	0.02	0.03	0.03
65–69	0.04	0.06	0.26	0.42	0.66	0.48	0.02	0.02	0.02	0.02
75+	0.04	0.07	0.18	0.33	0.71	0.54	0.03	0.02	0.04	0.05
Women										
65+	0.09	0.16	0.09	0.20	0.75	0.49	0.03	0.10	0.03	0.05
65–69	0.10	0.15	0.14	0.32	0.71	0.43	0.03	0.09	0.02	0.01
75+	0.08	0.16	0.03	0.08	0.80	0.55	0.04	0.11	0.05	0.09

Source: Japanese Census (*Kokusei Chōsa*) 1975, 1995.

2. *Improved economic status of older Japanese.* The increased coverage and benefit levels provided by public pensions along with the ability to amass substantial savings during their working years have dramatically improved the economic well-being of older Japanese in recent decades (Preston and Kōno 1988; Ogawa and Retherford 1993, 1997). Financial independence of aging parents eliminates one of the traditionally important motivations for coresidence.
3. *Increased economic opportunities for women.* The prevalence of coresidence may be influenced by greater economic independence for young women as well as the increasing labor force participation of middle-aged women. As the economic status and career prospects of young Japanese women improve, increased bargaining power vis-à-vis their husbands may allow them to insist on independent residence as a condition of marriage (see chapter 10). Furthermore, with middle-aged women (often the primary providers of care for old and frail coresident parents) increasingly less likely to be at home, one of the most important functions of coresidence (i.e., family caregiving) has become more difficult to fulfill (Maeda and Nakatani 1992; Retherford and Ogawa 1997).

Social factors include:

1. *Changing attitudes toward coresidence.* Attitudinal survey data consistently show declines not only in favorable attitudes toward filial provision of care for elderly parents, but also in the proportion of elderly and near-elderly who expect or hope to rely on support from their children (Kendig 1989; Martin 1989; Tsuya and Choe 1991; Ogawa and Retherford 1993, 1997; Economic Planning Agency 1994; Ogawa and Hodge 1994; Retherford, Ogawa, and Sakamoto 1996; Ogawa 1997). Perhaps reflecting these attitudinal changes, surveys also indicate that most Japanese (both older parents and their children) now plan to begin coresiding only when one parent dies or becomes seriously ill (e.g., Council on Population Problems 1991; Naoi 1996). These survey results are thought to reflect a trend away from obligatory coresidence in favor of strategic coresidence. That is, coresidence and provision of care to elderly parents is becoming less of a "natural duty" and more an arrangement of convenience.[1] In this arrangement, older parents typically provide housing, and perhaps childcare, in tacit exchange for the financial and physical support they may need as they age (Morgan and Hirosima 1983; Hirosima 1987; Martin and Tsuya

1991; Ohtake 1991; Tsuya and Martin 1992; Yashiro 1993, 1997; Ogawa and Ermisch 1996; Ogawa and Retherford 1997). The high cost of housing and the inadequate supply of child-care facilities in Japan are thought to play a particularly important role in this normative shift.

2. *Expanded provision and greater acceptance of nonfamilial care for the elderly.* As the provision of facilities (both public and private) for elder care increases and as the social stigma associated with their use decreases, some families that would have had no choice but to coreside in the past can now choose to live separately, with frail parents receiving institutional care (Maeda and Nakatani 1992; Maeda 1996).

In this chapter, we focus on demographic correlates of coresidence. This focus suggests three explanations for the decline in extended family residence among the elderly.

1. *Improvements in health and mortality.* Liu and colleagues (1995) show that older Japanese are expected to be functionally independent for 80 to 90 percent of their remaining life, suggesting that improvements in the physical well-being of the elderly may reduce the need for care provided by coresident children. Improvements in mortality, however, may be expected to work in the opposite direction, as years are added to the end of life when care requirements are greatest and the likelihood of coresidence is highest (Martin and Culter 1983; Martin 1989).

2. *Changing marital status distributions.* This is closely related to improvements in mortality in that reductions in mortality increase the likelihood that both spouses survive to older ages.[2] Because spouses are a primary source of care provision for frail elderly (Ministry of Health and Welfare 1992, 178–79), an increase in the likelihood of joint survivorship to older ages may reduce the likelihood of coresidence with children (Kojima 1989). This is particularly true in light of the attitudinal shifts mentioned above (Hirosima 1987). However, increases in the proportion of elderly men and women who are divorced might be expected to work in the opposite direction.

3. *Changing patterns of fertility and migration.* This can be restated more generally as changes in "kin availability." Declining fertility reduces the number of children with which aging parents could potentially coreside. Migration of children to urban areas, leaving older parents behind, has the same effect as declining fertility (Kojima 1989).

In this chapter, we have two primary objectives. The first is to document changes in the living arrangements of older Japanese between 1975 and 1995 and to evaluate the role of demographic factors in the declining prevalence of coresidence over this period. The second is to assess the importance of demographic factors in determining the likelihood that older Japanese coreside with a child at a single point in time.

To accomplish the first objective, we use information from the most abundant source of data on living arrangements, the national census (*kokusei chōsa*). After describing the available data, we use published tables of living arrangement distributions in conjunction with marital status life tables to create marital status-household type life tables. We then use these life tables to decompose the decline in coresident life expectancy between 1975 and 1995 into the contributions made by changes in mortality, changes in marital status distributions, and changes in living arrangements. Although it is also possible to incorporate the role of kin availability (i.e., fertility and migration) into this analysis, the procedure is a complex one involving several major assumptions. We therefore focus only on mortality and nuptiality in this aggregate-level analysis.[3] We do note, however, that although future cohorts of elderly are likely to have higher levels of childlessness, Hirosima (1987) finds that child availability has changed very little for older Japanese parents in recent decades.

To accomplish the second objective, we use information from one of the only publicly available sources of nationally representative data on older Japanese individuals, the 1987 National Survey of the Japanese Elderly (Liang and Maeda 1997). We apply standard statistical techniques to these data to examine the ways in which health, marital status, and kin availability are realted to the probability that Japanese over the age of 60 were coresiding with a child in the survey year.

Decomposition of Aggregate-Level Changes in Coresidence

Life-table analysis is a useful tool frequently employed by family demographers to study the lifecourse (e.g., Livi-Bacci 1982; Hofferth 1987; Watkins, Menken, and Bongaarts 1987; Zeng 1991). In the absence of longitudinal data at the individual level, the ability to simulate lifecourse experiences using cross-sectional data makes multistate life tables a particularly attractive tool for analyzing changes over time in demographic behavior.[4] In this analysis, we construct life tables that simultaneously classify marital status and living arrangements for the years 1975 and 1995. These life tables enable us to examine the relationship between changes in mortality and nuptiality and changes in the number of years that older Japanese are expected to live in different types of households.[5] More specifically, they enable us to calculate remaining life expectancy for all marital status-living arrangement combinations (e.g., remaining life expectancy widowed and living in a coresident household or remaining life expectancy never married and living in an institutional household).

Construction of these life tables consists of two steps. The first step is to create marital status life tables for 1975 and 1995. The marital status life table for 1975 is taken directly from Ikenoue and Takahashi (1994) whereas the table for 1995 is constructed using marital status-specific population data from the 1995 census and mortality and nuptiality data from the 1995 Vital Statistics of Japan. The second step is to apply age, sex, and marital status-specific household type distributions from the 1975 and 1995 censuses to the corresponding marital status life tables. Because these census data are available only by five-year age group, this procedure necessitates the assumption that the marital status-specific household type distribution for a five-year age group adequately approximates the distribution for each single year in that age group.

By simulating the experience of synthetic cohorts classified by age, sex, marital status, and household type for the two years, we are able to answer questions such as:

- Relative to 1975, how many more years can older Japanese expect to live in each type of household in 1995?
- How much of the reduction in the number of years lived in coresident households is due to changes in mortality?
- How much of this reduction is due to changes in nuptiality?
- How much is due to changes in living arrangements independent of mortality and nuptiality?[6]

Because the life tables are constructed using mortality rates, marital status transition rates, and household type distributions for the two years, we can calculate the answers to these counterfactual questions by sequentially replacing the 1995 mortality, nuptiality, and living arrangement data with their 1975 counterparts while holding the other two components constant. In other words, we use the life tables to calculate what household type-specific life expectancy in 1995 would have been if (1) mortality had remained at its 1975 level; (2) if nuptiality had remained at its 1975 level; and (3) if living arrangement distributions had remained unchanged from 1975. We then compare each of these counterfactual life expectancies to the observed life expectancies for 1995 to determine how much each factor contributed to the observed change in household type-specific life expectancy over the twenty-year period. In life table notation, we calculate:

$$e_{xi(j)} = e_{xi}^{95} - e_{xi}^{95(j)},$$

where $e_{xi(j)}$ is the change in the expected years lived (e) in household type i (i = single, couple only, coresiding with child, other, institutional) at age x (x = 65, 75) that is attributable to factor j (j = mortality, nuptiality, living arrangements, other) and $e_{xi}^{95(j)}$ is the counterfactual value of e_{xi}^{95} calculated by holding factor j constant at its 1975 level.[7]

This analysis requires consistent crosstabulations of marital status and household type by age and sex. The national census (conducted every five years) has published this information since 1975. The census provides information on four types of households: family households; non-family households; individual households; and institutional households. Within the category of family households, the following fourteen subcategories are identified:

1. Married couple only
2. Married couple and children
3. Father and children
4. Mother and children
5. Married couple and parents
6. Married couple and one parent
7. Married couple, parents, and children
8. Married couple, one parent, and children
9. Married couple and other relatives (i.e., not children or parents)
10. Married couple, children, and other relatives
11. Married couple, parent(s), and other relatives
12. Married couple, children, parent(s), and other relatives
13. Siblings
14. Other

We adopt Hirosima's (1998) classification scheme (depicted in Table 2.2) to collapse these fourteen family household types into three categories: couple-only households, coresident households, and other households.[8]

Table 2.2: Hirosima's (1998) Scheme for Census-Based Estimation of 65 and over Population Coresiding with Children

Household Type	Men			Women		
	Marital Status			*Marital Status*		
	Never Married	*Married*	*Widowed and Divorced*	*Never Married*	*Married*	*Widowed and Divorced*
Family Households						
1. Married couple only	Other	Couple	Other	Other	Couple	Other
2. Married couple and children	Other	**Coresident**	Other	Other	**Coresident**	Other
3. Father and children	Other	**Coresident**	**Coresident**	Other	Other	Other
4. Mother and children	Other	Other	Other	Other	**Coresident**	**Coresident**
5. Married couple and parents	Other	**Coresident**	**Coresident**	Other	**Coresident**	**Other**
6. Married couple and one parent	Other	**Coresident**	**Coresident**	Other	**Coresident**	**Coresident**
7. Married couple, parents, and children	Other	**Coresident**	**Coresident**	Other	**Coresident**	Other
8. Married couple, one parent, and children	Other	**Coresident**	**Coresident**	Other	**Coresident**	**Coresident**
9. Married couple and other relatives (not children or parents)	Other	Other	Other	Other	Other	Other
10. Married couple, children, and other relatives	Other	**Coresident**	Other	Other	**Coresident**	Other
11. Married couple, parent(s), and other relatives	Other	**Coresident**	**Coresident**	Other	**Coresident**	**Coresident**
12. Married couple, children, parent(s) and other relatives	Other	**Coresident**	**Coresident**	Other	**Coresident**	**Coresident**
13. Siblings	Other	Other	Other	Other	Other	Other
14. Other	Other	Other	**Coresident**	Other	Other	**Coresident**
Non-Family Household	Other	Other	Other	Other	Other	Other
Single Person Household	Single	Single	Single	Single	Single	Single
Institutional Household	Inst.	Inst.	Inst.	Inst.	Inst.	Inst.

Note: Bold entries represent coresident households, Couple represents couple-only households, Single represents single-person households, Other represents other households, and "Inst." represents institutional households.

Source: Hirosima (1998), 10.

Results

Before presenting the results of the decomposition procedure, we briefly examine changes in life expectancy by marital status and household type. Table 2.3 presents changes between 1975 and 1995 in the expected years of remaining life by sex, marital status, and household type at ages 65 and 75.[9] Improvements in mortality are readily apparent, with life expectancy at age 65 increasing by 2.4 years for men and by 4.2 years for women. For both men and women, these additional years are spent either never married or married. At age 65, men are expected to live two more years never married and slightly more than one-half year married. For women, the corresponding increases are respectively 2.3 and 3.8 years. The large increases in never-married life expectancy reflect declining first-marriage rates for both sexes whereas the increase in married life expectancy for women is primarily a reflection of improvements in male mortality. Similarly, the substantial decrease in the number of years that a 65-year-old woman is expected to be widowed or divorced reflects the improved chances of joint survivorship to older ages. Table 2.3 also indicates that, for both men and women, the largest increases in household type-specific life expectancy are in single-person households and couple-only households whereas the only decreases are in coresident households. In 1995, men aged 65 are expected to live 2.2 fewer years in coresident households

Table 2.3: Change in Life Expectancy between 1975 and 1995 by Age, Sex, Marital Status, and Household Type (unit=years)

	65 Years Old		75 Years Old	
	Men	*Women*	*Men*	*Women*
Total	2.37	4.22	1.89	3.33
Marital Status				
Never Married	2.03	2.25	1.16	1.38
Married	0.55	3.84	0.92	3.00
Widowed and Divorced	−0.22	−1.88	−0.19	−1.04
Household Type				
Single-Person	1.17	1.92	0.57	1.09
Couple	2.19	2.99	1.42	1.74
Coresident	−2.17	−2.90	−0.98	−1.12
Other	0.34	1.39	0.20	0.81
Institutional	0.84	0.82	0.69	0.81

than they were in 1975. The corresponding decline for women is slightly less than 3 years. The primary objective of the decomposition analysis described above is to evaluate the mechanisms behind this decline in coresident life expectancy.

Table 2.4 presents the decomposition results. The figures show the amount of the total change in years of household type-specific life expectancy that can be attributed to changes in mortality, nuptiality, and living arrangements for each of the five household types. Decomposition results at age 65 are shown in the upper panel while those for age 75 are shown in the lower panel. Positive

Table 2.4: Decomposition of Changes in Life Expectancy between 1975 and 1995 by Age, Sex, and Household Type (unit = years)

Sex, Age, and Household type	Total Change	Change due to Mortality	Change due to Nuptiality	Change due to Living Arrangements	Change due to "Other"
Men: Age 65					
Single–Person	1.17	0.33	0.19	0.72	−0.06
Couple	2.19	0.70	−0.71	2.05	0.15
Coresident	−2.17	0.74	−0.43	−2.40	−0.08
Other	0.34	0.26	0.34	−0.74	0.48
Institutional	0.84	0.41	0.31	0.38	−0.26
Men: Age 75					
Single–Person	0.57	0.19	−0.03	0.30	0.11
Couple	1.42	0.59	−0.26	1.16	−0.08
Coresident	−0.98	0.61	−0.03	−1.45	−0.11
Other	0.20	0.18	0.18	−0.44	0.27
Institutional	0.69	0.31	0.14	0.43	−0.20
Women: Age 65					
Single–Person	1.92	0.55	−1.07	1.79	0.65
Couple	2.99	0.79	0.89	2.12	−0.82
Coresident	−2.90	1.50	0.75	−4.19	−0.95
Other	1.39	0.44	−0.17	−0.28	1.40
Institutional	0.82	0.39	−0.30	0.56	0.17
Women: Age 75					
Single–Person	1.09	0.46	−0.71	0.98	0.36
Couple	1.74	0.71	0.64	1.10	−0.71
Coresident	−1.12	1.42	0.58	−2.46	−0.67
Other	0.81	0.37	−0.19	−0.24	0.88
Institutional	0.81	0.36	−0.32	0.63	0.14

values represent contributions to increasing life expectancy and negative values represent contributions to decreasing life expectancy. We focus our discussion primarily on changes in life expectancy at age 65.

For all household types, the largest contribution to changing life expectancy is made by changes in living arrangements independent of changes in mortality and nuptiality. This is particularly true for changes in coresident life expectancy. Had living arrangement distributions remained unchanged between 1975 and 1995, coresident life expectancy would have been 2.4 years longer for men and 4.2 years longer for women than was actually observed in the 1995 table. Net of the effect of changes in mortality and nuptiality is that there has been a shift away from coresidence of older Japanese with their children. Given the large increase in total life expectancy shown in Table 2.3, changes in living arrangement distributions necessarily contributed to increased life expectancy in non-coresident households, particularly single-person and couple-only households. In 1995, male life expectancies in single-person and couple-only households are 0.7 years and 2.1 years more than the counterfactual values calculated by holding living arrangements constant at their 1975 values. The corresponding figures for women are respectively 1.8 and 2.1 years. The importance of changes in living arrangements independent of changes in mortality and nuptiality is consistent with explanations of declining coresidence that focus on the importance of economic, normative, and social factors related to the desirability and feasibility of coresiding.

Although living arrangements are the most important factor in the decomposition, it is also clear that demographic factors, nuptiality in particular, contribute to changes in number of years older Japanese expect to live in different types of households. Reflecting age differences between spouses and differences in male and female mortality at older ages, the effect of changes in marital status transition rates differs dramatically by sex. For women, the primary effect is a reduction in the likelihood of widowhood (the result of improvements in male mortality). For men, the main effect is an increase in the likelihood of never marrying (the result of declining first marriage rates at younger ages). Therefore, when we hold marital status transition rates constant at their 1975 levels and calculate the difference between observed and counterfactual life expectancies, we see that women are expected to spend 1.7 more years of their remaining life in living arrangements common for couples (i.e., 0.9 years in couple-only households and 0.8 years in coresident households). Men, however, are expected to spend one year less in living arrangements common for couples (i.e., 0.7 years less in couple-only households and 0.4 years less in coresident households) and one half year longer in living arrangements common among the unmarried (i.e., 0.2 years in single-person households and 0.3 years in institutional households).

The effect of changes in mortality is the same for both sexes: an increase in life expectancy in all household types. The increase is particularly large for coresident life expectancy among the very old. The fact that the increases in coresident life expectancy due to mortality improvement are nearly identical at ages 65 and 75 indicates that the bulk of the extra life in coresident households is experienced at age 75 and beyond. This is a reflection of increased survival to older ages where the likelihood of coresiding with a child is greatest (see Table 2.1). As life expectancy after 65 and 75 increases, so does the time spent in household types common among the very old.

In sum, the decomposition results in Table 2.4 indicate that the effects of changes in mortality and marital status transitions across the lifecourse should not be ignored when proposing explanations for changes in extended family living among older Japanese. At the same time, changes in living arrangements, independent of changes in mortality and nuptiality, are the primary reason for the decline in the number of years that older Japanese are expected to live with their children. Although life table analysis is a particularly useful tool for understanding the relative importance of these components of aggregate-level change, there are inherent limitations to the information that this approach can provide. First, as a synthetic cohort measure, life expectancy does not represent the experience of any actual group of people. Second, the limited dimensions of published cross-tabulations preclude the incorporation of many substantively interesting characteristics such as health, labor force status, and economic well-being. These limitations can be addressed by examining individual-level data from cross-sectional or panel surveys to estimate regression models for categorical outcomes (i.e., different types of living arrangements). There is a vast body of research employing these techniques to examine the determinants of living arrangements among older individuals in various countries.[10] We follow this line of analysis in the next section to estimate models for the likelihood that Japanese men and women aged 60 and over in 1987 were coresiding with a child.

Individual-Level Correlates of Coresidence

As noted earlier, it has been argued that intergenerational coresidence in Japan has become primarily a strategic arrangement that commences with deterioration in the health of aging parents or with the death of one parent. This view suggests the importance of health and marital status as individual-level predictors of coresidence with older, less healthy, widowed elderly more likely to be living with adult children. Some support for these conjectures can be found in previous analyses of living arrangements (Kojima 1989; Martin and Tsuya 1991; Tsuya and Martin 1992; Kurosu 1994).

Attitudes toward coresidence and family obligations are a potentially important correlate of living arrangements that cannot easily be incorporated in demographic analyses. In aggregate analyses such as those presented above, it is difficult, if not impossible, to measure attitudes in a meaningful way. Most previous studies of the individual-level correlates of living arrangements at older ages have typically relied on crude proxies of attitudes such as educational attainment and area of residence (i.e., urban versus rural). Older Japanese with more education and those living in urban areas are thought to be less supportive of traditional family norms and therefore less likely to coreside with children (Kojima 1989, 1990; Tsuya and Martin 1992). Region of residence is also thought to reflect normative environment, with residents of Tōhoku and Hokuriku the most likely to coreside net of other factors, and residents of Kyūshū the least likely (Shimizu 1984, 1985).

Economic well-being, another hypothesized correlate of living arrangements, has typically been measured by home ownership and income, if data are available. As noted earlier, housing is thought to be a valuable asset that older individuals can exchange for tacit promises of care from coresident children. Previous studies have confirmed that home ownership has a strong positive relationship to the likelihood of coresidence. The expected effect of income is less clear. On the one hand, financial assets could also be exchanged for tacit promises of care, but on the other hand, greater assets eliminate one of the most pressing sources of concern for older Japanese. Some analyses have found that an elderly individual's (or couple's) income is positively related to the likelihood of coresidence (Ohtake 1991; Yashiro 1993) whereas others have found a negative relationship (Andō, Yamashita, and Murayama 1986). Educational attainment has also been viewed as a proxy for economic need, with the least educated elderly assumed to be less likely to possess the financial resources necessary for maintaining an independent household (e.g., Bumpass 1990).

In this section, we use data from one of the only publicly available sources of individual-level information on older Japanese, the National Survey of the Japanese Elderly, to examine these hypothesized correlates of the likelihood of coresiding with a child. This survey, conducted by the University of Michigan and the Tokyo Metropolitan Institute of Gerontology in November of 1987, contains information on 2,220 noninstitutionalized Japanese over the age of 60.[11]

Based on the household rosters collected in the survey, we classify respondents into two groups: those coresiding with a child and those not coresiding. Because we are interested in the correlates of coresidence, we exclude 118 respondents who reported no living children and were thus not at risk of coresidence. Based on the resulting sample of 1,882 observations, we estimate logistic regression models with a dichotomous classification of living arrangements (i.e., coresiding=1, not coresiding=0) as the dependent variable.[12] We estimate two models: one which includes only demographic characteristics (age, sex, marital status, health, and number of children) and one which adds several of the socioeconomic and geographic variables discussed above (educational attainment, occupational status, home ownership, area of residence, and region of residence).

Results

Before examining our results, we first describe the distribution of the sample with respect to the variables included in our models and present the bivariate relationships between these variables and coresidence. The characteristics of the sample are presented in the first column of Table 2.5. Sixty-four percent of the respondents in our sample were coresiding with a child in 1987, the same figure calculated by Hirosima (1998) for ages 65 and over using 1985 census data. The figures in this column further indicate that the majority of the respondents were married, not working, in good health, had three or more living children, lived in urban areas, and owned their own homes. For each category of each of these variables, the second column presents the proportion of respondents who were coresiding with a child at the time of the survey. We can see, for example, that women (67%) were slightly more likely than men (59%) to be living with a child and that, not surprisingly, the proportion coresiding increases with age. We can also see that, relative to other categories, the prevalence of coresidence is highest among the widowed, those with three or more children, the least educated, those working in family businesses, home owners, rural residents, and residents of Tōhoku and Hokuriku. The prevalence of coresidence does not differ greatly by health status as we have defined it.[13]

The results of the logistic regression models are presented in the third and fourth columns of Table 2.5 in the form of odds ratios. Odds ratios represent the odds of coresidence for a given category of an explanatory variable relative to the odds of coresidence for the reference category for that variable (the odds ratio for reference categories is thus 1.0). As in the bivariate analyses, the results of Model 1 indicate that women were slightly (5%) more likely to be coresiding than men and that the likelihood of coresidence increases with age. However, these differences are not statistically significant. The only significant correlates of coresidence in this model are number of children and marital status. Older Japanese with three or more children were 1.5 times more likely than those with only one child to be coresiding with a child in 1987. Relative to those with spouse present, divorced or separated elderly were 38 percent more likely to be living with a child while widowed elderly were twice as likely to be coresiding. These coefficients for marital status are therefore consistent with survey evidence suggesting that many Japanese plan to initiate coresidence when one parent dies. Our results are not consistent, however, with survey evidence indicating a desire to initiate coresidence when one parent becomes disabled or ill. The coefficients for functional status indicate that respondents with functional limitations are not significantly more likely than their healthier counterparts to be coresiding. Previous analyses based on different data have also reached this same, somewhat surprising, conclusion (e.g., Kojima 1989).

Model 2 adds several socioeconomic and geographic variables thought to be related to coresidence. The inclusion of these variables reverses the sign of the coefficient for sex, attenuates the association between age and coresidence, and strengthens the effect of being separated or divorced. All of the socioeconomic and geographic variables are significantly associated with the odds of coresiding. Home owners were 3.6 times (i.e., $1/0.28 = 3.6$) more likely than non-owners to be living with a child and respondents with less than six years of education were up to twice as likely as respondents with ten or more years of education to be coresiding. Relative to employed elderly, those in family businesses were also

Table 2.5: Correlates of Coresidence: Crosstabulations and Odds Ratios

Variable	Pct. of Sample	Pct. Coresiding	Odds Ratios Model 1	Odds Ratios Model 2
Living Arrangements				
Coresiding	63.69			
Not Coresiding	36.31			
Sex				
Male†	45.53	59.39	1.00	1.00
Female	54.47	67.28	1.05	0.97
Age				
60–64†	30.88	57.23	1.00	1.00
65–69	23.73	62.15	1.07	1.07
70–74	22.96	66.53	1.18	1.03
75–79	13.78	69.69	1.29	1.12
80–84	6.77	72.34	1.31	1.07
85+	1.87	79.49	1.90	1.67
Marital Status				
Married†	63.93	57.78	1.00	1.00
Divorced/Separated	2.93	65.57	1.38	2.20**
Widowed	33.14	74.93	2.00**	2.49**
Functional Status				
No Limitations†	74.64	62.48	1.00	1.00
Some Limitations	15.90	64.65	0.89	1.04
Major Limitations	9.46	71.57	1.11	1.15
Number of Living Children				
One†	13.98	59.45	1.00	1.00
Two	25.22	55.81	0.97	0.98
Three or More	60.81	67.93	1.49**	1.45**
Educational Attainment				
0–6 Years†	25.59	70.94		1.00
7–9 Years	40.56	66.43		1.07
10–12 Years	24.72	56.45		0.71**
13–14 Years	5.70	51.69		0.52**
15+ Years	3.43	47.89		0.54**
Occupational Status				
Working	25.61	61.54		1.00
Family Business	2.26	82.98		2.06*
Not Working†	72.13	63.89		0.97

continued on next page

Table 2.5 *(Continued)*

Variable	Pct. of Sample	Pct. Coresiding	Odds Ratios Model 1	Odds Ratios Model 2
Home Ownership				
Own Home†	83.98	68.18		1.00
Don't Own Home	16.02	39.46		0.28**
Region				
Hokkaidō	4.80	52.00		0.43**
Tōhoku	9.46	80.71		1.52*
Kantō†	24.06	64.27		1.00
Chūbu	20.32	74.47		1.24
Kansai	15.47	56.52		0.65**
Chūgoku	7.93	60.61		0.64*
Shikoku	4.33	66.67		0.77
Kyūshū	13.64	47.89		0.39**
Type of Area				
City†	69.12	61.29		1.00
Town/Village	30.88	69.05		1.21*
N	2,082	2,082	2,082	2,061
			−1.319	−1,199
Log Likelihood (df)			(12)	(27)

*p<.05, **p<.10, †omitted category in Models 1 and 2

twice as likely to be living with a child. Tōhoku residents had a significantly higher likelihood of coresiding than residents of the reference region, Kantō, whereas residents of Hokkaidō, Kansai, and Kyūshū were significantly less likely to be living with a child. Independent of these regional differences, rural residents were slightly (1.2 times) more likely than their urban counterparts to be living with a child. These results are consistent with both cultural and economic explanations of living arrangements. The higher probability of coresidence in certain geographic regions and in smaller towns and villages, along with the lower probability of coresidence among the more educated, is consistent with hypotheses that more "modern" ideas are associated with a reduced likelihood of coresidence. The higher probability of coresidence among home owners is consistent with hypotheses of tacit exchanges between generations.[14]

Unfortunately, the cross-sectional nature of the data available to us preclude analysis of temporal change in the relationship between coresidence and its correlates. If, however, we are willing to make the assumption that the relationships presented in the final two columns of Table 2.5 are relatively stable over time, inferences can be made about reasons for past declines in coresidence as well as the likelihood that the prevalence of extended family residence will continue to decline. Because the elderly population is comprised of successive cohorts whose characteristics (e.g., educational attainment, number of children, and main occupation) are either known or can be reasonably estimated, information about compositional change in the elderly population, in combination with the results in Table 2.5, can provide insight into the mechanisms behind changing living arrangements. For example, the negative relationship between educational attainment and coresidence in Model 2 suggests that declines in coresidence may be partly explained by the progression of successively better educated cohorts into the older population. Similar reasoning suggests that the increasing representation of intact married couples has also contributed to the decline in coresidence, a conclusion for which our decomposition analysis provides empirical justification. The results of Model 2 also suggest the possibility that urbanization, declines in self-employment, and declining fertility have contributed to lower proportions of older Japanese living with their children. To the extent that the baby boom cohort (born 1947–49) and subsequent cohorts have fewer children, more education, and are less likely to be either self-employed or living in rural areas, this line of reasoning also suggests the possibility of further declines in coresidence as these cohorts join the elderly population. Kojima (1989), among others, uses this logic of cohort succession in combination with models based on cross-sectional data to arrive at similar conclusions.

Summary and Discussion

With the baby-boom cohort now passing age 50, Japan is preparing for an unprecedentedly rapid increase in its elderly population. Searching for ways to help defray the costs of providing adequate levels of financial and physical support for rapidly growing numbers of dependent elderly, policy makers have come to view Japan's traditionally high levels of extended family residence as a potentially invaluable resource. This emphasis on intrafamilial support is a cornerstone of what has been promoted as a "Japanese style welfare society" (*nihongata fukushi shakai*) (Campbell 1992; Ogawa 1997). In this context, the substantial declines over the past twenty years in the proportion of older Japanese coresiding with their children is a subject of considerable interest.

Of the many possible explanations for this change, we have focused our attention on the role of demographic factors. In the first section, our decomposition analysis based on marital status-household type life tables indicated that changes in mortality and marital status transition rates are related to changes over time in the number of years that older Japanese expect to live in different types of households. We showed, for example, that an increase in the likelihood of never marrying contributed to the decline in coresident life expectancy for men while the decline in coresident life expectancy for women would have been even greater had mortality and nuptiality not changed over the twenty year period. These results are informative in showing the effects of changes in mortality, nuptiality, and living arrangements on changes in the number of years older Japanese expect to live in different types of households. They offer little guidance, however, in developing a substantive understanding of why coresident life expectancy has declined (i.e., why living arrangement distributions have changed). With nearly all of the decline in coresident life expectancy between 1975 and 1995 due to other factors independent of changes in mortality and nuptiality, results of the decomposition exercise are consistent with the many explanations of declining coresidence that focus on the importance of economic, normative, and social factors related to the desirability and feasibility of coresiding.

Rigorously differentiating among the many hypotheses that have been put forth would require either aggregate data cross-classified by far more variables than are available from the census or individual-level data covering a substantial period of time. Neither are currently available. In an attempt to further examine the role of demographic variables and to shed light on the relative importance of different socioeconomic variables, we used one of the few publicly available sources of individual-level data on older Japanese to estimate models for the likelihood that men and women over age 60 were coresiding with a child in 1987. The results of these models showed that, while some demographic characteristics (e.g., number of children and marital status) are important correlates of coresidence, socioeconomic and geographic variables such as educational attainment, home ownership, and region of residence are the primary predictors of which older Japanese live with their children. Assuming that these relationships are relatively stable over time, changes in the composition of the elderly population through cohort succession suggest that the decline in the prevalence of extended family living among older Japanese is likely to continue.

Notes

1. Ogawa and Retherford (1997) demonstrate a convergence between the proportion of married couples coresiding with husband's parents and the proportion coresiding with wife's parents as well as a relative decline in the proportion of first sons coresiding with parents. Both of these trends are suggestive of changes in the meaning of coresidence.

2. In order to distinguish between changes in own-sex mortality and changes in opposite-sex mortality, we choose to view changes in the likelihood of widowhood as changes in nuptiality (i.e., marital status transitions) rather than as changes in mortality.

3. Effects of changes in kin availability will be subsumed in the effects of changes in living arrangements and a residual category.

4. Life tables are also the source of many commonly cited demographic figures such as life expectancy, the total fertility rate, and the probability that a marriage will end in divorce.

5. For a formal explanation of marital status life tables and their uses, see Schoen and Nelson (1974), Schoen (1975), or Willikens (1987).

6. The term synthetic cohort (or hypothetical cohort) refers to the fact that, because they are based on cross-sectional data, life tables do not describe the lives of any "real" cohort. Rather, they describe what the life of a hypothetical cohort would look like if its members' age-specific behavior mirrored that of the various cohorts observed in the cross-section.

7. The fourth factor which we label "other" represents the interaction effect of the other three factors and is calculated as the difference between the observed change in life expectancy between 1975 and 1995 and the sum of the differences calculated based on the three counterfactual sets of life expectancies for 1995 (e.g., Kitagawa 1955; Smith 1992).

8. An important limitation of these data is the inability to distinguish households occupying the same structure or the same plot of land. Residents of two-household homes (*nisetai jūtaku*) will be classified as not coresiding although such arrangements probably do not differ substantially from coresidence in terms of intergenerational care provision.

9. Because a very small part of expected remaining life at age 65 and above is spent divorced and because the crosstabulations of household type by marital status in the 1975 census collapse widowed and divorced into one category, we do the same in this study.

10. See Wolf (1994) for a survey of recent literature.

11. Four subsequent waves of data have been collected (in 1990, 1993, 1996, and 1999), but are not yet available for public use.

12. Similar analyses have been conducted using different sources of data (Kojima 1989; Tsuya and Martin 1992; Ogawa 1997; Ogawa and Retherford 1997).

13. We define health status to represent the presence and severity of difficulties with eight activities of daily living (ADLs). Respondents were asked whether they had difficulty with a set of eight activities and, if so, how much difficulty. We have collapsed the responses into three categories: those having no difficulty with any activity, those having some difficulty with one or more activity, those having major difficulty with one or more activity.

14. Of course, it is possible that some respondents may have already transferred ownership of their homes to their coresident children, suggesting that the estimated effect of home-ownership is a conservative one.

References

Andō, Albert, Michiko Yamashita, and Atsuyoshi Murayama. 1986. Raifu Saikuru Kasetsu ni Motozuku Shōhi—Chochiku no Kōdō Bunseki [Analysis of consumption and saving behavior based on the life cycle hypothesis]. *Keizai Bunseki* [Economic Analysis] 101: 25–139.

Bumpass, Larry. 1990. A comparative analysis of coresidence and contact with parents in Japan and the United States. NSFH Working Paper no. 41. Madison: Center for Demography and Ecology, University of Wisconsin.

Campbell, John C. 1992. *How policies change*. Princeton, N.J.: Princeton University Press.

Council on Population Problems. 1991. *Nihon no Jinkō—Nihon no Kazoku* [The Japanese population—The Japanese Family]. Tokyo: Tōyō Keizai Shimpōsha.

Economic Planning Agency. 1994. *Kokumin Seikatsu Hakusho: Heisei 6* (White paper on the national life: 1994]. Tokyo: Ōkurashō Insatsukyoku.

Hirosima, Kiyosi. 1987. Recent change in prevalence of parent-child coresidence in Japan. *Jinkōgaku Kenkyū* [Journal of Population Studies] 10: 33–41.

———. 1997. Projection of living arrangements of the elderly in Japan: 1990–2010. *Genus* 53: 79–111.

———. 1998. Kōreisha no Setai Jōtai Henka no Yōin Bunkai: 1975–1990. [A decomposition of household status transitions of (Japanese) elderly]. *Keizai Kagaku Ronshū* 24: 1–41.

Hofferth, Sandra L. 1987. Recent trends in the living arrangements of children: A cohort life table analysis. In *Family demography,* edited by John Bongaarts, Thomas Burch, and Kenneth Wachter. Oxford: Clarendon Press.

Ikenoue, Masako, and Shigesato Takahashi. 1994. Kekkon no Tasō Seimeihyō [Multi-state marriage life tables]. *Jinkō Mondai Kenkyū* [Journal of Population Problems] 50: 73–96.

Kendig, Hal. 1989. Social change and family dependency in old age: Perceptions of Japanese women in middle age. NUPRI Research Paper Series no. 54. Tokyo: Nihon University Population Research Institute.

Kitagawa, Evelyn. 1955. Components of a difference between two rates. *Journal of the American Statistical Association* 50: 1168–94.

Kojima, Hiroshi. 1989. Intergenerational household extension in Japan. In *Ethnicity and the new family economy: Living arrangements and intergenerational financial flows,* edited by Frances K. Goldscheider and Calvin Goldscheider. Boulder, CO: Westview Press.

———. 1990. Correlates of postnuptial coresidence in Japan. IPP Working Paper Series no. 4. Tokyo: Institute of Population Problems, Ministry of Health and Welfare.

Kōno, Shigemi. 1996. Demographic aspects of population aging in Japan. In *Aging in Japan 1996,* edited by Japan Aging Research Center. Tokyo: Japan Aging Research Center.

Kurosu, Satomi. 1994. Who lives in the extended family and why? The case of Japan. In *Tradition and Change in the Asian Family,* edited by Lee-Jay Cho and Moto Yada. Honolulu, Hawaii: East-West Center.

Liang, Jersey, and Daisaku Maeda. 1997. National Survey of the Japanese Elderly, 1987 (computer file). ICPSR version. Tokyo: Tokyo Metropolitan Institute of Gerontology. Ann Arbor, MI: Inter-University Consortium for Political and Social Research.

Liu, Xian, Jersey Liang, Naoko Muramatsu, and Hidehiro Sugisawa. 1995. Transitions in functional status and active life expectancy among older people in Japan. *Journal of Gerontology* 50B: S383–S394.

Livi-Bacci, Massimo. 1982. Social and biological aging: Contradictions of development. *Population and Development Review* 8: 771–81.

Maeda, Daisaku. 1996. Social security, health care, and social services for the elderly in Japan. In *Aging in Japan 1996,* edited by Japan Aging Research Center. Tokyo: Japan Aging Research Center.

Maeda, Daisaku, and Youmei Nakatani. 1992. Family care of the elderly in Japan. In *Family care of the elderly: Social and cultural changes,* edited by Jordan I. Kosberg. Newbury Park, Calif.: Sage Publications.

Martin, Linda G. 1989. The graying of Japan. *Population Bulletin* 44: 1–42.

Martin, Linda G., and Suzanne Culter. 1983. Mortality decline and Japanese family structure. *Population and Development Review* 9: 633–49.

Martin, Linda G., and Noriko O. Tsuya. 1991. Interactions of middle-aged Japanese with their parents. *Population Studies* 45: 299–311.

Ministry of Health and Welfare. 1987. *Kōsei Hakusho: Shōwa 62* [White paper on health and welfare: 1987]. Tokyo: Kōsei Tōkei Kyōkai.

———. 1992. *Kokumin Seikatsu Kisō Chōsa* [Basic survey on the national life]. Tokyo: Kōsei Tōkei Kyōkai.

Morgan, S. Philip, and Kiyosi Hirosima. 1983. The persistence of extended family living in Japan: Anachronism or alternative strategy? *American Sociological Review* 48: 269–81.

Naoi, Michiko. 1996. *Kōreisha to Kazoku* [The elderly and the family]. Tokyo: Saiensusha.

National Institute of Population and Social Security Research. 1997. *Population projections for Japan: 1996–2100.* Tokyo: Author.

Ogawa, Naohiro. 1982. Economic implications of Japan's ageing population. *International Labour Review* 121: 17–33.

———. 1989. Population ageing and its impact upon health resource requirements at government and familial levels in Japan. *Ageing and Society* 9: 383–405.

———. 1997. Jinkō Hendō kara Mita Kazoku no Seikatsu Hoshō Kinō no Henyō [Population Change and Changes in Family Support Mechanisms] In *Kōreika Shakai no Seikatsu Hoshō Shisutemu* [Support Systems in an Aging Society], edited by Naohiro Yashiro. Tokyo: Tokyo Daigaku Shuppankai.

Ogawa, Naohiro, and John F. Ermisch. 1996. Family structure, home time demands, and the employment patterns of Japanese married women. *Journal of Labor Economics* 14: 677–702.

Ogawa, Naohiro, and Robert W. Hodge. 1994. Patrilocality, childbearing, and the labour supply and earning power of married Japanese women. In *The family, the market, and the state in ageing societies*, edited by John F. Ermisch and Naohiro Ogawa. Oxford: Clarendon Press.

Ogawa, Naohiro, and Robert D. Retherford. 1993. Care of the elderly in Japan: Changing norms and expectations. *Journal of Marriage and the Family* 55: 585–97.

———. 1997. Shifting costs of caring for the elderly back to families in Japan: Will it work? *Population and Development Review* 23: 59–94.

Ohtake, Fumio. 1991. Bequest motives of aged households in Japan. *Ricerche Economiche* 45: 283–306.

Preston, Samuel H., and Shigemi Kōno. 1988. Trends in well-being of children and the elderly in Japan. In *The vulnerable,* edited by John P. Palmer, Timothy Smeeding, and Barbara B. Torrey. Washington D.C.: Urban Institute Press.

Retherford, Robert D., Naohiro Ogawa, and Satomi Sakamoto. 1996. Values and fertility change in Japan. *Population Studies* 50: 5–25.

Schoen, Robert. 1975. Constructing increment-decrement life tables. *Demography* 12: 313–24.

Schoen, Robert, and Verne E. Nelson. 1974. Marriage, divorce, and mortality: A life table analysis. *Demography* 11: 267–90.

Shimizu, Hiroaki. 1984. Kōreika Shakai ni okeru Kazoku Keitai no Chiikisei [Regional differences in family structure in an aging society]. *Jinkō Mondai Kenkyū* [Journal of Population Problems] 7: 41–47.

————. 1985. Regional differences in family structure. *Jinkōgaku Kenkyū* [Journal of Population Studies] 176: 33–37.

Smith, David P. 1992. *Formal demography.* New York: Plenum Press.

Management and Coordination Agency. 1982, 1987. *Rōjin no Seikatsu to Ishiki ni kansuru Kokusai Hikaku Chōsa* [International survey on the lifestyle and attitudes of the elderly]. Tokyo: Ōkurashō Insatsukyoku.

Tsuya, Noriko O., and Minja Kim Choe. 1991. Changes in Intrafamilial Relationships and the Roles of Women in Japan and Korea. NUPRI Research Paper Series no. 58. Tokyo: Nihon University Population Research Institute.

Tsuya, Noriko O., and Linda G. Martin. 1992. Living arrangements of elderly Japanese and attitudes toward inheritance. *Journal of Gerontology* 47: S45–S54.

Watkins, Susan C., Jane A. Menken, and John Bongaarts. 1987. Demographic foundations of family change. *American Sociological Review* 52: 346–58.

Willekens, Frans. 1987. The marital status life table. In *Family demography,* edited by John Bongaarts, Thomas Burch, and Kenneth Wachter. Oxford: Clarendon Press.

Wolf, Douglas A. 1994. The elderly and their kin: Patterns of availability and access. In *Demography of aging,* edited by Linda G. Martin and Samuel H. Preston. Washington, D.C.: National Academy Press.

Yashiro, Naohiro. 1993. Kōreisha Setai no Keizaiteki Chii [The economic position of elderly households]. *Nihon Keizai Kenkyū* [JCER Economic Journal] 25: 34–57.

———. 1997. The economic position of the elderly in Japan. In *The Economic Effects of Aging in the United States and Japan,* edited by Michael D. Hurd and Naohiro Yashiro. Chicago: University of Chicago Press.

Zeng, Yi. 1991. Family dynamics in China: A life table analysis. Madison: University of Wisconsin Press.

3

Under One Roof: The Evolving Story of Three Generation Housing in Japan

Naomi Brown

The aim of this chapter is twofold: to discuss the changes that have occurred to the composition of private family homes in Japan and to analyze the discourse that accompanied these changes. The 1980s saw the rise and widespread adoption of a new form of housing in Japan embodied in the term *nisetai jūtaku*—two household family homes. This form of housing is designed to accommodate two related couples, where one is the parent couple and the other an adult child couple, under the same roof but with separate facilities for both. In the process of developing the new houses, housing companies noticed that more consumers were expressing a preference for living with their daughter's, as opposed to their son's, family. The latter combination was the more usual one, which accorded with the predominant prewar practice of patrilineal succession and inheritance. However, the abolition of the legal obligations of this system and the rise of nuclear families in the postwar period meant that although such a system may have remained the ideal it was no longer enforced; the "ideal" was ripe for reinterpretation to suit the changing times. As a consequence of the successful marketing of the housing companies' products, the financial incentives behind the choice of a *nisetai jūtaku*, and the reinterpretation of Japanese traditions to make the choice seem suitable to the society, the prefabricated housing companies have become a dominant force in the housing industry, and more elderly people are living with their children than ever before.[1]

Demographic trends have been a major stimulus to the prefabricated housing companies. In 1996 there were 13.6 million households in Japan with persons aged 65 and over, constituting 31 percent of all households in Japan.[2] These numbers were set to further increase as the aging of the population continued along its predicted course. For those in the business of providing special facilities for the elderly in the home, times were looking up even if the rest of the country was in recession. Their business acumen and resulting actions have had a direct effect on the way in which many Japanese families live today in terms of family structure and living patterns. It has also meant that standards of housing have risen such that it is now possible for the elderly, and incapacitated, to live in the comfort and safety of their own homes supported by the latest technological advances.

The Ethnography

The information in this chapter is drawn from research conducted on Japanese families over a course of fifteen years (commencing in 1985) during which I spent a part of nearly every year living and working in Japan. It was during this time that I was able to observe the changing family structures of several families in Tokyo, from the addition of a third, and occasionally fourth, generation to the retirement and death of the first generation members. Living with the families, on a rotating homestay basis, afforded an insider's view of the issues facing them at the various stages of the family's life cycle as they had to deal with the problems of finding an adequate living space for the growing numbers of family members as well as how to take care of the aging members.

Between 1992–94, I worked as a researcher and member of the sales teams of several housing companies that offered house designs capable of accommodating three or four generations of the same family within the same house. One of the marketing techniques used by the companies was to make an in-depth study of the customer by way of interviews with individual members of the family and visits to their existing home or homes (in cases where the married generations lived apart but were intending to live together again in their new home). Their intensive investigations were conducted in order to design a new kind of house that would be suitable for the family concerned. These interviews would be led by a main salesman, but a female member of the sales division would assist him in the discussions concerning the interior design. Together, they would both establish a connection with the family that would continue for at least a year beyond the completion of the house with visits to the new house as part of an after-sales service and information-collecting exercise. On average, sixty hours of interviews took place for each house sold; after-sales interviews with the families in their new homes averaged ten hours over the first year. A good salesman could work on six houses per month and a female assistant on twice that number.

In addition to the information collected from interviews that were specifically for the purpose of designing their new house, many of the families allowed me to stay with them. My objective was to discover what lifestyle they were leading before they moved to the new house, what "behind-the-scene" discussions were taking place without the presence of the housing company representatives, and to follow them through into their new house to see if their expectations were met. At first, I was surprised at the enthusiasm of the families to have me among their number especially as their old houses were often at an advanced stage of deterioration and space was at a premium—two of the main reasons they were considering a change. However, it soon became clear that the decision to build a new house was of such overriding importance to the family, they were keen to discuss the issue as much as possible; any initial embarrassment they might have had with regard to the state of their current home was soon dispelled once they began to describe the splendors of the house to be. Second, it often appeared that my presence acted as a legitimate reason for the members to voice an opinion on a subject that they might otherwise have had difficulty broaching, such as the expectations the older members had of their children. Once the move to the new house had taken place, it was to be at least several months before the cracks in the relationships began to appear; following these developments proved interesting, particularly as the family now rarely had the housing company representatives around to act as "family counselor" in the way they had at the start of the proceedings.

The Aging Population

If one is to believe the literature promoted by the private housing companies and supported by various government research bodies, the "ideal" Japanese society is composed of families that are self-sufficient in terms of taking care of themselves.[3] This means that rather than depending on the state to look after them as they grow old, responsibility for the older generation should fall upon the younger members of their own family. Thus the "ideal" family consists of two or three generations living in one house. Numerous mutual benefits are supposed to accrue from such an arrangement.

For example, the older person is able to fulfill a popular ambition which is "to die in one's own bed" (as opposed to a bed in a hospital or some other place). The younger person, on the other hand, is able to gain from the experience and knowledge of their elders who are steeped in a culture, which is periodically seen to be under threat from the encroaching Westernization of Japanese society. There are other aspects to the ideal as well, which each family has to consider. For example, the literature repeats a well-known sentiment that the individual should not have to rely on the state but should be supported, first and foremost, by their own family. Letting an older person depend upon outside help is seen not only as a failure on the part of that person to secure their own future while they were still able to, but also as a failure on the part of the younger generations in the family for not taking on the responsibility of looking after their own flesh and blood. However, although these ideals are used to shame those who do not follow them, it is apparent that the public condemnation of such antisocial behavior has not been strong enough to deter the deviation away from them.

The number of elderly persons living at home has been increasing alongside the general rise in the number of elderly persons in Japan.[4] In fact, elderly households have been increasing twice as fast as all other households and will continue to do so at a quicker rate in the future. There are three main types of household structures in which these elderly persons reside. In 1996, 17.4 percent were living on their own (i.e., in single-person households); 25 percent were living as a couple (where one or both are aged over 65); and, 45.4 percent were living with their children, of which 13.6 percent were living with their unmarried children and 31.8 percent were living with their married child or children.[5] Although the number of those living on their own or as a married couple have increased steadily, the majority of households were multi-generational, and just over half of all elderly people were living with their children.[6]

These statistics on continued coresidence excited the housing industry. This was an area in which they thought they could find a new market because they could tailor their prefabricated houses to the tastes of both generations within the same house. An example of this would be to offer a Japanese style of house, complete with tatami, sliding doors, and soft wooden furnishings on the lower level, while creating a bright, Western-style apartment on the second level. To further appeal to the sense that the new house would be perfectly in tune with the family's needs, the housing salesmen learned to make increasing use of new computer software packages that enabled them to plan a house that followed the geomantic principles seen in more traditional architecture.[7] Alongside the development of new products for sale, however, was the creation of a marketing strategy to justify the necessity for such goods.

The debate over Japan's aging society, which was becoming increasingly publicized towards the end of the 1980s, caught the attention of those in business looking for new markets for expansion in the domestic economy. They noted that the focus of the discourse was on Japan's social welfare system and whether it would be able to cope with the increasing demands being placed upon it. The supply of homes for the elderly, special institutions and hospital beds appeared completely out of balance with the anticipated demand. Yet this could not have been a sudden social phenomenon. Indeed, the government would have been aware of the figures since at least the 1970s census. Nothing concrete was proposed then and, even after the increased politicization of the debate twenty years later, it appeared that not much in the area of institutional care was being done either. Instead, the emphasis turned towards the responsibility of the family in taking care of itself. The elderly, it was argued, should depend upon family members first and choose to live at home before thinking of alternatives. To help with the care of the sick and infirm, the government stepped up its program to provide home-helpers and to improve and increase day care facilities for each neighborhood. At the same time it responded positively to suggestions from the prefabricated housing industry that they could play a significant role in providing suitable houses to encourage the family to depend on itself.

The way in which the prefabricated housing companies managed to get their houses for the elderly on to the market parallels the story behind the emergence of the industry. The key aspects of the companies' achievement include accurate readings of the direction of government social policy, careful negotiations with governmental bodies to gain special concessions and to create financial incentives for the consumer, and well-devised marketing strategies to launch the new products.

Two Generation Housing

Prefabricated housing companies have existed in Japan since the early postwar period, offering factory-built unit houses as an alternative to the more common wooden structures put together by local neighborhood construction companies (the *kōmuten*). It was not until the early 1980s, however, that the industry gained sufficient government approval to market their increasingly sophisticated prefabrication techniques and house models. They accomplished this by demonstrating to various government bodies that their houses would benefit two key areas of society: first, the improvement in housing quality and, second, the restoration of traditional social values that had weakened in recent years.

The issue of housing quality was a major concern in the 1980s. Almost anything had to be better than the poor, wooden-frame buildings erected after the war: the country was trying to pick itself up after defeat in the war, building material was scarce, and the attitude at the time placed the comfort of domestic housing low on the list of priorities. These weakening structures could not withstand the march of time for much longer. Advances in technology also meant that families wanted to take advantage of the sophisticated appliances now available, such as large gas stoves, electric heating, air-conditioning, and Western toilets and beds. Many of these did not fit well into the old house designs, whereas others, such as the new unit baths, could not be accommodated at all due to the advanced plumbing and electrical requirements necessary for their installment. The technological arguments had been won with relative ease. The Ministry of Construction had little hesitation in approving earthquake proof, fireproof, durable, and attractive house models. This was helped by the system in Japan that makes good use of its retired officials by placing them in directorships of large corporations. It was not a coincidence that the housing companies managed to secure their fair share of ex-officials from the departments and ministries with whom they were negotiating.

The second argument that the housing companies had to win in order to secure needed laws concerning construction rights and tax relief measures took more explanation. The task of housing the elderly offered the companies a powerful rhetorical basis for justifying their product to the state—the reunification of the extended family under one roof. In the process, the companies had to show that what they were offering was something that would contribute to society and be accepted by it. The increasing number of elderly persons living at home needed special functions to cater to their needs. Moreover, ideologically, the suggestion of a return to the "traditional" extended family responded to increasing concerns within the wider society.

The housing companies argued that the Japanese people needed to regain their faith in the family as the core of society. They suggested that their houses, by bringing back the union of the generations, could help relieve many of the burdens being placed upon contemporary society: the increasing number of elderly persons with no one to look after them due to the proliferation of the nuclear family; the changing expectations of women who wanted and needed to continue working outside of the home upon marriage as an expression of independence as well as financial necessity; and the disaffected youth whose numbers dropping out of school, causing violent incidents at home and at school, were seen to be part of the breakdown of the social fabric of society. Individualism and the nuclear family were targeted as the main causes behind the troubles. The case for a multigenerational house appeared persuasive and to fit in neatly with certain government directives of the time. By carefully wording the definitions that were adopted by the government to describe which houses would benefit from the special tax relief measures, the prefabricated housing companies assured themselves of the dominance of the market, to the detriment of any independent house-builders. This was largely due to factory specifications and technological details that nonprefabricated companies were unable to copy.

In addition to providing the consumer with an approved version of a manufactured house, the housing companies were also able to utilize their strength in size and connections to offer a total package surrounding the purchase of a house. On choosing a housing company, the consumer not only bought into the house product itself but also a whole range of services including advice on the purchase of real estate, financial services covering the entire deal, interior decoration, and "family advice" clinics that counseled families on how they could live harmoniously together. This latter idea, of offering an after-care service to the consumer, developed so quickly and extensively that an entirely new industry was formed to handle the maintenance and extensions of the prefabricated house (known as the "reform" companies).

It was one thing to find a new product to sell; the next stage was how to market that product to the consumer. Much as with any product, the housing companies had to find a suitable angle of sales. As they were dealing with houses, and families live in houses, they adopted a family friendly approach; that is, marketing strategies were developed to appeal to the consumer as a member of a family. At first the concentration was on meeting the demand of nuclear families. These were customers who, on the whole, owned their land but needed to replace their house which was reaching the end of its thirty year or so life. The new products available on the market—electrical items, cookers and so on—were also eyed

with desire. It became apparent, however, that the major landown-
ers belonged to the older generation, that is, a couple with grown
up and married children. The married children tended to live away
from their parents, following the postwar trend to start a new
home upon marriage in an apartment nearer their workplace. The
hurdle the housing companies had to clear was how to persuade
the younger generation that it was in their interest to live with
their parents. The companies accordingly stressed that, by returning to live with their parents, these children would enjoy more for
their money, maximize the land of their parents (by having two
households instead of one on the same property) and provide the
parents with some reassurance that help was near at hand if and
when they should need it.

It had been assumed all along that the older generation would
be willing to share their land and house space with their married
children. This was because the practice in Japan was for the parents to pass on their land after death (rather than, for example,
realizing its gains during their life by taking out reverse mort-
gages, or even selling their house and settling in a service apartment or home for the elderly). However, it soon became clear that
the elderly, who were living longer and beginning to enjoy many
more years after their official retirement, would also need to be
persuaded to forego some of this newly found independence in order to share their home with their children again. The figures that
pointed to the fact that 85 percent of houses with elderly persons
residing in them were privately owned, suggested that the real
power of house ownership lay with the elderly.[8] This meant that,
ultimately, they were the main target group and not their children.
Realizing this, the housing companies soon switched strategies and
started employing persuasive tactics to encourage the elderly to
"think of their future" and to grasp the opportunity of living with
their children before they became too infirm to even think of re-
building their homes.

It had been argued that living with one's children was the
ideal way of life; now, the companies showed that they were aware
that variations in families existed and that they had the right
products to meet that diversity. The *nisetai jūtaku* was a house
model that supposedly catered to the multigenerational family. This
was a model that provided each family with its own house unit,
while still under one roof; the legal obligation was that the two
families had to be related.[9] The degree of separation between the
families could be varied so that house plans might incorporate two
kitchens (one for each household) whereas everything else was

shared, or every room could be duplicated so that the family need never see each other. The stress on the independence of the households was reinforced by the existence of the two front doors; it was left to the family concerned as to the positioning of these side by side, front and back or upstairs and downstairs.

As the idea of the *nisetai jūtaku* spread, the sophistication of the plans on offer was also raised. A main distinction soon developed between those choosing to live with their son's family (*musuko fūfu dōkyo*) and those choosing to live with their daughter's family (*musume fūfu dōkyo*). It was seen that the mother-in-law/daughter-in-law phenomenon would necessitate a clear distinction between the households within the house, so that each would retain their independence. However, from the public perspective, the family would be represented by the one family name and so a "unified" front image had to be offered (one main front gate and door with a separate staircase at the back leading to the younger couple's house upstairs). On the other hand, it was suggested that mothers and daughters would cooperate more easily so that many parts of the house could be shared between the two households affording a more efficient use of space (one main dining and living area for example). Yet, because in most cases the daughter's husband would retain his own name the exterior of the house had to show this difference and, in these cases, two prominent front doors side by side were encouraged.

By the early 1990s, the prefabricated housing industry had managed to capture one-fifth of the housing market in Japan. The industry now constructs, in approximately equal proportions, private apartments as well as detached houses. The market is dominated by ten major housing companies of which Sekisui House, Misawa Home, and Daiwa House are the largest. In 1994, according to these housing companies, approximately one third of their orders were for *nisetai jūtaku*. Those choosing to live with their daughter's families had risen to comprise one half of the *nisetai jūtaku* because such a distinction first started appearing in the past ten years. It appeared that this trend would continue.

Case Studies: Theory versus Reality

The Tanaka family is a typical example of a *nisetai jūtaku* in the *musuko fūfu dōkyo* arrangement. The family started planning their new house in early 1990 with the help of a prefabricated housing company and had moved in by the end of the year. Mr. and Mrs.

Tanaka live downstairs in an interior decorated in the Japanese
style with *tatami* floors and sliding doors, while their son Ken'ichirō's
family live upstairs in a Western arrangement with carpets and
beds. There are two front doors on the ground level, but a staircase
immediately behind Ken'ichirō's front door leads directly up to their
section.

Ken'ichirō and his wife Masako started to consider the idea of
living with Ken'ichirō's parents after their second son reached primary school age. The two-bedroom apartment in which they were
living in Yokohama was getting rather cramped for their growing
family and they knew that the purchase of a bigger home would be
beyond their financial grasp. Masako was also beginning to tire of
making the long journey to see her parents-in-law every week, a
trip of at least one hour by car each way. In general her visits were
just courtesy calls, which she felt obliged to make as the wife of the
first son of the Tanaka's, but she sometimes had to call more frequently when either parent became ill or needed her help in some
way. Ken'ichirō's parents lived in a detached house in Setagaya, a
suburb of Tokyo, and appeared willing to demolish their old building in favor of a new, prefabricated one that would bring the two
families closer together. They seemed to agree that it would be in
their grandsons' best interest to live in a house, as opposed to an
apartment, and they were also pleased that they would be given
the opportunity of passing on some of their knowledge to the new
generation. Their second son and his family were living in Osaka
and it never occurred to them that there might be a problem in the
future over the inheritance of the estate.[10]

In order to accomplish the task of building a house that would
suit both families, the Tanakas decided that a prefabricated housing company might be the most suitable choice. They understood
from the advertising and marketing literature that the company
would be able to maximize the available space with their modern
house designs as well as to provide experience and advice in how
the house plan should be drawn so as to appeal to both generations. In addition, the family also realized that the prefabricated
housing company would be able to secure an advantageous "two
generation loan" to help finance the construction of the house.

The new house was completed in time for the New Year celebrations, an important family event in Japan. Both families appeared to blossom in each other's company and the grandsons, in
particular, enjoyed the traditional treats and activities that their
grandparents lavished on them. After a few months, however, the
initial euphoria had died down. Ken'ichirō and Masako continued

with their lives just as they had done when they had lived in their own apartment. In effect, this meant that Ken'ichirō left early to go to work and returned late so that he was rarely at home. In the meanwhile, Masako kept to her busy social calendar which involved a small circle of her university friends. The only variation to Masako's life was that she did not always need to rush home to meet her sons after school as one or both of their grandparents were usually at home to greet them. For the younger generation, therefore, the *nisetai jūtaku* was working according to plan. The same could not be said for the older generation.

"It's as if we don't exist," "Why did we go to all this trouble to build a *nisetai jūtaku*, it's the same as before when we were living separately," "I am more lonely now than before because people think I am living in a house full of people," "There's no time to enjoy my second life [i.e., life of retirement]." These were some of the comments made by the older Tanaka couple. In fact, rather than gaining from the new arrangement, they felt that they had lost both their space and their personal freedom as the upstairs of their house was no longer available for their use and they felt obliged to be at home for the sake of their grandchildren. Looking ahead to the future, Mrs. Tanaka did admit that her daughter-in-law might prove more helpful if either she or her husband became ill but, for the present, she missed the courtesy calls that Masako used to make every week because they had been times when Masako had made a special effort to be sociable. Now that they were living together, however, Masako hardly popped her head around the door to say hello, let alone stop and have a conversation.

The case of the Tanakas is by no means unique. Ironically, it appears that an increasing number of elderly couples are finding fault with the *reality* of the *nisetai jūtaku* even though the *idea* of the *nisetai jūtaku* was originally devised to appeal to them. In a couple of rare cases, the failure of the new *nisetai jūtaku* home has led to the elderly couple leaving the house and entering an apartment or accommodation catering to the elderly where they feel that they are able to regain some respect and attention.

The root of the problem lies in the fact that the elderly couple expects much more interaction with the younger couple than the latter are willing to provide.[11] Much of this has to do with time: the younger man is often busy at work and spends his leisure time asleep at home. In the past, he may have made the effort to visit his parents and spend time with them but now that they are in the same house, he feels there is less need for actual interaction because he is physically present all the time. Likewise, the younger woman is either busy at work or pursuing her own interests, which often include her children's nonschool activities or meetings with people of her own generation. She may do tasks for the elderly couple, such as shopping, cooking, or running errands for them, which she feels is sufficient demonstration of her respect and, in some cases, even beyond her duty as she is the one with the active life whereas the older generation have "nothing else to do." In fact, many younger women admitted that they purposely avoided getting involved with their mother-in-law's activities because it would be hard to extract themselves at a later date should they wish to do so.

It is the mother-in-law who, ultimately, feels betrayed by the idea of the *nisetai jūtaku*. In the "lead-up" to the building of the house, the housing company's literature emphasized the pleasures of living in a house with one's own children again. For many, this means that the younger married couple are moving back to live with them after several years apart and the older couple are excited at the prospect of the company of their children and grandchildren. The expectation of the mother-in-law is that she will have a companion around the house and that they will share in the management of the household. In reality, what tends to happen is that the older couple is left alone albeit provided for when necessary. To make matters worse, many are expected to act as babysitters on a regular basis when the younger couple goes out; this makes them feel as if they have been taken advantage of when they should be enjoying this free time in the later years of their lives. The younger couple, on the other hand, believes that they are giving their parents the opportunity of being with their grandchildren; they are also making full use of the *nisetai jūtaku* arrangement. Again, the anticipation of the elderly couple in the sharing of their grandchildren was not matched by the reality of being left alone with them.

In most cases, the expectations placed on the *nisetai jūtaku* were bound to lead to disappointment. In order to lure the customer to their company, the initial marketing ploys of the housing companies are pitched far beyond reality, both in what the customer can afford to build and the type of harmonious lifestyle that can be realized.[12] The inexperience of many people in the design and building of these new prefabricated houses results in delusions of grandeur, formed from two dimensional architect's plans and showpiece dream houses, that are shattered upon seeing their own, inevitably smaller and compact, home. Although this is not a complete disaster for those who come to terms with the physical disappointment, the self-delusion over the type of lifestyle they thought they would be leading is harder to face. After all, the *nisetai jūtaku* had promised both the elderly and younger couple that they would be able to live the lifestyles they each wished under the same roof. For many elderly couples, this meant enjoying more time with their children in a manner similar to their own experience thirty or forty years previously; for many younger couples, this meant enjoying their life as a nuclear family unit in a house that they would not have been able to afford on their own, while keeping an eye out for their parents who were now conveniently near. It was inevitable that such opposite viewpoints could not both be satisfied and, in practice, it has most often been the case that the older generation feels the most bitter.

In partial response to the problems being experienced by their consumers, the housing companies have created a new division in the business known as the "reform companies" that physically alter and repair the prefabricated houses. From the company's point of view, the successful realization of the *nisetai jūtaku* lifestyle lies in the structural layout of the house—two housewives under one roof need two kitchens so that each can have their own, independent area of control. Following this line of thought, the companies' natural response to any problems in customers' lifestyles is to apply different structures to the house. But for many consumers caught in the cycle of the housing company's philosophy there may be little escape apart from leaving the house altogether. New consumers, however, may be catching on to the drawbacks and so the companies have quickly turned to new sales strategies to attract their elderly clients.

Housing for the Elderly

After only ten years on the market, the very raison d'être of the *nisetai jūtaku* was under fire. The multigenerational household had to have a stronger reason for being together than the ideal concept of the "happy extended family." It was partly due to the increasing negative feedback from the older generation dissatisfied with their experience in the *nisetai jūtaku* that an adaptation in the marketing strategy started to emphasize the technological improvements made to cater to the elderly at home. It was also quickly calculated that the elderly were, in the majority of cases, the dominant financial partner in the two household relationships, mainly by virtue of their possession of the land the house was on. Thus, it was crucial to cater to their needs if the housing companies were to remain in business.

The realization of the importance of the elderly consumer as a potential growth market also spurred the industry into improving dramatically the sophistication of their houses to cope with the demands of the elderly living at home. Their ability, both perceived and actual, to provide for this section of the population is proving a major consideration in their business strategies for growth and survival in the changing demographics of the consumer market.[13]

Houses aimed specifically at the elderly began to appear in mid-1994. These concentrated on technological innovations that would make living at home much safer as well as more convenient for the elderly person. New design features included leveling the floor between rooms so that the elderly person does not trip on the ridge of the door-frame (especially into the bathroom), making corridors wide enough to take a wheelchair, attaching railings along walls for people to grasp as they walk around the house, making all buttons and switches extra large, and including emergency buttons around the house. A major area of concern is the bathroom; this has been altered so that the elderly person can easily maneuver into and out of the bath or be lifted by an electronic arm. The toilet has also been improved so that it can clean the person while the person is still sitting on it. The installation of these last two items has meant that many elderly, who would otherwise have had to be taken care of in an institution, can now live at home, with a regular visiting nursing unit making house calls where necessary.

"Granny, we've considered your needs!", "Look Granny. We've got big light switches—easy for you to see," "I like living with Granny. She tells us about the old customs." The advertisements, in which the above statements appear were written by the relatively young members of the housing company sales teams, trying hard to show that they were considering the elderly consumer market. In practice, many elderly consumers appreciated the attention that the salesmen paid them, as well as the recognition that they were the ones with the economic power. However, the main complaint that almost always emerged was that the salesman had little real knowledge of house-building and was, therefore, unable to answer many fundamental questions they had to ask. These complaints were well-founded because the salesmen are not technical experts and are only trained in putting together a prefabricated house which, ultimately, has to receive the approval of the in-house architect and engineer. If the elderly consumer had any experience of house-building in the past, it would have been with a local carpenter who would have built the house himself and, therefore, possessed the knowledge to satisfy the consumer.

Another complaint against the company has to do with being told how to live one's life. "He actually told me that I should use the staircase rather than the elevator as this would be good for my health" is how one flabbergasted elderly woman responded after a young salesman had left the house. "He can tell me how to live with my daughter-in-law because they are the same generation, but not how to take care of myself," she continued. In this case, the salesman overstepped the boundary by giving advice on a subject which he obviously knew little about. As the housing companies step away from *nisetai jūtaku* marketing techniques into focusing on housing for the elderly, they are coming to terms with a different market.

It appears that it was acceptable to advise the elderly on lifestyle matters when two generations were involved as the older generation lacked knowledge in this area and were ready to listen to the suggestions of the housing companies on how to cohabit successfully with the younger generation. It also seems that the older generation was ready to leave the construction details of the house to the younger generation. In the case of the *nisetai jūtaku*, in particular, it was the younger generation that contributed a large part of the construction costs and so they assumed the greater responsibility in considering the technical aspects. As the housing companies focus solely on the elderly consumer, however, those consumers are beginning to find a voice, and their demands are those of a different generation from the salesmen responsible for their needs. A more successful approach has been to emphasize the safety features that can be installed in the house and how their use can improve the lifestyle of the elderly.

The housing companies continue to stress the lifestyle aspects of their prefabricated houses in their marketing strategies, but the trend has been toward day-to-day improvements rather than ideological arguments that have proved hard to win. In order to cater to the burgeoning elderly market, the way that prefabricated houses can improve their living conditions is the main selling point; whether this is achieved in a *nisetai jūtaku* arrangement or not is no longer the priority.

Conclusion

The rise of the prefabricated housing industry in the postwar era of Japan's history so closely mirrors the pattern of the society at a

given time that it is often difficult to distinguish whether it is
responding to the demand or creating it. The houses sold have
ranged from cheap, standard model structures catering to the postwar nuclear family to the fully automated, Western-influenced
designs specially created to match the daily movements of the
members of a multigenerational family. It is clear from the variety
of models the industry has offered over the years that Japanese
families, as consumers, react very quickly to the latest change.
This leaves one wondering whether the latest movement portrays
a knee-jerk reaction to the latest trend or a long-term shift in
behavior. Whatever the house type of the day may be, the growth
pattern of the prefabricated housing companies has been following
an increasingly steep upward curve as the industry matures and
becomes more aware of its potential strengths. At the same time,
it is quickly learning how to change its rhetoric in order to match
the ever-changing trends of the consumer market. In the space of
a little over a decade, housing salesmen have learned how to utilize, and in some ways direct, the country's prolific output of data
and academic research with regard to Japanese families and their
lifestyles. The "ideal" house has developed from being one in which
three generations can live happily to one in which the elderly can
be safe and comfortable. The industry has had to consider and
react to the socioeconomic and political environment in which it
first appeared in order to survive; thus far it has proven a quick
learner. But it is the demographic circumstances of the country
today, and of the future, that may determine the long-run success
of this fledgling industry.

Notes

1. The main research for this chapter was conducted in Japan between 1992–94 under the auspices of the Ministry of Education (Monbushō)
and the University of Tokyo. I wish to acknowledge the support of the
Housing Division of Asahi Chemical Company, Misawa Home, and Daiwa
House as well as the numerous customers with whom I planned their
house designs and experienced life in their old and new homes.

2. Unless otherwise indicated, all statistics given are quoted from
the 1996 "Report on Comprehensive Survey of Living Conditions of the
People on Health and Welfare," Statistics and Information Department,
Minister's Secretariat, Ministry of Health and Welfare.

3. In the early years of the promotion of *nisetai jūtaku*, the housing
companies relied on theories and definitions as outlined in works on the

Japanese family and family life by such academics as Y. Yuzawa (1975), T. Okazaki (1992, 1st edition 1987) and T. Watanabe (1983). The research institute of the Housing Division of Asahi Chemical Company developed its own "definitive" work on *nisetai jūtaku* in 1990 in which it promulgated its own interpretation of the "ideal" Japanese family lifestyle.

4. The "elderly" are defined as those persons aged 65 years and above.

5. In Ōe's (1991) study of the population composition in Setagaya ward, he discovered that although the statistics showed that a majority of elderly persons were living on their own, most were also within walking distance of a younger relative who was looking after them on a daily basis. He suggests that such arrangements are common in other locations and, therefore, cautions against misleading interpretations of statistics that purport to show that "modern Japanese society" has left elderly people to manage on their own just because they are living in single person households.

6. As a proportion of the total number of persons aged 65 and over (as opposed to the number of households with persons aged 65 and over in them), the percentages divide as follows: 12.6 percent (of all elderly persons) live on their own; 30.6 percent live as a married couple; 53.1 percent live with their children; and 3.7 percent in other types of households.

7. The software would indicate where certain key features of the house should be placed such as the fire and water elements. A convincing interpretation of the principles had to be conveyed to the customers and works such as Seike (1989) and Tomizuka (1994) were required reading for any good salesman.

8. Prime Minister's Office, Statistics Bureau, Report on Housing Statistics, 1993.

9. The government's concern was that a family might build this type of semi-detached house and rent out one half for profit. Thus, they adopted various suggestions put forward by the prefabricated housing companies that clearly distinguished by the house plan and construction materials used which houses would be classified as *"nisetai jūtaku."*

10. Unfortunately, the second son was insulted by this lack of consultation by either his parents or his older brother. He threatened to pursue his legal rights for an equal share of the inheritance of his parents' land when they pass away. If an agreement cannot be reached between the two brothers, this could mean that Ken'ichiro and his family would have to sell their house and land in order to realize the value of half of the property on which the new house is standing. (The implications for future succession and inheritance practices as a result of these new *nisetai jūtaku* are explored in more detail in Brown [1997]).

11. Authors such as F.Sakakibara, M. Yoshioka, M. Fukushma (1993), M. Sugawara, (1993) and A. Yanaga (1992) explain the changes in attitude of the contemporary Japanese towards their families.

12. A glance at the in-house magazines produced by such housing companies as Asahi Kasei and Misawa Home reveal the idealistic tendencies of the writers proposing housing solutions that, more often than not, prove to be unrealistic.

13. As always, the housing companies keep a close eye on government publications for an indication of the current trend, such as those produced by the Ministry of Health and Welfare, the Ministry of Construction (e.g. their annual White Papers), the Prime Minister's Office, and related offices such as papers by the Planning Department of the Tokyo Metropolitan Government (see references for influential examples); this is especially important if new designs and technological innovations are to be approved by the various departments involved.

References

Nisetai Jūtaku Kenkyūjo. 1980 to 2000. Collected data on reports concerning *nisetai jūtaku*. Asahi Kasei Kōgyō Kabushiki Kaisha.

Brown, Naomi. 1997. The Nisetai Jūtaku phenomenon: A study of changing family patterns in contemporary Japan. Ph.D. diss., Oxford University.

Ministry of Health and Welfare. 1996. Japan. *Report on Comprehensive Survey of Living Conditions of the People on Health and Welfare.* Statistics and Information Department, Ministers' Secretariat.

Institute of Research and Development, 1983 to 1994. Reports concerning multi-generational family homes. Misawa Home Kabushiki Kaisha.

Nisetai Jūtaku Kenkyūjo. 1990. *Shin Oyako dōkyo, dōkyo o kangae hajimeta kazoku tachi no tame* [Living with one's parents. For those families who have begun thinking of living together]. Tokyo: Daiyamondosha.

Ōe, Moriyuki. 1991. *Tanshin kōreisha setai no kazoku kankei to kyojyū jōtai—Setagayaku o jisturei toshite* [Family relations and the state of dwelling of one-aged person households in Setagaya ward]. Tokyo: Nihon Kenchiku Gakkai Daikai Gakujutsu Kōen Kenkyūshū.

Okazaki, T. ed. 1992. *Kōreika shakai no jūtaku* [Housing for an aging society]. Tokyo: Ichiryusha.

Prime Minister's Office, Japan. 1993. *Report on Housing Statistics.* Statistics Bureau.

Sakakibara, F. Yoshioka and M. Fukushima, eds. 1993. *Kekkon ga kawaru kazoku ga kawaru* [Marriage is changing, families are changing]. Tokyo: Heibonsha.

Seike, Kiyoshi 1989. *Gendai no kasō* [Contemporary house geomancy]. Tokyo: Shinchosha.

Sugawara, Mariko. 1993. *Shin kazoku no jidai* [The new era of the family]. Tokyo: Chūkō Shinsho.

Tokyo Metropolitan Government. 1991. *Tōkyōjin no seikatsu purofairu—deta de miru toshi shakai no kadai* [Profile of lifestyles in Tokyo—urban society future tasks as analyzed from the data]. Tokyo.

Tomizuka, T. 1994. *Kasō no yoku naru sekkei to madori* [Designs and plans for better house geomancy]. Tokyo: Narimodo Shuppan

Watanabe, Takenobu. 1983. *Sumaikata no shisō* (Ideology on how to live). Tokyo: Chūō Kōronsha.

Yanaga, Akira. 1992. *Korekara no oyako dōkyo no sumaikata to sumai* [Lifestyles and housing for future parent/child cohabitation] in *Kōreika shakai no jūtaku* edited by T. Okazaki. Tokyo: Ichiryusha.

Yuzawa, Yasujiko. 1975. *Kazoku kankeigaku* [Studies on the family]. Tokyo: Koseikan.

Coping with
Demographic Change

Changes in demographic behavior are not necessarily experienced passively by those who live through them, but are also the object of contestation, improvisation, and negotiation by people as they attempt to come to terms with new circumstances as they age. Human beings are active agents who respond to the changes they experience in society and, in their responses, direct and redirect the course of change. In Japan, trends in demographic behavior over recent decades—particularly reduction in the total fertility rate and decreased mortality—have challenged both the government and citizens to develop novel ways of coping with and adjusting to those changes. The authors in this section look at a variety of ways in which governments and individuals respond to the difficulties that arise from such rapid demographic change.

In her chapter, Leng Leng Thang describes an alternative to traditional institutional care for both the elderly and for preschool aged children. Both forms of care have been stigmatized in Japanese society—nursing homes as dumping grounds for elderly who lack caring children and child day care centers as a poor substitute for motherly attention, accessed only by the poor or by inadequate mothers. Thang suggests that combined elder/child care facilities can contribute to destigmatizing old age institutions by providing a new alternative to institutional care that expressly promotes closer intergenerational ties. She argues that such age-integrated institutions have the potential to improve attitudes towards the elderly among younger generations by challenging stereotypes—such as that the old are sick, backward, difficult—that inhibit contact among generations. Given the strong tendency in Japanese society towards age segregation, such age-integrated facilities are a particularly interesting approach to coping with changes in demographic behavior.

In their chapters, Christopher Thompson and John Knight turn their attention to one of the most pressing demographic problems facing contemporary Japan—rural depopulation. For several decades, Japan has experienced a large-scale out-migration trend in which young people depart rural areas to pursue education and work in cities; destinations include regional cities such as Sendai in northern Japan, Fukuoka in Kyūshū, and especially the great metropolis of Tokyo. Rural depopulation is an acute problem for the municipal governments affected not only because of the economic ramifications of losing young workers to the cities, but because the outflow of younger people contributes to the top-heavy character of the population pyramid in these areas. This depopulation problem has particularly serious implications for the largely elderly populations residing in rural regions. In a society that continues to emphasize in-home, family-provided care of the elderly, the loss of younger generations able to provide that care becomes a major dilemma.

Thompson describes an example of a community attempting to stem the tide of rural out-migration through the practice of what he calls "population politics"—the public presentation, discussion, or interpretation of local population figures and related demographic data by the mayor and other town hall bureaucrats to attract outside resources. Thompson shows how demography itself becomes politicized in the context of power relations between the central government and local politicians. "Population politics," or a variation thereof, has become a development tool used by many small, depopulated municipalities with minimal resources fighting for social and economic survival in a political environment that encourages locally designed solutions to local problems.

The struggle with depopulation is also the theme of Knight's chapter, which focuses on a mountainous municipality of western Japan. Knight considers another approach to tackling the problem of depopulation—the attempt to repopulate depopulated areas by appealing to those living in the city to come and settle locally. He shows how, in the face of large scale out-migration trends, municipal governments attempt to maintain or restore their populations both by promoting return-migration on the part of city-based migrants and by encouraging urbanites in general to consider residing in the country. But he also casts doubt over whether these efforts to satisfy this "population hunger" on the part of remote areas will succeed.

Finally, Satsuki Kawano considers how a declining total fertility rate, delayed marriage, and shrinking household size intersect with the system of ancestor veneration that requires successors in the stem family to provide ritual care for the family dead. She considers the question: How do people cope with the requirements surrounding ancestral rites and burial practices when the supply of healthy descendants is insufficient to care for the dead in traditional ways? She addresses this question by considering alternative approaches to burial and ancestral care that have emerged to address the problems associated with a limited supply of successors to care for graves.

Each of these chapters examines the creative, and sometimes contested, approaches that Japanese people are taking to cope with changes in demographic behavior. What emerges is a complex, heterogeneous picture of Japanese life, one that reveals considerable creativity and invention in the ways in which Japanese people draw on long established values and ideas while engaging with new ones.

4

Generational Reengagements: Changing Demographic Patterns and the Revival of Intergenerational Contact in Japan[1]

Leng Leng Thang

Like all advanced nations, Japan at the beginning of the twenty-first century is faced with an era of demographic imbalance as the population pyramid expands at the top and shrinks at the bottom to resemble a bell shape. The bell-shape age structure is a consequence of industrialization and modernization, which have, among other things, brought about mass longevity and concerns over coping with population aging on all levels of the society. One important response to the surplus of elderly in Japan is an increase in the supply of old age institutions to accommodate the growing and varying needs for long term living and care environments. However, despite the growing recognition that homes for the elderly represent one viable solution to caring for the aged, cultural and social norms of expecting an older person to be cared for by the family remain strong. Coupled with the sometimes negative media reports and criticisms of institutions as dehumanizing their residents, these old age institutions are commonly stigmatized as *obasuteyama*[2]—a dumping ground for the elderly where they are alienated from the society.

In this chapter, a new alternative institutional care facility—where services for the old and young are established within close proximity to each other—is described and evaluated. Besides potentially destigmatizing old age institutions, these new alternatives to the stereotypical image of homes for the elderly as bleak and hopeless also provide opportunities for the revival of the intergenerational contact in Japan, which has been endangered by social, cultural, and demographic changes in the recent decades.

Changing Demographic Patterns
and Generational Disengagement

The era of demographic imbalance in Japan is characterized by *shōshika* (trend towards fewer children) and an expanding number of elderly in *kōreika shakai* (aging society). As noted by Kaneda and Raymo in chapter 8, Japan has experienced an exceptionally rapid demographic transition since 1945. It was the first nation among the industrialized countries to experience a postwar fertility decline. Fertility in Japan has declined sharply after recording an average total fertility rate (TFR) of 4.42 during the baby boom in 1947–49. By 1960, the TFR had already fallen by more than half, to 2 children per woman. Since 1974, the TFR in Japan has fallen below replacement level, reaching a record low of 1.38 in 1998 (Kono 2000).

At the same time, age-specific mortality rates at birth have also declined sharply. In 1947, life expectancies for men and women were 50.1 and 54 years respectively. They rose to 67.7 and 72.9 respectively in 1965. By 2000, the life expectancies for both sexes had risen to a world-record high of 77.64 years for men and 84.62 years for women. Japan has maintained the record for attaining the world's highest level of life expectancy since the early 1990s.

Such combined effects of an extremely low fertility rate and an exceptionally high life expectancy rate are resulting in a new phase of demographic evolution as indicated by the elderly/child ratio[3] (Kono 2000). Although the elderly/child ratio was only 13 elderly per 100 children between 1930-50, it has increased rapidly thereafter; to about 50 per 100 children in 1986 and reaching equal number of elderly and children by 1997. It is estimated that by the year 2050, the ratio will soar to 247 where elderly will outnumber children by two and a half times (Kono 2000, 17).

The demographic imbalance is already having an effect on both educational and welfare institutions dealing with both populations. On the one hand, with fewer children born each year, schools and kindergartens are left with more empty classrooms as they continue to experience a decline in enrollment. On the other hand, despite the negative perceptions that one may have of homes for the elderly, there are pressing demands for more such facilities to cater to the elderly. The demand is to a large extent triggered by the lack of caregivers at home. Although family care remains the norm in Japan, various factors such as a decline in multigenerational living arrangement, a fall in the number of children available to provide care as the birthrate decreases, an increase in the number of women in the workforce, and mother-in-law and daughter-in-law conflicts have reduced the availability of caregivers at home.

The combination of this demand, attitudes towards old age institutions, and the overall demographic context thus sets the stage for the emergence of the new alternatives to age-integrated facilities. Defined as facilities that combine services for the elderly and the young, age-integrated facilities have distinct advantages. Apart from solving the problem of space shortages for old-age services by locating them in the empty classrooms, more significantly, these facilities break away from the image of homes for the elderly as a congregation of elderly lost in a lifeless world to one in which the laughter of children can be heard, and new opportunities for intergenerational contact are possible.

Age-Integrated Facilities in Japan and Generational Re-engagement

Age-integrated facilities are an emerging new alternative in Japan (Kaplan et al. 1998). Services can become age-integrated either by moving into an existing facility or by constructing new projects with the goal of integrating services for different generations in mind. For the former, the most common combination is the setting up day-service centers or other elderly services in the empty classrooms of schools and nurseries. Establishing services for the elderly in the school compound is a major "breakthrough" in bureaucracy; schools come under the purvue of the Ministry of Education, whereas elderly welfare belongs to the Ministry of Health and Welfare. Until the pressing need for increased elderly welfare was felt, transferring the "property" of one Ministry to another was almost impossible.

The possibility for elderly services to move into schools reflects the direct consequence of *shōshika* and *kōreika*. More than 50,000 classrooms in elementary and junior high schools nationwide were vacant as a result of *shōshika* (Yomiuri Shinbun June 23, 1994). At the same time, the shortage of land in major metropolitan areas has forced many old-age services to be established in the suburbs or the country, removing the elderly from the communities in which they have lived much of their lives. In addition to opportunities for interactions with children, the setting up of day service centers or other elderly services inside the schools and nurseries thus allows easy access for the elders in the community. With the anticipated increase in elderly service centers in the New Gold Plan, more schools will see elders in their compound in the near future.

The latter type of age-integrated facilities are those that were deliberately constructed from the beginning to accommodate both generations. There have been few studies or surveys conducted on such facilities nationwide. From information gathered in various sources (such as various government agencies, news reports, and newsletters from welfare service organizations), I identified thirty-nine age-integrated facilities in Tokyo in 1996.[5] They represent a wide range of combinations, from the more usual day service for the elderly and nursery combination, to others such as a senior house combined with a dormitory for college students, and a nursing home combined with a secondary school and nursery.

One of the pioneers in age-integrated facilities is located at Edogawa Ward of Tokyo. The aged-integrated facility, named Kotoen, includes a Special Nursing Home for the Aged, a Home for the Elderly, a Day Care Center for Elders, and a nursery for children from the neighborhood.[6] Because of the multiple services offered, Kotoen resembles a community filled with people of various ages. On a typical day, there will be eighty children ranging from 1 to 6 years old who come in the morning and stay till as late as 6:30 P.M. at the nursery. At the Home for the Elderly, there are fifty ambulant resident elders. Another fifty semi-ambulant or bed-ridden elders reside in the Special Nursing Home. In addition, twenty elders from the community attend day care service on the weekdays with transport provided by the center. The center also offers short stay service for bedridden elders rehabilitation and bath services for elders in the community as well as regular seminars for caregivers in the community. Its effort to reach out to the community illustrates the center's attempt to change the negative image of old age institutions to a positive one that shares its existence with the wider society.

Kotoen started as a *yōrōin* (old age asylum) in 1962 and changed its name to *yōgo rōjin hōmu*—home for the elderly[7]—in accordance with the 1963 Welfare Law for the Elderly (*Rōjin Fukushi Hō*). The nursery was initially built next to it in 1976 and became combined under one roof since 1987. Since the coexistence of both populations, Kotoen has set up a committee called the *fureai sokushin iinkai* (committee to promote interactions), which meets monthly to discuss events and evaluate their intergenerational programs. There are various programs to promote interactions, including daily activities such as morning exercises, engaging the elderly's help to dress the children, and joint activities such as arts and crafts and story-telling. There are also monthly events such as the "open childcare program" where groups of elderly from the Home for the Elderly take turns spending a day with the children and annual events including the "beginning childcare" program where elderly are invited to help in babysitting the newly enrolled one-year-old toddlers. In addition, almost all cultural and annual events such as the nursery's graduation and opening ceremonies involve both the elders and children. Besides the planned programs, children are encouraged to visit the elders whenever they feel like it. It is not uncommon to see nursery teachers bringing their little ones for a walk to greet the elderly residents. Kotoen represents an age-integrated facility that maximizes its unique combination to reengage the generations through active promotion of intergenerational interaction both in planned programs and casual contacts.

Benefits of Age-Integrated Facilities

Opportunities for elderly and children to interact have decreased as fewer children are staying with their grandparents today. As Raymo and Kaneda discuss in chapter 2, Japan has been witnessing a decline in the proportion of multigenerational households in recent decades. Coupled with this decline in traditional households is an increase in the number of single elderly and elderly couple households. Japanese have been found to have less contact with their children (and grandchildren) than other nationalities when they do not stay together. Only 14.3 percent of Japanese 60 years and above reported that they see their children everyday, and 17.2 percent said they meet them more than once a week. This is significantly lower than the U.S. samples, which recorded 21.2 percent and 40.8 percent respectively (Sōmuchō 1990). Outside the family, elderly-children contacts are similarly limited as most education, recreational, and social opportunities are set up on an age-specific basis, limiting intergenerational contact (Traphagan 1998). It is ironic that in an aging society where more grandparents and great-grandparents than ever are present, interaction between elderly and children appears to be declining in frequency.

One of the negative consequences of generational disengagement is an increase in "ageist" attitudes towards the old among the younger generations. An overview of studies on the perception of high school and college students has concluded that the attitudes of Japanese youth towards the elderly are characterized by negative attitudes (Koyano 1989). An international comparison of college students' perceptions of elderly among Japan, United States, Britain, and Sweden has further shown that more young Japanese perceive elderly as grouchy and stubborn and fewer see them as kind and honest than do peers in the other three countries (Koyano 1993). Age-segregation and the consequent negative perception of aging and old age, therefore, foretell concerns on different levels, from personal concerns about the children's attitudes toward their own aging parents in the future, to wider social implications on the future survival of the aging society.

Age-integrated facilities offer hope for generational reengagement pertinent to the development of more positive attitudes towards old age among the young. Children in Kotoen, for instance, claimed that they enjoyed the elders' presence. As a result of daily "skinship" with the elders, the children feel more attached to their own grandparents. All replied they would love to live with their grandparents: "How nice if Grandpa and Grandma could live with us!" one girl said.

To elderly living in an institution too, the presence of children enlivens an otherwise monotonous age-segregated environment. Children give elderly residents an opportunity to play the role of surrogate grandparent in various ways. At Kotoen, an announcement by the children every afternoon defines the role of the elderly, "Grandpas and grandmas, little children have awakened; please come down to help us get dressed. . . ." Upon hearing this, interested elderly will head for the nursery to help the 1 and 2-year-olds that are still too young to dress themselves. Every April when a new batch of 1-year-olds comes in, some elderly will volunteer to be babysitters for the month. Individual attention provided by the elderly has eased the transition from home to an institution for the toddlers. After a few days as babysitters, the elderly will each tend to "adopt" a particular child and gradually, he/she will come to be known as the "grandchild" of certain "grandpa" or "grandma."

Although the nursing home elderly do not participate as babysitters, they are equally excited with the new toddlers. When they come down for a rehabilitation session, some will request the caregiving staff to bring them to the toddlers and have one of the kids sitting on their laps for a while. Presence of the children have been said to encourage some frail elderly to attend physiotherapy regularly in the hope to walk again and resume active interaction with the children.

Like any eager grandparents, elderly residents enjoy imparting their knowledge to the children. For example, they teach the children about nature as they go on strolls together. The elderly are also invited to talk to the children about traditional customs and folktales during festive celebrations. The learning experience is mutual, as elderly also learn about contemporary youth culture, such as comic book characters and new vocabularies from the children. The children help promote interaction among the elderly too, as they become a subject for conversation among them. In joint activities with the children, elderly sometimes end up teaching each other how to make items that interest the children. Such opportunities instil among them a sense of usefulness and satisfaction.

Problems and Criticisms

Age-integrated facilities such as Kotoen have received frequent media attention praising them as playing a positive role in reviving intergenerational reengagement. These institutions, however, are small in number and therefore atypical. Although they could be understood as a kind of "flagship" response, rather than typical instance of elderly care in Japan, it should be noted that they indeed receive little formal support from the bureaucracy. There is no department in the ministries to coordinate these facilities; each service in an age-integrated facility is treated as a separate entity in administrative terms. As age-integrated facilities are simply seen as "built together" due to "limited land," their merits of enhancing the ties between the old and young are merely seen as a secondary effect of the combination (Rōjin Hoken Fukushi Jānaru 1993, 8). As a result, many age-integrated facilities faced initial difficulties in trying to convince the different departments involved of the benefits of such a complex combination.

Kotoen's open design on the first floor of the complex to promote intergenerational contact was initially frowned upon by the authorities. The director recalls how they were forced to include in their architectural plan a mobile wall in the multipurpose hall to separate the elders from the children—a wall that they have never put up—in order to obtain approval for construction.

Besides opposition from the state, many administrators also faced opposition from parents—the middle-generation—when age-integrated facilities were first proposed. Parents objected on the grounds of hygiene, and worried that elders would transmit diseases to the children. The director of a day service center combined with an elementary school in the center of Tokyo blamed the initial objections from the PTA members on the negative portrayal of elders by the media, which influenced the public's stereotypical image of elders as senile and therefore potentially harmful to children. Their opposition delayed the interaction between the elders and the children for two months. Kotoen, too, faced the same apprehensive response from parents when they first merged. Nonetheless, the parents soon discovered the benefits of age-integration and many of these facilities today pride themselves on this unique characteristic.

Many facilities also face the constraints of failing health among their elderly residents. Although some facilities would encourage intergenerational interaction only among the healthy elderly and children, an increasing number of administrators are recognizing passive interaction—such as watching the children at play, and nonverbal touch—as being equally significant and therapeutic to the elderly.

Not all age-integrated facilities take advantage of the opportunities provided by their unique combination. In one facility combining after-school care and day service for elderly (run by two different organizations), the children and elderly hardly meet since the children use outside stairs to enter their premise, which is located just above the day service. The administrator said they have joint events only twice a year: during the summer *bon* (festival of the dead) dancing and fire drill. Another similar combination, however, reported active interaction between the two generations, especially during school vacations.

Interactions between school children and elderly who are using the empty classrooms also depend on cooperation between the schools and the elderly services. Although there are those which exist as clear-cut separate entities, there are others that organize frequent get-togethers and lunch for both the students and the elderly and even conduct joint lessons (e.g. in Hiroshima Prefecture) (Tokyo Volunteer Center 1993a).

Sometimes, favorable reports on intergenerational interaction in age-integrated facilities manifest the ideal rather than reality. One "ambitious" combination of a nursing home, a nursery, and a junior high school established in the center of Tokyo in 1991 has appeared regularly in the media reporting frequent interactions between the elderly and children, as well as junior high students who serve as volunteers in the nursing home. Interviews with the administrator of the nursing home, however, showed that interactive activities with the children occurred only about once a month; interaction with the junior high students is even more limited. Many students visit the home only once as part of their curriculum during their first year. Very few students serve as volunteers, and they are also not particularly encouraged by the school to do so, as students are expected to spend most of their time preparing for examinations.

The efforts and attitudes of the administrators thus determine the level of interaction between elderly and children in these facilities. Due to the additional work involved in planning joint activities for different ages, it is common for many facilities to confine age-integrated programs to a weekly or monthly event. Moreover, without support groups and programs for age-integrated facilities to get together and share ways to promote intergenerational interaction, many administrators find their staffs and themselves lacking adequate knowledge and training to formulate effective programs.

Many age-integrated facilities also fail to maximize their potential in sharing utility spaces and generating cost savings. Some share an entrance, but many have separate entrances. Among the facilities observed for this study, Kotoen has explored and benefited most from the combination: it has saved in overhead costs from sharing common spaces and utilities such as kitchen, office, and an activity hall among different services.

Reviving Intergenerational Contact in Changing Demography

Despite the problems and criticisms that have surfaced, the significance of the new alternative in a *shōshika* and *kōreika* Japan should not be underestimated. Although fewer children in the population, coupled with nuclearization of the family and increased mobility of family members, implies diminishing opportunities for elderly to grow old with children and grandchildren around them, Japan's record long life expectancy also means that grandparents in their 60s and 70s will remain comparatively young and energetic, and many may still be in the workforce and lack the free time to interact with their grandchildren.

In Kotoen, for instance, the majority of the nursery children live in nuclear families (justifying their application to the nursery) like most urbanites in Japan. Many of their grandparents live out in the country, which means they get to meet only once or twice a year during festival seasons. Even when some grandparents are staying nearby, many children claim that their grandparents are too busy working and have no time to play with them. This parallels with Bengston's (1985) analysis of the variability in grandparenting, which warns that natural grandparents may have their own jobs, leisure, and family activities. Lebra's study (1979) on Japanese women has also shown some grandmothers to be too preoccupied with their own activities to have time for grandchildren. Thus, if not for the presence of age-integrated facilities, some children will have limited opportunities to interact with the elderly.

Parents agree that the opportunities to interact with elderly individuals have provided "precious experience in a nuclear family." In fact, the age-integrated facilities, in offering a chance for children to have surrogate grandparents, also benefit the middle generation of parents. In Kotoen, three-generational contact is also evident in some cases as mothers of the children develop relations with the grandparents whom their children befriend. A few mothers still bring their children to visit the "grandparents" who have been transferred to the nursing home during the New Year.

In short, age-integrated facilities thus have great potential in helping to solve the problems of generational disengagements and to "humanize" old age institutions in an era of demographic change.

Notes

1. This chapter is derived from materials from my book *Generations in Touch: Linking the Old and Young in a Tokyo Neighborhood* (2001). Portions of the chapter are reprinted from this work and are used by permission of the publisher, Cornell University Press. My research was funded by a Japan Foundation Dissertation Fellowship (1995–96), for which I am very grateful.

2. *Obasuteyama* (literally "granny-abandoning-mountain") is a legend about the ethic of filial piety and describes the dilemma of a man who must bring his aging parent to die in the mountains. There are many versions of the story (see Bethel 1993). The name of the legend, *Obasuteyama* has become a label for old-age institutions in which the residents are viewed as having been abandoned by their family.

3. Elderly-child ratio refers to the number of elderly (population aged 65 and over) divided by the number of children (population under 15), multiplied by 100 (Kōno 2000, 15).

4. Among them, I visited five (in addition to my field site) and surveyed twelve other facilities by telephone. They represent a good cross-section of various combinations—age-integrated facilities combining nursery, nursing home, day service centers (3); a nursing home with nursery and junior high school (1); nursing homes with nurseries (4); an old-age home with nursery (1); day service centers with nurseries (2), with children's after-school centers (2), or with elementary school (1); elders' rest-centers with nursery (1), with children's after-school center (1), or with both a

children's after-school center and "silver pia" housing (1); an elder care house with university students' dormitory (1).

5. I did fieldwork in Kotoen for ten months from 1995-1996, where I worked as a volunteer at the center. Besides participant observation, interviews and surveys were conducted with various people related to the center or involved in age-integrated facilities.

6. Under the 1963 Law, *yōrōin* was changed to a new name, *rōjin hōmu*, an attempt to reduce the stigmatization of institution for the aged. The Law also divides *rōjin hōmu* into three types, namely *yōgō rōjin hōmu* (home for the elders), *tokubetsu yōgō rōjin hōmu* (special care home for the elders), and *keihi rōjin hōmu* (low cost home for the elders).

References

Bengston, Vern. 1985. Diversity and symbolism in grandparental roles. In *Grandparenthood* edited by Vern Bengston and Joan Robertson, Beverley Hills, Calif.: Sage Publications 11–25.

Bethel, Diana. 1993. From abandonment to community: Life in a Japanese institution for the elderly. Ph. D. diss., University of Hawaii.

Kaplan, Matthew et al. 1998. *Intergenerational programs: Support for children, youth, and elders in Japan.* Albany: State University of New York Press.

Kōno, Shigemi. 2000. Demographic aspects of population. In *Aging in Japan,* edited by Shigeyoshi *Yoshida.* Tokyo: Japan Aging Research Center.

Koyano, Wataru. 1993. Age-Old stereotypes. *Japan Views Quarterly.* Winter: 41–42.

———. 1989. Japanese attitudes towards the elderly: A review of research findings. *Journal of Cross–Cultural Gerontology.* 4: 335–45.

Lebra, Takie Sugiyama. 1979. The dilemma and strategies of aging among contemporary Japanese women. *Ethnology* 18(4): 337-353.

Rojin Hoken Fukushi Jānaru. 1993. *"Hitotsu Yane no Shita" ni Atsumareba.* [Journal of Elderly Health and Welfare]. October:4–17. 1993. Let's gather "under the roof" p. 4–17. October 1993 Issue.

———. 1990. *Rōjin no Seikatsu to Ishiki ni kansuru Kokusai Hikaku Chōsa.* Tokyo: *Sōmuchō Chōkan Kanbō Rōjin Taisaku Honbu.* Somūcho [Japanese Office of General Affairs]. *1990.* International Comparative Survey on livelihood and consciousness of elderly. Tokyo: Headquarter of measure for Elderly, Japanese Office of General Affairs.

Thang, Leng Leng. 2001. Generations in touch: Linking the old and young in a Tokyo Neighborhood. Ithaca, N.Y.: Cornell University Press.

———. 1999. The dancing granny: linking the generations in a Japanese age-I integrated welfare centre. Japanese Studies 19 (2): 151-62.

Tokyo Volunteer Center. 1993. Senior Volunteers' Activity Manual. Tokyo: Tokyo Volunteer Center.

Traphagan. 1998. Contesting the Transition to Old Age in Japan. *Ethnology* 37(4): 333–50.

5

Depopulation in Rural Japan:
"Population Politics" in Tōwa-chō

Christopher S. Thompson

> *When I was a child, there were many large families, the crops were good, and the future looked bright. Now, we can't even grow what we want, the population is dwindling, and everybody is old. It's hard not to get depressed, but I try to think positively.*

—45-year-old Tōwa-chō farm wife

Depopulation has been a major problem for many small rural municipalities in Japan during the postwar era. Hardest hit have been towns and villages located in the *chihō*, or geographical regions furthest from the nation's political, economic, and cultural center in Tokyo. Nowhere has postwar depopulation been more pronounced than in the Tōhoku region of northeastern Honshu (Liaw 1992). Many agricultural municipalities in Tōhoku continue to be affected. In this chapter, I examine the added burden that national demographic trends have placed upon an already depopulated agricultural community, and show how the resulting socioeconomic impediments and national level policy changes have continued to affect the lifestyle of farm families while compelling local bureaucrats to implement a new style of local politics.

The negative long-term effects of depopulation on Tōhoku agricultural communities has been well documented by Japanese and North American ethnographers alike (Bailey 1991; Hashimoto 1986; Kelly 1990; Moore 1990; Shimpo 1976). The scarcity of young people, the disproportionate number of senior citizens, unequal access to educational opportunities, the lack of good jobs, and the deficiency of funds to provide needed health and social services are but a few of the symptoms. Current demographic trends nationally such as declining fertility and the unprecedented rapid aging of the general population (see chapter 2), as well as new welfare policies designed for long-term care (see chapter 9), place added pressure on local governments to furnish solutions to local problems. Shifts in the public discourse of filial obligations and care for the elderly make finding solutions even more difficult. All of these factors are reflected within Japan's postwar interprefectural migration patterns, which have been predominantly a movement from rural areas to urban Japan (Fukunari 1991).

In the past thirty years, depopulation and state sponsored municipal consolidations have had a pronounced effect on the transformation of rural social space (Knight 1994b). During this period, two major patterns have characterized the response of depopulated agricultural *shichōson* (cities, towns, and villages) to their demographic plight. Communities unable to maintain adequate municipal operating budgets while providing needed public services have struggled quietly, some succumbing to amalgamation (Brown 1979). Other small municipalities have chosen instead to fight to retain their vibrancy and local autonomy (Obara 1998).

In this chapter, I focus on an example of the latter type of community, the small Tōhoku municipality of Tōwa-chō, where local bureaucrats fight for municipal survival by practicing a community development technique I call "population politics" to combat the burdens of demographic change. By examining the practice of "population politics" in Tōwa-chō, this chapter will demonstrate how demography and development are interrelated in the small nonindustrial agricultural towns of Japan. I argue that "population politics" is one result of a renegotiation of power relations between the central government and local political leaders regarding the implementation of development policies designed to solve local socioeconomic problems in rural municipalities. This shift can be attributed to national level policy changes during the late 1980s that have enabled local governments to exercise more freedom than ever before in determining local policy. This new freedom in turn influences the way local politicians in some small nonindustrial agricultural communities address development issues rooted in population decline.

Briefly defined, "population politics" is the public presentation, discussion, or interpretation of local population figures and related demographic data by the mayor and other town hall bureaucrats to attract outside resources or to justify the implementation of municipal policies and projects designed to develop the community economically and demographically by projecting a positive image of the facts. Tōwa-chō bureaucrats practice "population politics" in order to counter the historical, economic, and political causes that perpetuate population decline and underdevelopment in their town. "Population politics," or a variation thereof, has become a development tool used by many small, depopulated municipalities with minimal resources fighting for social and economic survival in a political environment that encourages locally designed solutions to local problems.

The chapter begins by offering a brief description of the postwar circumstances that brought about the depopulation of Tōwa-chō. After analyzing the political economy of population figures in rural municipalities, I present the repopulation strategies generated by town hall bureaucrats in Tōwa-chō who have problematized local population figures through their use of "population politics." As will be shown, "population politics" enables local bureaucrats to facilitate new patterns of consumption both inside and outside the community. However, this strategy also saddles them with a great deal of responsibility and accountability for their policy initiatives. For Obara Hideo, who became Tōwa-chō's mayor in 1986, a perhaps overly entrepreneurial approach to "population politics" resulted in his resignation from office before the completion of a third term. [1] In the conclusion of this chapter, I will argue that Obara's resignation signals more than his own political decline. It also reflects the delicate balance between breaking and sustaining the socioeconomic cycle that perpetuates population decline in the nonindustrial agricultural communities of rural Japan today.

Before addressing the history of depopulation in Iwate, it is important to situate the data presented here within the broader ethnographic study of demography and residence patterns in Japan. Dating back to Embree's study of Suye Mura (1939), demographic analysis has been a pillar of village and community studies. However, demographic studies have rarely examined the contradictory ways in which local residents (some of whom work for the town hall) use population figures to represent themselves. This reflexive use of population figures underscores the importance of qualitative analysis in demographic inquiry. If we fail to understand the sociocultural factors that produce these figures, we will not understand their true significance. More importantly, comprehending the sociocultural significance of population figures is a prerequisite for understanding the context in which families (a major demographic focus in this volume) living in agricultural communities in rural Japan are experiencing national demographic change.

When contextualizing the significance of population fluctuations in rural Japan, it is not only important to understand how policies made at the national level trickle down to the local level (see Brenda Robb Jenike, chapter 9), it is also necessary to recognize policy adjustments at the local level that help local residents to benefit from national policies. An examination of "population politics" provides a window through which to view this process. This development technique has theoretical implications for the conventional wisdom concerning local politics in Japan as well. During a better part of the postwar era, U.S. scholars have described the unitary system of the Japanese government to be very different from the United States (Steiner 1965). By assuming that much of the independent thinking and legislation in Japanese politics happens at the national level, with local politicians having little room to exercise originality or independent thought, insufficient attention has been given to policy making at the local level. Policies designed to counter demographic fluctuations are no exception. The actions taken by Tōwa-chō bureaucrats will show that the top down model is far from an accurate view of local politics in rural Japan today (Samuels 1983).

Since 1990, the central government's renewed emphasis on economic and political decentralization has resulted in more abundant funding opportunities for local development projects. The *mura okoshi undō* (village revival movement) and the *furusato sōseiron* (the hometown creation plan) of the late 1980s are well known (Knight 1994a). Taking advantage of opportunities made possible through such programs, many depopulated towns throughout Japan have initiated a host of unprecedented and sometimes unorthodox town development schemes during the late 1980s and 1990s to bring back residents and to jump start their economies. In this regard, Tōwa-chō's repopulation strategies are not especially unusual. Yet what is happening in Tōwa-chō represents a new wrinkle of change in small town development. No longer are local bureaucrats content with prefectural or regional solutions to their problems. Instead they seek answers that are national and international in scope.

Research for this chapter was conducted during fieldwork in Tōwa-chō from 1994-96 and on subsequent visits to the community in 1998 and 1999. Tōwa-chō is located forty kilometers north of Kanegasaki and Mizusawa, towns discussed by Naomi Brown (chapter 3) and John Traphagan (chapter 10). Data for this chapter were collected from primary documents and via participant observations, interviews, and focus group sessions with local residents on pertinent issues. I also owe a debt of gratitude to a certain Tōwa-chō policeman whose introduction of key informants was invaluable.

The History of Depopulation in Tōwa-chō

Postwar population decline in the small towns and villages of Japan can be traced to Japan's economic take-off period in the 1960s and to the national agricultural reform policies that were enacted at that time. During the early 1960s, often referred to by economists as Japan's income doubling decade (Kosai and Kaminski 1981), factories and construction companies in Japan's major cities were desperate for labor. For many successive years, thousands of young people were recruited annually from rural regions to work in the cities. Entire graduating classes of junior high school students were hired by factories desperate for labor. Men and women were drawn to the cities as well, taking their children with them. The resulting loss of so many adolescent children caused towns and villages to consolidate or shut down many of their primary schools. In this way, macroeconomic circumstances caused major levels of out-migration, resulting in the depopulation of largely agricultural prefectures and the break-up of what had been three generation natal households. The economic boom of the 1960s left older farmers trapped on their land and their children tied to jobs far away (Kelly 1990).

Historically, Iwate and other outlying prefectures have supplied not only labor but also food, especially rice, to the urban areas of Japan. However, structural reforms (i.e., rationalization initiatives) within the Japanese agriculture system during the years spanning from 1965–80 changed rice agriculture forever. During this period, farms were rebuilt into larger plots more suited to mechanized tilling. Mechanization was supported by loans from the national government. This soon led to overproduction and mandatory national *gentan* policies that restricted the amount of rice that could be grown. Following this move, the national government established *tensaku* (crop rotation) policies, demanding that farmers should place more effort on growing fruits and vegetables instead of rice (Moore 1990).

The loss of income resulting from the mandatory agricultural cutbacks during the 1970s and 1980s caused more out-migration and resulted in a growth in the practice of *dekasegi* (seasonal employment of males outside of the home village), which has a long history in Japan, but which is often perceived as a social problem. It has also led to the *hanayome mondai*, the practice finding brides, often from countries such as the Phillipines, for sons who stay behind and inherit the family farm. When living on an agricultural income alone became difficult, small farm towns such as Tōwa-chō lost even more residents to the cities. The state had hoped that its reforms would encourage farmers to give up individual farms and move toward cooperative farming, but this didn't happen. Although individuals left farming in great numbers, most households held onto their land and used farm machinery to allow one or multiple members of the household to continue small-scale farming on a part-time basis (Kelly 1990).

In a massive effort to address the growing social and economic problems of agricultural Japan, the national government launched an initiative called the *Furusato Sōsei Undō* (Movement to create hometown identity) in 1989. Block grants of ¥100,000,000 were given to every town and village in rural areas to promote *furusato-zukuri* (hometown-making) as local bureaucrats saw fit. For many small agricultural communities in Iwate, this block grant launched them into the age of hometown revival in what came to be known as the *chihō no jidai* (age of the regions), a national movement highly touted during the later half of the 1980s by the administration of Prime Minister Takeshita Noboru. The *Furusato Sōsei* grants were also a symbolic acknowledgment by the national government that it was no longer sure what to do with farmers when addressing the endemic problems of depopulation, jobs, and aging in rural Japan (Media Production Group 1991). Small rural communities now had no choice but to fend for themselves.

In the 1990s, the national government has promoted the cultivation of specialty crops, but has also encouraged farmers to get out of agriculture altogether by promoting the service sector, thinking that rural Japan should develop more resorts and a tourism industry. Such policy changes at the national level in the 1990s have left rural nonindustrial municipalities dependent on agriculture, depopulated, and disillusioned.

Consequently, four major obstacles to socioeconomic development characterize the predicament of small agricultural communities in rural Japan today. As I have established, many agricultural towns have yet to recover from the depopulation that occurred in the 1960s and 1970s. Government mandated agricultural restrictions produced a part-time farming lifestyle in agricultural communities that has left many families tied to their land and limited in their potential for earning outside income. These first two obstacles have been exacerbated by national demographic trends such as low fertility rates and the rapid aging of the general population in the local context. Also, a new emphasis on decentralizing the national government has led to the shift of responsibility for local development from the national to the local level.

The Political Economy of Population Figures

A strong relationship exists between local population figures, the local economic base, and the municipal treasury. A closer examination of Japan's national tax system shows how delicate the balance is between these three factors. In brief, a fixed percentage of the revenue collected by the national government is returned to the local level in the form of subsidies and grants. These moneys are called *chihō kōfuzei*, or provincial support funds.

The amount of provincial support funding allocated to a municipality is determined through a simple formula. A municipality's expected tax income is subtracted from the estimated income needed to support city facilities and services. Part of expected income includes provincial support funding that a municipality automatically receives. This funding is determined in large part by local population figures. A population census is conducted every five years to determine the annual level of population funding a municipality receives. Currently in Tōwa-chō, each resident represents a potential provincial support funding value of approximately ¥3,000,000 (roughly $30,000) every five years. Theoretically, for every resident that leaves Tōwa-chō, ¥3,000,000 is lost every five years from the town treasury.[2] Therefore, population figures have a major and direct impact on the operating budget of a municipality. Only if expected income is less than needed income does a municipality becomes eligible for additional provincial support funds to supply what is lacking in the general operating budget. However, local politicians do not receive this funding automatically. They must travel to Tokyo to lobby for these funds with no guarantee of securing the entire amount needed (Hashimoto 1991; Media Production Group 1991).

Competition for funding among small, depopulated towns is fierce. In order to receive the maximum amount of subsidies possible, local bureaucrats utilize all the universal political lobbying techniques and public relations ploys they can muster to influence financial award decisions in their favor. Name recognition, reputation, and the activation of personal political connections in the home prefecture and in Tokyo are crucial to distinguish the local bureaucrat, and the municipality for which funds are being sought. Since the passage of the Decentralization Promotion Law in 1995 (Muramatsu 1997), the national government had been more likely to reward municipal efforts designed to solve local problems through efforts to increase the local tax base. Full funding of such projects is most likely if a municipality shows signs of progressive leadership and creative policy making. "Population politics" is the process by which depopulated agricultural communities demonstrate they have these qualities.

In Tōwa-chō, the inadequacy of the local tax base to provide for its social and economic needs has been evident since the early 1980s when the local population fell to approximately 13,000. Due to depopulation and agricultural policy changes that reduced the amount of income possible from farming, the Tōwa-chō treasury became unable to sustain a majority of its operating budget from the collection of local taxes alone. Since this time, Tōwa-chō bureaucrats have been dependent upon additional provincial funding for a majority of their annual operating budget. It is in part for this reason that in the mid 1980s, Tōwa-chō bureaucrats began stepping-up efforts to promote their town's social and cultural appeal to attract new residents and draw former residents back. Also related to Tōwa-chō's need for additional provincial funding was the mayor's move to implement a series of new and often flamboyant economic development strategies designed to attract national attention while addressing the town's financial woes and demonstrating a proactive leadership style.

According to Aqua (1974), municipal dependence upon regional subsidy funding is nothing new in the postwar period. The government considers agricultural municipalities that can generate 30 percent of their operating costs from their tax base and population-based automatic provincial support funding to be in the "acceptable" range. Tōwa-chō's expected income from local taxes for fiscal year 1997 was approximately 21 percent of needed income. Approximately 10 percent of its operating budget came from population-based provincial support funds. Consequently, Tōwa-chō had to lobby to procure roughly 70 percent of its general operating budget from provincial support funds. Still, Tōwa-chō's combined figure of 31 percent places it among agricultural municipalities with an "acceptable" percentage of tax and population-based income, but with little breathing room. Thus, from an economic standpoint, population figures are a significant factor in determining the potential level of revenue that can be gained by a municipality. Consequently, the need to compete for funds at the national level transforms the issue of local population decline from a mere socioeconomic issue into a politically charged process. The practice of "population politics" at the local level enables farm town bureaucrats to compete for funding with municipalities with better economic potential.

Problematizing Population Decline:
The *Yakuba* Perspective

There are two major facets of "population politics" used by the Tōwa-chō Yakuba (Town Hall) to combat population decline. The first facet involves organizing local population data in a way that reveals possible sectors of growth in the community. The process of problematizing population decline is grounded firmly in Tōwa-chō's community development plan (TCDP). This is a document required by law that is submitted to the Prefectural Office every ten years in which the administration in office at the time must outline and justify current policies and initiatives.

In the 1996 TCDP, Tōwa-chō's latest, the *yakuba* identifies three significant demographic trends at the root of the town's depopulation and related problems. The first trend is based on a *yakuba* analysis that shows although the local population has steadily declined from a high of 16,851 residents in 1955 to 11,685 in 1990, the number of households (2,961 in 1955) has actually increased during the same period (2967 in 1990). According to *yakuba* analysts, these figures indicate that although young people continue to move away from Tōwa-chō, the households remain because their parents remain on the farms while first time residents migrate in, creating new households. Thus, the most efficient way to curb local population decline is to focus on finding ways to attract new residents while deterring younger current residents from moving away (Obara 1996a).

Secondly, the TCDP identifies the percentage of Tōwa-chō residents over age 65 as having increased from 19.5 percent of the population in 1990 and to a level estimated to be over 28 percent as of 1999 (Obara 1996a). This estimate is used to show that ensuring adequate welfare provisions for senior citizens is a critically important priority of the *yakuba*.

Next, the argument is made that neither strategies to keep young residents in the community nor the needs of senior citizens can be addressed adequately by the *yakuba* without some kind of major economic development initiative to produce jobs for the young and finances for the care of seniors. In the third section of the TCDP, the occupational categories of working aged residents from the 1950s to the 1990s is examined. The data show that not only have levels of employment off the farm among Tōwa-chō residents risen in the last two decades (indicating that Tōwa-chō residents are willing to work), but the Tōwa-chō economy, which was once based on primary occupations, has now changed to one based on tertiary jobs. The data indicate that secondary occupations were never prevalent in the community, making the point that if the *yakuba* were to initiate economic development initiatives, the most beneficial plan would be one that could produce primary and tertiary sector jobs (Obara 1996a).

Finally, the TCDP reports that based on the results of local opinion polls, Tōwa-chō residents are overwhelmingly in favor of *yakuba* sponsored economic development initiatives that could retain young people, create more care options for seniors, and create jobs that would allow them to remain on their farms (Obara 1996a). In this way, the skillful deployment of "population politics" to present Tōwa-chō demographics within the TCDP enables the *yakuba* and local bureaucrats to give local residents hope for the future, create a justification for a certain type economic development while projecting an image of Tōwa-chō as a town full of possibilities to potential public and private sector funders outside the community.

Large Scale Policy Initiatives: 1986–96

The second major facet of "population politics" in Tōwa-chō, as in many other depopulated municipalities in Iwate, involves the implementation of concrete large-scale strategies designed to specifically address the economic and social problems in a community as outlined in its community development plan. Successful large-scale projects draw new resources to the community. They also have immense public relations value. For a local town hall initiative to gain exposure in the local, regional, or national media strengthens a mayor's political influence and makes fund raising easier in Tokyo.

Driving the Tōwa-chō Yakuba's efforts toward community development since 1986 has been Obara Hideo. As Mayor of Tōwa-chō from 1986–97, Obara put into motion a large-scale town development scheme designed to increase local tax revenue, create new jobs, and stimulate demographic transition aimed at creating a town that could retain younger residents and care for the old. Obara outlined and updated a version of his plan in the 1996 TCDP.

The trademark of Obara's large scale development strategies have been the *jisaku shuen jigyō* (self-initiated development projects) for which outside support is secured and in which the initiator plays a starring role. Starting in April 1986, Obara brought multiple *jisaku shuen* projects to fruition in Tōwa-chō. Among his most famous has been the Four Tōwa Alliance. Obara knew well that

Tōwa-chō's economy could not be improved without outside resources, and thus forged an economic alliance between four towns in Japan with the same name (Tōwa-chō) but located in different prefectures (Yamaguchi, Fukushima, Miyagi, and Iwate). Pooling the towns' resources, Mayor Obara engineered the use of a cousin's residence in Tokyo to establish a "Tōwa Tokyo Office," which became the retail outlet for marketing the local farm products from each Tōwa-chō.

Pointing to the success of the Tōwa Tokyo Office, Mayor Obara persuaded his mayoral colleagues to open a second shop, then located in Yoyogi (in Tokyo's Shibuya Ward), as a showroom for Tōwa-chō local products. Called the "Antenna Shop," the showroom was used to hold lectures and seminars to advertise Tōwa products and to inform Tokyoites of the sightseeing and recreational possibilities available in the four Tōwas. Mayor Obara also established a third sector restaurant sponsored by Iwate Tōwa with the help of Tokyo investors on the Ginza, called "Masuhachi," which served the local dishes of Iwate Tōwa using local products that were also offered for sale near the cash register at the entrance to the store.[3] The Four Tōwa alliance, the Tōwa Tokyo Office, the Antenna Shop, and "Masuhachi" were all economic development projects initiated by the *yakuba* under Obara's guidance to expand Iwate Tōwa's economic base in a way that would attract the attention of national level politicians. These new ventures were also designed to offer young residents in each Tōwa-chō new and exciting professional opportunities that were made available through the town halls in each municipality.

Many other memorable large scale *jisaku shuen* projects took place during my two years of fieldwork in Tōwa-chō. One such project was initiated during the aftermath of the Hanshin earthquake in January 1995. At this time, then Mayor Obara suddenly announced that Tōwa-chō was opening its doors to any earthquake survivors who were interested in relocating to Iwate Tōwa. To make this possible, Mayor Obara secured funding from the Ministry of Home Affairs for a free housing allowance and a daily stipend lasting for up to one year or until the individual or family was successful in finding local work. Mayor Obara even offered the services of his *yakuba*'s planning and finance division in the job search to help earthquake refugees relocate permanently.

The "Great Hanshin Earthquake Relocation Project" did wonders for promoting Tōwa-chō and helped local bureaucrats to project an image of their town as small but progressive and resourceful to a national audience. Funding for this project was made available

by the Home Affairs Ministry in Tokyo, whose top officials knew
well the Masuhachi restaurant on the Ginza and were well aware
of Mayor Obara's town development exploits through the regional
and national media. Three Hanshin families eventually took-up
residence in Tōwa-chō. Obara's invitation to the earthquake survivors became one of the top ten news stories in Iwate for 1995.

A major attempt to create an income generating community
resource came in the form of drilling for a hot spring in Tōwa-chō.
In January 1996, Tōwa-chō became the first Iwate town in the
Kitakami Range to have a hot spring. After securing the necessary
outside funding from a major Japanese bank impressed by the
Mayor's record of high-profile development initiatives, Obara and
his planning and finance division hired a Japanese-American joint
venture company to conduct the drilling with special equipment
designed for boring oil wells.

As soon as the hot spring began to flow, the financial benefits
of the project seemed obvious. Japan Railway East (JR East) immediately completed negotiations with Tōwa-chō and a local land-
owner to build a hotel. In addition a well-known real estate
company entered into a partnership with Tōwa-chō to develop a
hot spring resort complex, which was to include a host of new
facilities utilizing the hot spring. Plans for a public swimming
pool and a brand new senior citizens' health care and residential
facility, funded partially by JR East and Tōwa Hot Spring income
were also made.

Similarly, many other Iwate communities practice their own
forms of "population politics" by instituting large scale development strategies to bring people into the community and to boost
the local economy. Ohasama-chō, located north of Tōwa-chō, focuses on wine making and its traditional *kagura* (Shinto dance)
folk performances to attract people. Tōno, located on Tōwa-chō's
west side, is known for being Japan's national folklore capital. One
town, Yuda-chō, has even gone so far as to build a hot spring in the
local JR East railroad station hoping that travelers will take a
break in their travel schedules to stay and take baths.

Large Scale Policy Initiatives: 1997–99

According to local informants, community enthusiasm generated
by the Obara policies was beginning to wane by the fall of 1997. By
this time the inadequacies of Obara's flamboyant development
projects were becoming apparent. Although Obara was successful

in building a new senior citizens' heath care facility featuring "hot spring therapy," none of the large scale development projects had significantly increased primary or tertiary sector jobs, nor had they stopped, or even slowed, population decline.

The stringent financial demands of maintaining an office in Tokyo caused the Four Tōwa Alliance to close its Tokyo office. Without the business that the Tokyo office generated, Masuhachi and the Antenna Shop became casualties as well. Though macro-level domestic economic fluctuations undoubtedly had some influence on the outcome of these projects, many local residents blamed this result on the over ambitiousness of their creator, Obara Hideo.

Locally, the outlook was not much better. The company that drilled the Tōwa Hot Spring filed for bankruptcy shortly after successfully drilling a second well on the edge of Lake Tase on the outskirts of Tōwa-chō. This canceled the maintenance contract that was negotiated at a reasonable cost. The unanticipated financial burden of maintaining both hot spring wells through a new company affected profits from the main hot spring in town.

By the end of 1997, Obara himself was in even more political trouble. In a major effort to move Tōwa-chō in a more positive direction, he had decided to investigate creative income generating possibilities in the primary sector. His solution was to argue against the national laws that require municipal offices to work with the local agricultural cooperative to enforce *gentan* (restrictions on growing rice) policies. Furthermore, Obara suggested that local municipalities should be allowed freedom to grow unrestricted amounts of rice and should be allowed to develop their own markets to sell their products. Obara's unprecedented move frightened local farmers, shocked and embarrassed prefectural level bureaucrats, and infuriated national level legislators. In the words of a 35-year-old Tōwa-chō male full-time farmer:

> Unfortunately, many Tōwa-chō farmers didn't like Mayor Obara's plan. Many of us feared that by participating, we would lose the subsidies we already received. Some farmers worried about their lack of equipment to grow increased quantities of rice. Others feared they would not have the labor power to increase rice production. I think that latently there were supporters, but they never spoke up because of the social pressure for farmers to present a united front.

On December 11, 1997 Obara resigned from his post as mayor of Tōwa-chō, an office he had held for eleven years (Nichi Nichi

1997). Obara's resignation put into motion an interesting surge in local politics. National election laws require that when a mayor resigns, an election must take place within fifty days to determine a successor. Two candidates quickly emerged: Odashima Mineo, the incumbent deputy mayor, and Kikuchi Norio, the retired president of Iwate Cleaning Center. Kikuchi was a local product who had been living and working outside of Tōwa-chō for much of his career. He ran on a platform promising to strive for "a fair and open town government in which residents are central" (Nichi Nichi 1998a). Odashima countered by promising "a town government in which residents participate," and to "clean up town finances and use public moneys more efficiently" (Nichi Nichi 1998b). The two mayoral candidates campaigned feverishly during the two week campaign period.

On January 25, 1998, Odashima was elected and his administration moved to a considerably more conservative tack. The Odashima led Tōwa-chō government distanced itself from the large-scale projects aimed at retaining and attracting population that had characterized the Obara administration. This shift suggests that the problematization of demographic change operates within the confines of people's willingness to experience major changes in their lives. In the words of a forty-three-year-old male Tōwa-chō shop keeper:

> Since Odashima became mayor, there have been no new policy initiatives that have attracted the attention of the national media. I am sure there are residents that feel relieved about this. You have to like his philosophy of meeting with local residents directly by attending the small block association meetings.

Conclusion

Demography and development are closely tied in the depopulated agricultural towns of Japan. In towns such as Tōwa-chō where the population continues to decline, local bureaucrats must rely on their knowledge of the Japanese political system and their individual creativity to generate solutions to local problems against almost insurmountable odds. In this sense, "population politics" enabled Hideo Obara to launch an impressive list of initiatives in an attempt to fight against the single largest reason that residents leave his community—a lack of secure, long-term employment.

We have also seen that local development is much more than reviving the village through *machiokoshi* initiatives, or creating hometown identity with a grant of ¥100,000,000 from the *Furusato Sōsei Undō*. To Mayor Obara, local development was a serious matter that required a serious commitment on his part and in the community. If there is a connection between the degree to which a community allows its leader to pursue town development and the extent to which a town can be developed, as Bailey (1991) suggests, Obara exposed the limits of this theory.

To a large extent, Obara may have been a casualty of his own policies. Many in the Tōwa-chō community feel that Obara Hideo was a political maverick who became a nail that stuck out too far. His dictatorial approach, overconfident and overbearing manner, and propensity for creating horizontal ties across social, economic, and political structures normally considered to be vertically insular offended many. Obara's policy on unrestricted rice cutbacks is the prime example of his actions that led directly to his political demise.

Yet, Obara's resignation represents much more than his own political motivation or style. His willingness to challenge the national *gentan* policies reflects his understanding that a major factor perpetuating population decline in Tōwa-chō and in other agricultural communities is the subjugation of rural Japan to the policies of the state. Obara understood that only major changes at the local level were going to break the socioeconomic cycle that perpetuates population decline in rural Japan. His brand of "population politics" provided Tōwa-chō residents with opportunities to make those changes.

Two years after Obara's resignation, some residents were reexamining their response to Obara's actions. As a Tōwa-chō male part-time farmer in his early 40s confided to me in September 1999,

> Perhaps our previous mayor [Obara Hideo] with his multiple large-scale development projects seemed too revolutionary and flamboyant at the time. As a town, we voted to curtail this type of development. But as I think now, things have been pretty dead around here since. We are maintaining a status quo that is getting us nowhere. As the situation stands now, we are on a course that will result in amalgamation with Hanamaki in the next ten years. I think more and more of us [farmers] are feeling like we'd like to pursue a more aggressive development plan, such as with the previous administration. Right now I'd estimate that 30% of us feel this way, and the numbers are growing.

The future of small agricultural towns in Japan is uncertain. The demographic dilemmas of rural farm families may not change drastically any time soon. However, as the example of Tōwa-chō has shown, many rural municipalities are far from stagnant political entities waiting to be amalgamated into a neighboring town. The bureaucrats in these towns have much more local autonomy than ever before in the postwar period. If Tōwa-chō is any indication, the future of local agricultural communities in Japan will not be determined solely by the state, but is at least partially in the hands of local residents and in the abilities of those they choose to represent them in their local town halls.

Notes

1. For Japanese names in this chapter, I use the Japanese convention of family name first.

2. The information was obtained via an interview with current Tōwa-chō Mayor, Odashima Mineo, on September 30, 1999.

3. A third sector enterprise is one in which a government institution such as a town office and a private sector partner pool their capital to invest in a business venture (Bailey 1991).

References

Aqua, Ronald. 1974. Local Institutions and Rural Development in Japan. Rural Development Committee Center for International Studies. Cornell University. Ithaca, New York 14853.

Bailey, Jackson H. 1991. *Ordinary people, extraordinary lives: Political and economic change in a Tōhoku village.* Honolulu: University of Hawaii Press.

Brown, L. Keith. 1979. *Shinjō: The chronicle of a Japanese village.* Pittsburgh, Pa.: University Center for International Studies, Publication Section, University of Pittsburgh.

Embree, John. 1939. *Suye Mura: A Japanese village.* Chicago: University of Chicago Press.

Fukurai, Hiroshi. 1991. Japanese Migration in Contemporary Japan: Economic Segmentation and Interprefectural Migration. *Social Biology* 38(1): 28–50.

Hashimoto, Ryoji. 1986. "The women speak: Rikuchū Tanohatamura." *Aruku, Miru, Kiku* 238 (12): 5.

Kelly, W. W. 1990. Regional Japan: The Price of Prosperity and the Benefits of Dependency. *Daedalus* 119: 209-27.

Knight, John. 1994a. Rural revitalization in Japan: Spirit of the village and taste of the country. *Asian Survey* 34: 634-46.

————. 1994b. Town-making in rural Japan: An example from Wakayama. *Journal of Rural Studies* 10(3): 249–61.

Kosai, Yutaka, and Jacqueline Kaminski. 1981. *The era of high speed growth: Notes on the postwar Japanese economy.* Tokyo: Nihon Hyoronsha.

Liaw, Kao-Lee. 1992. Interprefectural migration and its effects on prefectural populations in Japan: An analysis based on the 1980 census. *Canadian Geographer* 36(4): 320–35.

Moore, Richard H. 1987. Land tenure and social organization in a rice-growing community in Tōhoku Japan. Ph. D. diss., University of Texas at Austin.

————. 1990. *Japanese agriculture: Patterns of rural development.* Boulder, Colo.: Westview.

Media Production Group. 1991. *As Iwate goes: Is politics local?* (video) Center for Educational Media Institute for Education on Japan. Earlham College, Richmond, IN 47374.

Muramatsu, Michio. 1997. Local Power in the Japanese State. Trans. Betsey Scheiner and James White. Berkley: University of California Press.

Nakane, Chie. 1970. *Japanese society.* Berkeley: University of California Press.

Nichi Nichi. 1997. Tōwa Chōchō Nennai de Yūtai [Tōwa to voluntarily retire by year's end]. *Iwate Nichi Nichi Shinbun*, 9 December.

————. 1998a. Odashima Mineo, Kikuchi Norio Tōwa Chōchōsen Ikkiuchi ga nōkō [Odashima and Kikuchi battle over farm policy for Tōwa mayoral seat]. *Iwate Nichi Nichi Shinbun*, 1 January.

————. 1998b. Odashima Hatsutōsen [Odashima attains first election victory]. *Iwate Nichi Nichi Shinbun*, 26 January.

Obara, Hideo. 1996a. *Tōwa-chō Sōgō Kaihatsu Keikaku* part I. [The Tōwa-chō comprehensive development plan part I.]. March 3. Tōwa-chō Town Office. Iwate-ken, Waga-gun, Tōwa-chō.

————. 1996b. *Tōwa-chō Sōgō Kaihatsu Keikaku* part II. [The Tōwa-chō comprehensive development plan part II.). March 3. Tōwa-chō Town Office. Iwate-ken, Waga-gun, Tōwa-chō.

Obara, Hideo. 1994. *Chiisana Machi no Ookina Choosen* [Small town, big challenge]. Morioka, Japan: Totos Planning.

———. 1998. *Sonoki Ni Nareba "Mura" Wa Kawaru* [Spirit willing the "village" will change]. Tokyo: Fūunsha.

Samuels, Richard J. 1983. *The politics of regional policy in Japan: Localities unincorporated.* Princeton, N.J.: Princeton University Press.

Shimpō, Mitsuru. 1976. *Three decades in Shiwa: Economic development and social change in a Japanese farming community.* Vancouver: University of British Columbia Press.

Steiner, Kurt. 1965. *Local government in Japan.* Stanford, Calif.: Stanford University Press.

Tōwa Kōhō (Tōwa Town Newsletter). 1998. "Building a Healthy Community Full of Hope with 6 Billion 360 Million Yen." October issue, 2. Tōwa-chō Town Office. Iwate-ken, Waga-gun, Tōwa-chō.

6

Repopulating the Village?

John Knight

The phenomena of rural depopulation and rural abandonment have been widely documented. The rural exodus that has occurred throughout the industrialized world has affected remoter, forest-edge peripheries with particular severity. This trend has been well-documented, especially in Europe.[1] In many cases, this process of rural abandonment has become irreversible, with abandoned areas reverting to (secondary) forest, and even becoming redefined as places of natural heritage in the context of national parks (Romano 1995, 129). There have also been state attempts to halt and reverse the trend of rural depopulation (Pallot 1990, 660–69). But typically priority is given to more proximate parts of the countryside at the expense of the remoter areas which have tended to be written-off as too expensive to integrate and modernize. In this chapter, I present an example of attempted rural repopulation from upland Japan in the 1990s, with specific reference to direct interventions in population management by the municipal government.

Since the 1960s rural depopulation—the theme of "the dying Japanese village"—has assumed a high profile in Japan (Hiraike 1985; Kanzaki 1996, 26). The other side of the rapid economic growth and development in and around the cities has been the demographic decline and economic stagnation of remoter rural Japan. Although lowland rural areas have often been effectively integrated with metropolitan Japan through transport links and industrial relocations, upland areas have not. Ultimately, the depopulation and abandonment of these forest-edge settlements results in their reclamation by the adjacent forest. This is a fate which has claimed many of Japan's small upland villages in the course of the twentieth century, and seems set to account for many more in the next one. "If the wave of depopulation continues, will

107

not villages throughout Japan become forest in which all that remains are the ruins of where people once lived?" (Kitsu 1990, 94).

For some writers, this scenario amounts to a national disaster. For the economic geographer Yūki Seigo, the depopulation of Japan's upland periphery represents the release of nature from human control, with potentially calamitous consequences. "Nature which has been liberated from the control of human productive labour is like a wild animal freed from its cage. The great increase in flood damage in recent times is one face of depopulation" (Yūki 1970, 146-47). For the rural sociologist Hasegawa Akihiko, the depopulation of upland Japan means that "territory is being lost which has been established as a place of human dwelling over hundreds, even thousands, of years of human history during which Man did battle with nature. Man has become weary and tired in the war with nature, he has abandoned the war, he has conceded defeat" (Hasegawa 1996b, 25). It is as though depopulation, through the consequent reforestation that occurs, represents a de facto loss of national territory and a diminution of national strength.

Efforts are being made to resist rural depopulation in Japan. This applies to the level of national government, where considerable resources have been provided to tackle the depopulation problem, but also to the level of local government. In this chapter, I document the efforts made by a municipal government on the Kii Peninsula in western Japan to expedite repopulation. Data is drawn from the mountainous municipality of Hongū-chō in Wakayama Prefecture, where ethnographic fieldwork has been carried out in a number of stages in the late 1980s and in the 1990s.

Depopulation

The municipality of Hongū-chō was formed in 1956 from the merger of five old municipal units (the *mura*). This rural town consists of fifty mountain villages, ranging from concentrated downstream settlements made up of hundreds of households to sparsely populated upstream settlements of only a few. It covers an area of just over 200 square kilometres, and consists largely (93%) of forest land, most of which lies on smaller mountains and hills, with farmland accounting for only 1 percent of the land area. Accordingly, forestry has been the dominant local industry, and farming of relatively little importance.

In the postwar period, Hongū has been afflicted by large scale outmigratory depopulation. In 1955 the population of

Hongū-chō was 10,276, but by 1995 it had fallen to 4,310. Post-war depopulation in Japan can be broken down into a number of phases characterized by markedly different rates of decline. In the period 1965–70 alone, Hongū lost no less than one-fifth of its total population! Since this time the local population has continued to decline, but at much slower rates. Postwar depopulation has also been marked by a discrepancy between the figures for individuals and for households. The individual population of Hongū fell by over half, whereas the number of households declined by around 20 percent, from 2,263 households in 1956 to 1,754 by 1995. This indicates that, in general, depopulation has been due to the outmigration of younger family members rather than the departure of whole families. Consequently, there remains a large number of households, but they mostly consist of older people.

Depopulation is caused, in the first instance, by large scale outmigration. Official records show that in the period 1965–95, 12,356 people outmigrated from Hongū. Although this averages out at just over 400 outmigrants each year, the figure conceals enormous variations within the period. The peak of outmigration was in 1967 when more than 1,000 people left, and the trough in 1991 when 177 people left. However, there is a second phase of rural depopulation in which population decline is principally accounted for by the low fertility rates arising from the removal of the reproductive age bands from the local population by outmigration. The birth-rate in Hongū declined from 210 births in 1956 to 27 births in 1995. The mortality figure, by contrast, has remained relatively stable: 88 deaths in 1956, compared to 61 deaths in 1995. Eventually, a threshold is passed whereby fertility rates fall below mortality rates; in Hongū this point came in 1970, the first year when local deaths exceeded local births—69 to 65. This natural reduction of population is one of the features of rural areas in advanced states of depopulation (Mitsuhashi 1989, 23).

One of the characteristics of depopulated rural Japan is the population structure that emerges. First, there are few children. In Hongū in 1960 there were 3,548 children aged 0-14; by 1996 the number had fallen to 518, one-seventh of the 1960 total. In 1960 children aged 0–14 made up 37 percent of the Hongū population, but by 1996 this had diminished to 12 percent. Second, the number of young adults falls. In 1955 there were 1,546 people in their 20s, making up 15 percent of the population; but by 1996 there were only 318 people in their 20s, just over 7 percent of the population. On the other hand, the proportion of the elderly increases. In 1955 people aged over 65 made up 6.7 percent of the local population, but by 1995 this proportion had increased to 33 percent.

One of the problems for younger adults who do remain in the village, rather than migrate, is marriage. Surveys have shown that a great many Japanese municipalities are "short of brides" or *yomebusoku* (see Shukuya 1988, 40–41; Itamoto 1994, 144). In Hongū in 1994 31 percent (55 out of 178), of men in their 30s were unmarried compared with a national figure of around 25 percent. There is also a growing number of rural bachelors in their 40s and 50s. Many of these unmarried men are farmers, foresters, and construction workers, and the problem tends to affect white collar workers, such as those in the town hall, much less.

Another feature of depopulated Japan is that, in addition to its (diminished) residential population, it has attached to it a secondary population of migrant sons and daughters. Although Hongū has lost most of its natal population through outmigration, many of these migrants remain connected to their hometown economically, ritually, communicatively, and through return visits. The main occasion for return-visiting is *bon*, the great midsummer festival, during the three days of which the village populations swell to three times their normal size. Such migrant ties can make an important contribution to mountain village life—by helping local families to continue farming where otherwise they might abandon it; by reinforcing, through ritual, the sense of family unity, despite the reality of dispersion; and, insofar as they bind migrants to their natal localities, by expediting future return-migrations. However, the migrant connection can also contribute to the demoralization of the village. At the end of *bon* the village returns to its earlier state of depopulated normality. Within a few short days, the excitement of the crowded village gives way to silence and stillness, a change which can produce a palpable sense of sadness and loneliness among villagers.

Another source of demoralization in depopulated areas is the environment. There is a proliferation of *akiya* (empty houses): my own 1989 survey (of four Hongū villages) showed that 31 of the 148 houses, or 21 percent, were unoccupied. There is also much abandoned farmland. In recent decades the area of farmland in Hongū has diminished by two-thirds, from 508 hectares in 1960 to 179 hectares in 1995. One consequence of this trend (accelerated by the government policy of ricefield acreage reduction, known as *gentan*) has been a large drop in the area of ricefields, many of which have been transformed into dry fields for the cultivation of vegetables and other crops, whereas the old dry fields at the forest edge have become scrubland or planted with conifer saplings to become, in effect, an extension of the forest. Consequently, the forest has expanded throughout upland Japan. In Hongū, forest has increased from 90.7 percent of the municipal area in 1970 to 92.7 percent in 1995. Although the increase in the forest area is proportionately small (in the case of Hongū only 2%), this extra forest has a considerable visual impact, making the village feel a dark, lonely (*sabishii*) place.

Depopulated villages, with their proliferation of empty, rundown houses, closed-down schools, abandoned farmland, encroaching forest, grown-over footpaths, and unkempt graveyards, are typically viewed as depressing, spooky (*bukimi*) places, places with no future, places forgotten by the rest of the nation—"villages of death" (*shi no shuraku*), in the words of one observer (Aoyama 1994, 19–20). The decline of the timber forests, many of which were in effect commissioned by the nation in the aftermath of the war to regenerate the national timber resource, are a a striking visual testament to the present-day national indifference to the domestic forestry industry and the forestry villages dependent on it in places like Hongū.

Depopulated areas are also afflicted by social fragmentation and depression. "Human relations have collapsed, individuals are dispersed and isolated, and there is a loss of social cohesion" (Hasegawa 1996b, 37). As one rural mayor put it, "what is frightening is when depopulation reaches the hearts of [local] people" (in Takahashi 1984, 6). Commentators refer to "depopulation consciousness" (*kaso ishiki*), where residents lose confidence in their way of life and develop an inferiority complex (Yūki 1970, 131–32); to "psychological depopulation" (*shinriteki kasoka*) where the residents of depopulated villages "become depressed and irresponsible" (Hasegawa 1996a, 13); and to "depopulation of the heart" (*kokoro no kaso*) where local people lose pride in their village and wish that they were in Tokyo or some other large city (Hiramatsu 1990, 151–52; Hasegawa 1996b, 23; Senboku 1998, 17-20). High rates of clinical depression have been reported for depopulated areas (Ogino 1977, chap. 2). Depression especially affects young men unable to get married because of the bride shortage (Yūki 1970, 153–55; MSAS 1988, 16–17), and involuntary bachelorhood in rural areas has also been linked with high rates of suicide (Uchiyama 1990, 154).

It is against this background that the town hall desperately seeks to stem the population decline and attract people back to Hongū. One of the features of the town hall in depopulated rural Japan is an institutionalized optimism whereby it constantly talks up the future. A key expression in the case of the Hongū town hall is that of the *akarui machi* or "bright town" that Hongū is set to become, an implicit reference to the present-day "dark" state of depopulation that must be tackled. As part of the programme of *akarui machizukuri* (Creating the Bright Town), the town hall has undertaken a range of initiatives to foster identification with the town and to promote optimism and enthusiasm about its future (see Knight 1994). But these efforts tend to be undermined by ongoing population decline. This is the background to the more direct attempts to boost the local population.

Revitalization Initiatives

Formally, the mountain villagers of Hongū are *chōmin* or town citizens. The institutional locus of the town is the town hall which, with eighty-seven full-time municipal employees (all of whom are local people), is by far the largest employer in Hongū. The town hall is responsible for the general administration of the town, especially in the areas of registration, health, welfare, public works, and education. In addition, the town hall takes on responsibility for tackling the depopulation trend and maintaining the municipal population.

The municipality exists to administer a certain scale of human population in a delimited area. Administrative efficiency was one of the main reasons behind the 1956 municipal mergers. One governmental commission cast doubt on the viability of all municipalities with populations less than 8,000—something that in 1950 implied the redundancy of 85 percent of them (Steiner 1965, 187)! The threat of administrative merger still hangs over many of Japan's depopulated municipalities. In Hongū town hall, there is much anxious talk about a further municipal amalgamation in which the town would become administratively incorporated into Shingū City on the coast. Accordingly, for the town hall, the very survival of the municipality as a distinct entity depends on halting the depopulation trend.

Infrastructural improvement is one of the main ways in which the local state has attempted to secure repopulation. Enormous resources have been put into building and improving the rural road infrastructure, and into constructing buildings and facilities such as new administrative offices, new community halls, new schools, new clinics, and new recreational facilities such as gymnasia and sports grounds. There have also been attempts at attracting private sector economic investment into remote areas, and many remote municipal governments have been active in soliciting factory relocations to their areas. In addition to these measures, local governments have embarked on efforts to manage the rural population through pronatalist measures.

Pronatalism

In the past, the Japanese state has attempted to secure population increase by pronatalist policies, such as promoting marriage and encouraging married couple to have more children. Pronatalist policies are evident in present-day depopulated areas too. There is official encouragement of marriage. Municipal governments in Japan have become involved in the area of marriage brokerage. From the mid-1970s on, prefectural and local governments responded to the growth of rural bachelorhood with a range of measures designed to assist local men in their search for brides, including the establishment of municipal marriage consultants, marriage awards to young couples, and go-between incentive schemes (i.e., a finder's fee system). In 1993, 408 municipalities offered monetary "marriage awards' to newly married couples, and 419 municipalities had go-between incentive schemes (KKTK 1994, 29–30).

Another initiative has been the establishment of meeting clubs (*kōryūkai*, Contact Societies); these are intermunicipal associations—usually with urban municipalities—that hold events (popularly referred to as *shūdan omiai* or group dates) in holiday resorts and other venues at which rural men have the opportunity to meet women. But these events have failed to secure many actual marriages. In the case of the *kōryūkai* of Wakayama Prefecture, between 1982 and 1994, 6,231 people participated in the various gatherings, but only 184 were successful in finding a marriage partner through the scheme. Some rural municipalities in Japan have sought to assist local men in getting married by establishing links with foreign municipalities (in southeast Asia) in order to provide a new source of brides.[2] No such initiative has been launched in Hongū, even though there are in fact a small number of foreign brides (from the Philippines and Thailand) in the municipality.

There is also official encouragement of childbirth and other schemes to boost the numbers of children. In Japan 462 depopulated municipalities offer childbirth awards (*shussan shukkin*) to citizens who have babies (KKTK 1994, 30), and some waive medical fees for children under the age of 6 (MSAS 1988, 30). However, in the case of these childbirth awards (as with the marriage awards), the small sums of money involved would appear to make little difference. Despite these pronatalist policies, there cannot really be fertility campaigns in depopulated areas as there have been at the national level simply because the reproductive demographic or age-band has often ceased to exist locally. Municipal efforts to secure social reproduction tend rather to be focused on encouraging re-turn-migration and in-migration—in other words, on the bringing-in of a reproductive population (importing fertility).

Return-Migration

The second area of direct population management is return-mi-gration. Hongū town hall registration figures show that 2,018 people return-migrated between 1985–95, on average 200 each year. Since the 1970s, municipal and prefectural governments in Japan have actively encouraged return-migration. This has largely taken the indirect form of promoting economic development in the expectation that greater local job availability will, in itself, induce return-migration. There are examples where this strategy has proved successful (Okahashi 1984, 428–30). However, in recent years more direct measures have been employed to promote return-migration. Prefectures have opened offices in Tokyo to publicize the return option and to handle inquiries from the public. Advert-izing campaigns have been carried out—through, for example, posters in the Tokyo subway, print advertisements, television commercials—exhorting migrants from the regions to return to their *furusato*. Rural municipalities have even offered monetary incentives to encourage migrants to return to their villages (Nozoe 1994, 88–89).

     Some rural municipalities have formed migrant associations aimed at consolidating links with migrants and encouraging would-be *yūtānsha* or "U-turners" (e.g., MSAS 1988, 25; cf, Yasui 1997, 66-68). An example of this is the establishment of the Sasayuri Kōryūkai by Hongū in 1993. An annual gathering of the Hongū *kōryūkai* takes place in Osaka, attended by Hongū migrants in the Keihanshin area (the metropolitan area embracing the cities of Kobe, Osaka, and Kyoto) and by Hongū residents, and features a banquet, folk art performances by Hongū citizens, the (subsi-dized) sale of Hongū produce ranging from farm produce to folkcrafts, and speeches by Hongū leaders and migrant representatives. The attendance of these gatherings is between 400 and 500 people, the great majority of whom are migrants; in the 1993 gathering, for example, there were 350 migrants and 60 Hongū residents present.

The gathering is an opportunity for migrants considering return-migration to consult informally with town hall staff and with local residents. The *kōryūkai* represents a concrete instance of the town reaching out to its migrants and becoming a sponsor of the *furusato* tie. Since 1960 Hongū has passively suffered urban outmigration, but it is now becoming more assertive by actively encouraging return-migration. The Hongū town hall estimates that there are up to 8,000 people of Hongū origin in the Keihanshin area—twice the current population of Hongū itself. Through the *kōryūkai*, the town is attempting to institutionalize this link with a large pool of potential future citizens. It is hoped that, by consolidating hometown ties, the *kōryūkai* will help to reduce the tendency among migrants to lose touch with the hometown, and that it will therefore make easier the decision to return. However, doubts have been expressed as to the effectiveness of the *kōryūkai* in stimulating return-migration. According to one view, people in the city will either return-migrate or not depending on their own circumstances, regardless of such gatherings.

One main obstacle to return-migration is the shortage of appropriate local housing. Formally, rural heirs would be entitled to dwell in their family house, but in practice many are reluctant to live with their parents under one roof. Rural municipalities respond to this problem by providing extra housing for return-migrants in this situation. Some rural town halls have produced inventories of empty houses, with a view to encouraging resettlement or at least to putting them to some other (public) use. The National Land Agency offers subsidies to rural municipalities for the renovation and reutilization of empty houses and old school buildings (KKTK 1994, 239–41). Hinoemata-mura in Fukushima Prefecture, for example, has built "'U-turn housing" and singles apartments in order to make return-migration to the village easier for non-successors (Kai 1997, 181). In Hongū too, a housing shortage is recognized; in some cases, return-migrants have been unable to reside in the actual town area and forced instead to go to neighbouring municipalities that do provide rentable housing. This situation has led to demands in Hongū for public funds to be used to establish public housing for return migrants or for the town hall to buy up empty houses and make them available for return-migrants.

The Furusatokai

There is a further dimension of the village-migrant relationship that should be considered. The *furusato* relationship of the migrants can serve as a powerful social model, one which makes possible new, wider forms of affiliation with, even recruitment to, the village. The prime example of this is the *furusatokai* (hometown association). The *furusatokai* is a rural-based mail order food enterprise that sells local farm products (often garden produce) directly to urban consumers in a seasonal, low-volume food trade (for a fuller account, see Knight 1998b). The enterprise is explicitly modeled on the migrant-hometown tie: consumers adopt the rural locality as their *furusato*, becoming *furusato menbā* or hometown members. Some associations explicitly characterize their locality in kinship terms, such as the Country Relatives Village (*inaka no shinseki mura*). The food package that is transacted is known as the *furusato kozutsumi* or village parcel—a reference to the food parcel traditionally sent by village mothers to migrant sons.

The Hongū Town Country Taste Society of Friends (*Hongū-chō inaka no aji tomo no kai*) was established on November 12, 1984 by a former schoolteacher who had recently return-migrated to Hongū from Tokyo. The launch received considerable national publicity, and by 1985 the Society had 120 members. The membership figures have subsequently fallen—by 1994 membership had dropped to half of this figure (and has since declined even further). The enterprise sends out quarterly parcels of local food produce, including game meat, freshwater fish, wild herbs, fruit, vegetables, rice, *tsukemono* pickles, and *miso* bean-paste. The parcel also contains a (hand-written) newsletter informing the urban membership of news and developments in Hongū, including introductions to and descriptions of named local producers of the *furusatokai* produce.

There have been a variety of initiatives aimed at deepening the tie of the *furusatokai* member to his or her adopted hometown. Members of the Hongū *furusatokai* are invited to local festivals and other events (and offered special discount rates at local guesthouses). Some *furusatokai* overlap with "owner schemes" whereby, in addition to the quarterly food deliveries, members become "owners" of citrus, apple or other fruit trees which they come to harvest themselves (see FJS 1988). *Furusatokai* members are also the object of various forms of rhetorical inclusion. They may be designated or proclaimed by their adopted locality to be special villagers (*tokubetsu sonmin*) or special citizens (*tokubetsu chōmin*). They may also be offered other forms of institutional inclusion, in an effort to reinforce their allegiance to the host locality. In the Winter 1992 newsletter of the Hongū *furusatokai*, reporting the forthcoming Osaka *furusato kōryūkai* gathering (see above), the urban *furusatokai* "members" are invited to join the *kōryūkai* gathering—in effect merging the symbolic migrants with the real migrants.

Furusatokai members are also invited to settle in the locality. The founder of the Hongū *furusatokai* initially believed that the city members, because of their strong attraction to the countryside, could become a source of repopulation for Hongū. The Spring 1991 newsletter of the Hongū *furusatokai* carried an invitation to the city "members" to come and live in Hongū, along with the promise of assistance with finding housing and land. Subsequent issues of the newsletter followed up on the theme by describing the problems of local schools faced with the prospect of mixed-year classes (and by implication, eventual school closure), and by encouraging city families with young children to settle locally and thereby help to maintain single age classes.

To what extent are these overtures successful? There are examples from other Japanese consumer-producer co–partnerships of consumers who eventually do opt to migrate and live in the producers' village, crossing the line to become one of the producers themselves. In his report on the Miyoshi-Tokyo Copartnership, Darrell Moen mentions the example of a Tokyo family who decided to move to Miyoshi where they took up farming (Moen 1997, 21–22). Some members of the Hongū *furusatokai* have expressed a strong interest in settling in Hongū in the future. To date, however, none have actually made the move.

New Settlers

Although none of the *furusatokai* urbanites have settled in Hongū, other urbanites have. Since the 1970s people of urban origin have been migrating to the countryside to take up rice farming, dairy farming, woodcrafts, charcoal burning, and timber forestry, or to pursue artistic vocations such as poetry, painting, sculpture, and calligraphy. Many of the settlers are young, recently married, and starting a family. These rural settlers, known as "I-turners" (as opposed to "U-turners" and "J-turners"), are, in many cases, actively invited to come and settle locally by rural municipalities, which see them as a potential source of repopulation. Prefectures have established offices in the big cities to field inquiries from would-be "new farmers," as well as assistance and training programs to help them settle (see Hidaka 1996, 188–97).

According to the 1997 Farming White Paper (*Nōgyō hakusho*), in 1996 inquiries about rural resettlement were made by 3,570 people (to the National New Farmers' Guide Center and Prefectural Advice Centers), and 384 people actually began farming (NTK 1998, 174). In the period 1988–96, the same source records that 1,556 people took up farming. These figures undoubtedly understate the phenomenon of rural resettlement because much of it tends to bypass official channels, and occurs instead through networks of people committed to organic farming and alternative lifestyles and through informal word-of-mouth communication. Since 1980 approximately twenty new families have come to settle in Hongū-chō. They originate from Tokyo, Kyoto, and Osaka, as well as regional cities, and their past occupations include company employee, computer programmer, gardener, livestock farmer, baker, Buddhist priest, and artist. Most have come to practice organic farming, in some cases exclusively so. In the 1990s a number of incomers have joined the labor force of the Hongū Forestry Cooperative, whereas others have taken up charcoal-burning and woodcrafts. They usually rent vacant houses at very low cost.

This recent rural resettlement trend in Hongū originated independently of the town hall, and should be understood in relation to certain counter-cultural currents in modern Japanese society. However, the Hongū town hall soon lent its support to the trend, providing assistance to newcomers with finding property and settling in. There are a number of reasons for this official welcome. First, the infusion of these young adults is seen as a benign demographic addition to the aged municipality; in some cases, their young children boost the rolls of village schools. Second, the newcomers' interest in organic farming is seen as something that could contribute to development initiatives aimed at reviving farming and establishing new local products. Third, the newcomers are to be seen as a valuable contribution to the forestry industry (as Forestry Co-operative employees).

The new settlers may not, however, be a long term replacement population for outmigrants. Some incomers react to frictions with locals by leaving. Some find their new way of life harder than anticipated and give up after a few weeks or months (cf., Hidaka 1996, 164). Others have no permanent commitment to begin with, and come only to obtain a one-off experience of country life—a phenomenon that has been likened to that of the young Japanese who go abroad to get experience of living and working in a foreign country (Kitsu 1993, 115). There are also what might be called "serial settlers" who, while pursuing the same lifestyle, periodically move from one new region to another. Some refer to themselves as "travellers" (*tabi no hito*) or "ramblers" (*yūhosha*) (Takahashi 1984, 34); one family (in Fukui Prefecture) depicted themselves as "guerrilla peasants" (*gerira nōmin*) who must constantly move rather than remain tied to one place (Yamashita 1993, 113).

Attracting the Elderly?

In recent years some rural municipalities have pursued another repopulation strategy. Known as Revitalization through Welfare (*fukushi de kasseika*), rural areas across Japan have actively sought to attract old people as a means of boosting their populations. According to an NHK documentary, 241 out of Japan's 3,237 municipalities have *kaigo ijūsha* (care migrants)—older people who have migrated to these localities on account of their superior welfare provision. Across Japan, rural municipalities have established what are variously known as Silver Areas and Welfare Villages: special zones consisting of advanced welfare provision (e.g., home helpers, visiting nurses, special housing, customized medical facilities) aimed at attracting elderly migrants to their areas.[3] The municipality of Shimizu-chō, lying to the northwest of Hongū-chō, has plans to establish a welfare village (*fukushi no sato*), consisting of assorted care facilities for the elderly, into which it hopes to attract retired couples from outside (Wakayama-ken 1996, 28–29). The first phase of the plan envisages twenty-five new households in the village.

The background to this new trend is the change taking place in Japan's system of elderly care provision. A new National Care Insurance scheme (*kokumin kaigo hoken*) began in 2000. This system is aimed at stimulating and improving welfare provision in order to meet the demands of the aged society that Japan is projected to become in the twenty-first century. Hongū town hall staff view this scheme as heralding a revolution in the provision of welfare for the elderly, in particular by allowing for much greater choice among the elderly as to where they receive care and welfare services. The head of the Residents Section (Jūminka) in the Hongū town hall, Matsumoto Junichi, believes that welfare is becoming "one industry among others" (*sangyō no hitotsu*) and that rural municipalities will come to compete with each other to attract elderly people. Increasingly, municipalities like Hongū must give some thought to the strategy of Revitalization through Welfare.

However, in Hongū-chō the strategy of Revitalization through Welfare strikes many people as strange, if not bizarre. One common local quip is that Hongū does not need old people's homes because it already is one. When raising the issue of the Revitalization through Welfare, I have also encountered strong hostility among some Hongū people. "It's the same as disposing of rubbish! It's the same as the *obasuteyama*," said one Hongū man in his 50s, referring to the famous *obasuteyama* legend of elderly abandonment in which grandmothers are left to perish in the mountains. The reference to "rubbish" (*gomi*) expresses the perception that remote areas such as Hongū, which are already burdened with a disproportionately large local elderly population, are being treated as a dumping ground for the nation's elderly.

Until now, "village revival" and "revitalization" have been defined in terms of *recovering a balanced population* (such as by providing a sufficient local employment base). The strategy of attracting elderly settlers through improved welfare, although it may slow or halt population decline on paper, appears to do little to stem the outmigration of local youth. Moreover, until now, the dominant discourse of rural decline has been one which pairs depopulation with aging—*kasoka* with *rōreika*. Old people have tended to be viewed as part of the problem—the "aging problem" or *rōreika mondai*. Suddenly, a new official orthodoxy is emerging of Revitalization through Welfare, in which the elderly are redefined as a "resource," and therefore as part of the solution to depopulation. The reactions above indicate that this new perspective is likely to take some time to gain popular acceptance within depopulated areas like Hongū.

Conclusion

The initiatives examined in this chapter point to two alternative images of the future in upland areas of Japan like Hongū. The first is that of a kind of return to the *status quo ante:* to the demographically balanced rural society of the past, to which the missing younger age bands are restored. The realization of this state of demographic normality will of course depend on the establishment of a commensurable economic base. In this connection, much hope is placed on the revival of the forestry industry in the coming decades, as the ubiquitous timber plantations established in the 1950s and 1960s reach maturity. In forestry circles in Japan there is much talk about a forthcoming "era of domestic timber" (*kokusanzai jidai*) in the first decades of the twenty-first century in place of the present-day situation in which foreign timber satu-rates the Japanese timber market. No doubt there will be an in-crease in the level of domestic timber production, but it is not clear what lasting difference this will make to the employment base in the upland areas of Japan. Even in conjunction with the recent growth of the tourist sector in upland areas of Japan, the likely increase in employment in forestry will not necessarily be of an order that will support the scale of population of the 1950s.

However, the widespread idiom of *kōryū* or contact suggests an alternative image of rural society in the future. At the end of the twentieth century, rural Japan has ceased to be a true *lifecourse* space for most of those born into it. The great majority of natal villagers will leave it, to live most, if not all, of the rest of their lives outside it. They have become *lifephase* spaces into which people are born and raised but then leave, perhaps to return later in life. Whether as a place of study, of work, or of settling down, the city becomes part of the normative lifecourse for *all* present-day Japa-nese, urban-born and rural-born, and, to this extent, there no longer is a "rural Japan" in the conventional sociological sense of the term. The above examples of *kōryū* in Hongū-chō suggest that at least some rural municipalities in Japan are coming to terms with this new reality. The *kōryūkai* can be seen as an attempt to exploit the appeal of the village as a *furusato* or place of origin, whereas the Hongū *furusatokai* represents an example of the fictive ex-trapolation of the rhetoric of *furusato* beyond actual migrants to unrelated urbanites. The Revitalization through Welfare strategy suggests a further recognition of these new patterns of residential behavior. In other words, despite the obvious municipal nostalgia for the return of the rural lifecourse space, in practice there ap-pears to be an increasing acceptance of and adjustment to the new ways in which demography cross-cuts locality in the modern world.

Notes

1. See Pallot (1990) for Russia; Stasiak (1992) for Poland; Vartiainen (1989) for Finland; Romano (1995) and Batzing et al. (1996) for the Alps; and Preiss et al. (1997, 51–52) for France.

2. For extended discussion of municipal matchmaking in rural Ja-pan, see Knight (1995).

3. Well-known examples, which have received much media coverage, include Goshiki-chō in Awajishima, Ōmori-machi in Akita Prefecture, and Minami Shinano-mura in Nagano Prefecture.

122   *John Knight*

References

Aoyama, Hiroshi. 1994. Tenryū ringyōchi kara no hōkoku [A report from the Tenryū forestry region]. In *Sanson ga kowareru mae ni* [Before mountain villages are destroyed], edited by Sanson Keizai Kenkyūsho. Tokyo: Nihon Keizai Hyōronsha.

Batzing, Werner, Manfred Perlik, and Majda Dekleva. 1996. Urbanization and depopulation in the Alps. *Mountain Research and Development* 16(4): 335–50.

FJS (Furusato Jōhō Sentā). 1988. Furusato jōhō [Home village information]. Tokyo: Author.

Hasegawa, Akihiko. 1996a. Joron—chiiki kasseika no shiten to mondai [Introduction: Issues and problems in regional revitalization]. In *Kaso chiiki no keikan to shūdan* [Landscape and groups in depopulated areas], edited by Hasegawa Akihiko, Fujisawa Kazu, Takemoto Tamotsu and Arahi Yutaka. Tokyo: Nihon Keizai Hyōronsha.

1996b. Kasoka no shinkō to kasotaisaku no suii [Ongoing depopulation and trends in depopulation countermeasures]. In *Kaso chiiki no keikan to shūdan* (Landscape and groups in depopulated areas), edited by Hasegawa Akihiko, Fujisawa Kazu, Takemoto Tamotsu and Arahi Yutaka. Tokyo: Nihon Keizai Hyōronsha.

Hidaka, Kunio. 1996. *40 sai kara no inakagurashi* [Country Life after Forty]. Tokyo: Tōyō Keizai Shinpōsha.

Hiraike, Yoshikazu. 1985 The dying Japanese village. *Japan Quarterly* 32(3): 316–19.

Hiramatsu, Morihiko. 1990. *Gurobaru ni kangae, rokaru ni kōdō seyo* [Think globally, act locally]. Tokyo: Toyo Keizai Shinpōsha.

Itamoto, Yōko. 1994. Sanson seikatsu to kekkon mondai [Mountain village life and the marriage problem]. In *Sanson ga kowareru sono mae ni* [Before mountain villages are destroyed], edited by Sanson Keizai Kenkyūsho. Tokyo: Nihon Keizai Hyōronsha.

KKTK [Kasochiiki Kasseika Taisaku Kenkyūkai]. 1994. *Kasochiiki kasseika handobukku* [Handbook on revitalization of depopulated areas]. Tokyo: Gyōsei.

Kai, Taketo. 1997. "Bunka shihon" to shite no sukii to "chiiki no kyōikuryoku" [Ski-ing as "cultural capital" and the "standard of regional education"]. In *Sanson no kaihatsu to kankyō hozen* [Mountain village development and environmental preservation], edited by Matsumura Kazunori. Tokyo: Nansōsha.

Kanzaki, Noritake. 1996. Muraokoshi no haikei [The background to village revival]. *Nihon Minzokugaku* 206: 25-36.

Kitsu, Kōichi. 1990. *Kore kara wa inakagurashi ga omoshiroi* [From now on country life is interesting]. Tokyo: Hato Shuppan.

Kitsu, Kōichi. 1993. *Inaka urimasu* [Selling the countryside]. Tokyo: Daiyamondosha.

Knight, John. 1994. Town-making in rural Japan: An example from Wakayama. *Journal of Rural Studies* 10(3): 249–61.

———. 1995. Municipal matchmaking in rural Japan. *Anthropology Today* 11(2): 9–17.

———. 1998a. Wolves in Japan? An examination of the reintroduction proposal. *Japan Forum* 10(1): 47–65.

———. 1998b. Selling mother's love: Mail order village food in Japan. *Journal of Material Culture* 3(2): 153–73.

MSAS (Mainichi Shinbun Akita Shikyoku), ed. 1988. *Kaso* [Depopulation]. Akita, Japan: Mumeisha.

Mitsuhashi, Nobuo. 1989. Kaso shichōson ni okeru jūmin ishiki ni tsuite— kyōju no chūshinsei to no kanren. [Residents' attitudes in depopulated municipalities]. *Nōson Seikatsu Sōgō Kenkyū* 7: 23-42.

Moen, Darrell Gene. 1997. The Japanese organic farming movement: Consumers and farmers united. *Bulletin of Concerned Asian Scholars* 29(3): 14-22.

NTK (Nōrin Tōkei Kyōkai). 1998. Nōgyō hakusho [Agriculture white paper]. Tokyo: NTK.

Nebuka, Makoto. 1991. *Yama no jinsei: Matagi no mura kara* [Mountain life: From the village of Matagi]. Tokyo: NHK Books.

Nozoe, Kenji. 1994. *Furusato no saisei no michi* [The road to the rebirth of the hometown]. Tokyo: Ochanomizu Shobō.

Ogino, Kōichi. 1977. *Kaso chitai no bunka to kyōki—Okunoto no shakai seishin byōri* [Culture and insanity in depopulated regions: The social psychopathology of Okunoto]. Tokyo: Shinsensha.

Okahashi, Hidenori. 1984. Kaso sanson, Ōita-ken Ōyama-machi ni okeru nōgyō seisan no saihensei to sono igi [Reorganization of agricultural production in the depopulated mountain village of Ōyama-machi in Ōita Prefecture and its wider significance]. *Jinbun Chiri* 36(5): 413–32.

Pallot, Judith. 1990. Rural depopulation and the restoration of the Russian village under Gorbachev. *Soviet Studies* 42(4): 655–74.

Preiss, Eric, Jean-Louis Martin, and Max Debussche. 1997. Rural depopulation and recent landscape changes in a Mediterranean region: Consequences to the breeding avifauna. *Landscape Ecology* 12(1): 51–61.

Romano, Bernadino. 1995. National parks policy and mountain depopulation: A case study in the Abruzzo region of the Central Appennines, Italy. *Mountain Research and Development* 15(2): 121–32.

Senboku, Toshikazu. 1998. *"Nogyō" kibō sengen* [Declaration of Hope for "Agriculture"]. Osaka, Japan: Mainichi Shinbunsha.

Shukuya, Kyōko. 1988. *Ajia kara kita hanayome: mukaerugawa no ronri* [The brides who came from Asia: The receiving side's logic]. Tokyo: Akashi Shoten.

Stasiak, Andrzej. 1992. Problems of depopulation of rural areas in Poland after 1950. *Landscape and Urban Planning* 22: 161–75.

Steiner, K. 1965. *Local government in Japan.* Stanford, Calif.: Stanford University Press.

Takahashi, Yoshio. 1984. *Inakagurashi no tankyū* [Investigating country life]. Tokyo: Sōshisha.

Uchiyama, Masateru. 1990. *Gendai nihon nōson no shakai mondai.* [Social problems of present-day Japanese villages]. Tokyo: Tsukuba Shobō.

Vartiainen, Perttu. 1989. The end of drastic depopulation in rural Finland: Evidence of counterurbanization? *Journal of Rural Studies* 5(2): 123–36.

Wakayama-ken. 1996. *Aritagawa ryūikiken kasseika keikaku* [Revitalization plan for the Aritagawa Valley area]. Wakayama City, Japan: Prefectural Offices.

Yamashita, Sōichi. 1993. *Datsusara nomin wa naze genki* [Why are new farmers doing well?). Tokyo: Ie no Hikari Kyōkai.

Yasui, Manami. 1997. "Furusato" kenkyū no bunseki shikaku [The analytical vision of furusato research]. *Nihon Minzokugaku* 209: 66–88.

Yūki, Seigo. 1970. *Kamitsu kaso: yugamerareta nihonrettō* [Overcrowding and depopulation: The distorted Japanese archipelago]. Tokyo: San'ichi Shinsho.

7

Finding Common Ground: Family, Gender, and Burial in Contemporary Japan

Satsuki Kawano

In opposition to the prewar ideals that emphasize the continuity of the family line and three-generational households, present-day Japanese society is facing a dramatic demographic shift, characterized by a falling birth rate, a shrinking household size, postponed marriages, and the spread of single-person households. This chapter provides a cultural analysis of such demographic shifts and their impact on ancestor veneration in Japan.[1]

The system of ancestor veneration in Japan requires that successors in the stem family (*ie*) provide ritual care for the family dead. During the thirty-three–year ritual cycle, the family dead gradually lose their individual characteristics and finally join the collectivity of ancestors as their contemporaries die out (Plath 1964). The Japanese idea of *en* (connections) is embodied in the continuous exchange of ritual care between the living and the family dead. What happens to ancestor veneration and the associated idea of connections when the society is no longer ensuring the healthy supply of descendants to care for the dead? In order to answer this question, this chapter first describes the system of ancestor veneration and the family grave system, then identifies the increasing number of people who are disadvantaged in such a system in the present demographic context. Third, this chapter examines creative solutions—new burial systems—that have emerged to cope with the lack of grave successors. Finally, the chapter examines socioeconomic factors that surround the prospect of new burial systems.

The data used in this chapter were collected during my fieldwork in the Tokyo Metropolitan Area and in Kyoto between May 1998 and June 1998. During my fieldwork, I visited funeral homes, Buddhist temples, citizens' groups, and cemeteries. Semi-structured interviews were conducted with funeral home employees, Buddhist monks, members of citizens' groups, salesmen of graves, as well as my informants in Kamakura City, with whom I already had research connections from my previous fieldwork conducted between 1995–96.

The Dead in Japanese Society

In Japanese society, the dead are dependent on the living—typically their descendants—to become full-fledged ancestors.[2] The dead who have no descendants to provide such care become *muenbotoke*, pitiable "homeless souls" (Plath 1964) or, literally, the "disconnected" dead. The division between these two kinds of the dead is visible in every Japanese cemetery—whether it is a Buddhist temple's cemetery, a public graveyard, or a private cemetery: there are the family graves for ancestors and *muenbaka* (the "disconnected" graves) for homeless souls.

The cultural idiom of "connection" (*en*), which reveals the "relational" nature of the Japanese personhood (Smith 1983; Kondo 1990), helps explain the stratification between ancestors and homeless souls. The term "connection" is often used to refer to, but is not limited in its usage to, kinship and marital ties. It may be used to refer to relations in general, both interpersonal and human-object relations. Connections bring persons, families, objects, and even the dead into interactive states. For example, arranged marriages are called *endan*, whereas unmarried persons are said to have no connections (*en ga nai*). The term disconnection, on the other hand, refers to the state in whereas persons, families, objects, and the dead are set apart and cease interacting. When a child is discharged from a family, his or her ties to parents are said to be severed (*oyako no en o kiru*). The disowned child no longer takes part in familial interactions. The expression "severing connections" is also used for a divorce.

Unlike the disconnected dead, ancestors are part of the culturally valued continuity—generations of successors and their spouses. Ancestors continue to maintain social identities and participate in the social life among the living (Plath 1964, Smith 1974, Hamabata 1990). They are permanently enshrined at a domestic altar and at the family grave, receive regular offerings and greetings, and are thanked for ensuring the well-being of their descendants. Ancestors are talked to or about as if they were alive—often in the present tense. Meanwhile, the disconnected dead are liminal souls; they have no homes to return to. Unlike ancestors, the disconnected dead are usually not enshrined at a domestic altar (*butsudan*) or at the family grave. However, they are not entirely denied ritual care. Family members, communities, or religious organizations occasionally venerate them as a group. Homeless souls are venerated not because they ensure the well-being of the living, but because they are pitiable souls and may harm the living.

The Family Grave System

The division between ancestors and homeless souls has been built into the family grave system, both legally and conventionally. The right to use a grave is indivisible under the Meiji Civil Code (1896–8) as well as the New Civil Code (1947). Only one child—most frequently the eldest son—inherits the right to use the family grave; therefore, all the other children who set up branch families have to build their own graves. Those who are married-out will have the right to be buried at their spouses' family graves.

The family grave is a place that embodies the prewar ideology of the *ie*, or the stem family, characterized by frequent primogeniture and the legal privileges of the successor over the other family members. Under the Meiji Civil Code, inheritance of the family grave was defined to be one of the privileges of the successor of the *ie* (the stem family).[3] Although the New Civil Code legally terminated the *ie* defined by the Meiji Civil Code, it drags a ghostly shadow of the *ie* (Takeuchi 1993) and specifies that the successor of the grave is determined according to the "custom" (*kanshū ni yori*, in Article 897).[4] The "custom" is not clearly explained and thus easily evokes the old custom under the Meiji Civil Code.

The presence of such old "custom" is evident in Tokyo's Public Cemetery Regulations[5] (1971, in Fuji 1991, 226), which set up parameters for choosing a grave successor. These regulations value a blood relative (*ketsuzoku*) over an affine, a linear (*chokkei*) over a nonlinear (*bōkei*), descending generations (*hizoku*) over ascending generations (*sonzoku*), male over female, elder over younger, and the main family line over the branch family line. These parameters resemble those for choosing the *ie* successor in the Meiji Civil Code (Article 970). In this system, women and younger siblings are clearly disadvantaged in inheriting the right to use their family graves.

In principle, the family line should continue and the family grave is permanently tended by the generations of successors in the stem family. When graves have no successors to provide financial and ritual care for the dead, the grave becomes "disconnected,"[6] and the dead are reburied at the graves for homeless souls, usually located in the shady corner of a temple's cemetery. Its disadvantaged location speaks to the misery of the nameless disconnected dead. People without successors are seriously disadvantaged in the family grave system.

Recent Demographic Contexts and the Family Grave System

The media as well as government reports have highlighted demographic contexts behind the "grave problems" (*hakamondai*). Until the late 1980s, growing urban centers were producing a serious shortage of cemeteries in the Tokyo Metropolitan Area (Fujii 1993, 10–11). Since the Meiji Period, public cemeteries have been built every several decades. Aoyama, Yanaka, Zōshigaya, and Somei Cemeteries opened in Tokyo in 1872; Tama Cemetery opened in 1923 away from the central city; Yahashira Cemetery in 1935, Kodaira Cemetery in 1948; and Hachiōji Cemetery in 1971. In spite of their scale, these cemeteries scarcely met the needs of the increasing urban population in the Tokyo Metropolis; Hachiōji Cemetery became full in 1987. In order to deal with the shortage of cemeteries, Tokyo Metropolis started two committees on "grave problems" (*Tōkyō-to reien mondai chōsakai* in 1986 and *Shin reientō kōsō iinkai* in 1988). This stimulated administrators at the national level; the Ministry of Health and Welfare organized two committees and considered future prospects for cemeteries.

However, as the 1998 national survey conducted by the Ministry of Health and Welfare (1998) shows, in addition to a lack of cemeteries (34.2%) and rising cost of graves (43.7%), the lack of successors (27.4%) has emerged as a new social problem in recent national demographic contexts. The national survey reveals "grave problems" beyond those commonly associated with urban settings—such as a lack of cemeteries and the rising cost of graves. Under the family grave system, which stratifies souls with and without successors, the rising number of people without successors—such as permanently single people, childless couples, and couples having only married-out daughters—promise to become the disconnected dead. The total fertility rate is continuously falling (1.35 in 2000), people are marrying later (in 2000, the average age for first marriage was 28.8 years old for men, 27 years old for women), the size of the household is becoming smaller (2.76 in 2000), and the number of single-person households is rising (26.4% in 2000) (See Table 7.1).[7] These demographic trends sharply contrast with the pre-war ideals that stress the continuity of the family line and three-generational households.

Because the conventional family grave system presupposes the continuity of the family line, an increasing number of people without successors are denied their right to buy a grave, to receive proper ritual care, and to follow the path leading to full-fledged ancestorhood. Particularly, with the current low birth rate, many people will be the eldest son or daughter. Since the bride or the groom has to become a member of the spouse's family at the time of marriage, some families will surely lose successors for their graves. People's fear of becoming the "disconnected dead" is spelled out in surveys, mass media, advertisements of cemeteries, and popular culture.

For example, *"Ohaka ga nai!"* (I have no grave for myself!) is a 1997 movie that comically addresses today's grave-related problems (*haka mondai*). In this movie, a famous, single actress in her forties believes that she will die of cancer within half a year. On

Table 7.1: Recent Demographic Trends

	Birth Rate	*Average Age for First Marriage*	
		Male	Female
1925	5.11		
1940	4.12	—	—
1955	2.37	—	—
1975	1.91	27	24.7
1985	1.76	28.2	25.5
1995	1.42	28.5	26.3
1999	1.34	28.8	27
	Household Size	*Proportion of Single-Person Households*	
1960	4.14	16.5%	
1975	3.28	19.5%	
1985	3.14	20.8%	
1995	2.82	25.6%	
2000	2.76	26.4%*	

Source: Based on Ministry of Health, Labour, and Welfare (http://www.mhlw.go.jp) except for Number of Single-Person Households 1960–95 (Japan Statistical Yearbook 1997). *The figure was obtained from the latest report on 2000 National Census (http://www.stat.org).

the festival of the dead (*obon*), the director of the film tells everybody, both actors and staff, to visit their family graves (*hakamairi*) because the film makers are making a movie about death and therefore should pay respect to the dead. (The actress is playing the role of a mother whose daughter will die of cancer within half a year.) In the film, one of the characters says: "I wonder what it's like for those who have no graves for themselves. What a pity—they'll become homeless after death." The actress feels shocked, realizing that she will be dead soon but has no grave. In fact, the 1998 national survey indicates that the majority of the respondents (81.4%) already have graves for themselves, and respondents often inherit their family graves.[8] If the actress were married, she would have the right to be buried in her husband's family grave. Yet, she is unmarried. The actress does not even have a natal family—she has told everybody that she is from a well-to-do family, but in fact, she is an orphan. She belongs to no family; thus, she has no family grave. Her quest to find her ideal grave begins.

The actress first visits a renowned Buddhist temple in central Tokyo and encounters the most typical grave-acquisition rules. When the actress asks the priest if she may buy a grave, the priest asks her, "Do you have somebody who can take care of the grave after your death? Do you have any family members who live with you?"[9] After finding out that the actress lives alone and has no family, the priest tells her that without a successor or a family she cannot buy a grave. The persons who promise to be "disconnected"—including successful, single women like the actress—are anomalies in Japanese society, where marriage and childbearing are taken for granted. A Japanese person is conceptualized to be shaped by a web of interpersonal relationships (See, for example, Smith 1983; Lebra 1976 and Kondo 1990), and one of the most fundamental connections is based on his or her belonging to the family and house, *uchi*. It is not hard to imagine that homeless souls are seriously in trouble in such a society.

Moreover, the system of recycling grave lots, which costs a significant amount of time and money for grave providers, further disadvantages persons without successors. Public cemeteries in Tokyo declare a grave to be disconnected when the annual maintenance fee has not been paid for ten years (Inoue 1990, 108). According to the Ministry of Health and Welfare, in order to conduct reburials of the dead in disconnected graves[10] and to recycle grave lots, the following procedures should be taken:

1. Potential successors[11] must be sought by referring to the administrative districts where the dead resided or the dead's original family registry is located, and verification needs to be obtained that no successor was found; or

2. Advertisements have to be published more than three times in more than two kinds of daily newspapers, and verification must be obtained that no query was made by a potential successor.

Advertisements two columns by five centimeters in size (typical for an advertisement for reburials) in a national and a regional newspapers are estimated to cost approximately ¥400,000 (=$3,600; Takeuchi 1993, 121). A male informant in his sixties told me that since the family grave is very important, the process of reburials is made to be complex and difficult. However, such a system further disadvantages the increasing number of people without successors, because, considering the cost and the time required for renovating a grave, it makes sense for grave-providers to avoid customers without successors in the first place.

The Grave as a Place

Why does the actress in the film mentioned earlier badly need a grave? A grave is considered a place to memorialize the dead (*shisha o shinobu*).[12] A grave has to be maintained and visited regularly, most commonly during the festival of the dead in August, on the two equinoxes, and on the annual deathday(s).[13] In addition, my informants typically visit their family graves for the New Year, when their social ties with others—including family, friends, clients, deities, and ancestors—are renewed. Some informants visit their family graves more often, for example, on the monthly deathday(s) or whenever convenient. To visit a grave is a culturally valued act of maintaining the connection between the dead and the living.

My informants told me that when they visit family graves, they can "meet" their close kin, such as their parents and grandparents. At a family grave, my informants interact with the family dead. They wash the gravestone; purify the grave; burn incense; and make offerings, such as flowers, food, and drink, to the ancestors. A female informant in her late forties told me, "I used to bring my mother's favorite food to her grave, a bag of rice crackers." Another informant, a male engineer, offered a can of beer to the grave of his father, who used to enjoy drinking with other family members. The beer was then circulated among the family members to be shared. The communal nature of a grave visit is also evident in the following case. A female architect in her late thirties told me that she designed a grave for her deceased father-in-law. She said, "I designed a bench by the gravestone for visitors to sit and spend time with the dead." Similarly, spreading a plastic picnic sheet and a lunch box, a salesman tells the actress: "A good thing about a Western-style lawn cemetery is, we can have a picnic with *hotoke-sama* (ancestors)."

The actress in the film has no family to memorialize her, but, instead, she wants her fans to visit her grave and keep her alive in their memories. After visiting graves at a Buddhist temple in central Tokyo, a large, suburban private cemetery, and a locker-style grave in a building, the actress states that she wants something more "lively" (*ikiikishita*). She comments on a famous singer's grave covered with bouquets and incense offered by fans: "Misora Hibari, Ishihara Yujiro, and Ozaki Yutaka—all the famous stars are remembered after death because we have their graves to visit!"

The actress also wants a grave because the wealth and fame of the family or the individual is often translated into a grave. The actress wants a grave that represents her fame. Representing herself as being from a wealthy family, she states that her natal family grave is probably larger than a small apartment where a young movie staff member lives. In fact, my informant, whose ancestor is a renowned medieval warrior, has a grave as large as an eight-mat-*tatami* room, certainly larger than a tiny efficiency in Tokyo. Those who want to show off may spend millions of dollars to build large, elaborate graves. In search of her ideal grave, the actress even takes a flight over the ancient tomb of Emperor Nintoku; it is a good example that ostentatiously displays the authority and wealth of the deceased.

In addition to being a place for memorialization and displaying fame, a grave is considered a house of the dead. Preferable spatial conditions of a grave and a house overlap to a great extent. A salesman of graves told me: "Just like houses, people like a grave with a good view in a sunny location facing south, while they dislike a small grave in a wet and shady spot." Images of graves are changing from dark, scary places to bright, park-like places.[14] Like a house, a grave is expensive; a typical grave in Tokyo costs ¥3,000,000 (=$27,300). This usually includes a gravestone, engraving services, ritual utensils, a fence, an underground structure for storing the urn of ashes, and the permanent right to use the grave lot (as long as the family line continues). Frustration, laments, and anger often characterize narratives surrounding grave-hunting. In an article entitled "New Residents in Tokyo in Search of Graves,"[15] the writer compares graves with houses in Tokyo. Then he laments, "Considering that we have all endured small rabbit-huts before our death, the present situation of graves seems to suggest: 'why can't we stand small graves as cremated remains.'" A 67-year-old man stated that he spent two years looking for a reasonably priced and located grave. When he finally bought a grave for ¥2,000,000 (=$18,200; this excludes the cost of the gravestone) in a suburb of Tokyo,[16] he commented, "Since I've bought a grave, I am not worried about dying any more. Yet, I wonder what the government is doing; ordinary people today cannot afford dying since graves are so expensive."

A grave is a house in material terms. The grave is a place where the dead people "sleep" (*nemuru*). Just as a house accommodates a family, a grave accommodates the bodily remains of a family. Bodily remains are more than mere material objects but are reference points where the dead's spirits reside.[17] In the film mentioned earlier, the actress feels shocked when she realizes that her bodily remains will be placed in a tiny urn in a small underground structure under the gravestone. She becomes horrified: "Since I am claustrophobic, my cremated remains will be too!" Similarly, an unmarried female informant in her fifties told me:

> My family can trace back their ancestry for seven hundred years in Hiraizumi, and we have our own graveyard on a hill. When my family had to renovate our graves, we found old bones of my grandparents. These bones come from the time when the bodies were not cremated. I touched the bones with gloves, and greeted my ancestors. I had a feeling that I finally met the grandfather I never knew—but heard many stories about.

In short, a grave is a house of the dead, regularly maintained and visited by the living to memorialize the dead. The actress needs a grave to sustain her social identity after death—to remain connected to the living.

Seeking Connections after Death

Since a grave is considered a house of the dead, burial partners matter. A couple with marital problems may want to "get a divorce after death." Partners in extramarital affairs may try to be buried

together and "get married after death." The children by the deceased
first wife may refuse their step-mother's entry into their family grave,
and create their "ideal" family after death. A grave is not a passive
reflection of society, but is actively shaped by social actors.

Following Caudill and Plath's work on sleeping patterns (1966),
let us now examine sleeping patterns after death: who wants to be
buried with whom. In choosing coresidents of the house after death,
the conjugal tie is most frequently sought, second is the future-
oriented linear tie with children, and third is the past-oriented
linear tie with ancestors. According to the 1998 national survey,[18]
70.1 percent of the respondents reported that they want to be buried
with their spouses, 41.1 percent with their children, 25.7 percent
with ancestors of their *ie* (*senzo daidai*), and 24.9 percent with
their own parents (See Table 7.2).

Women are increasingly voicing their wishes to be buried with
their own parents and/or ancestors of their natal families.[19] Some
women do not want to be buried at their husband's family graves.
Others wish to have their cremated remains split and a portion
buried in their natal family graves. These women are questioning
the ghostly shadows of the prewar gender ideologies behind the
family grave.

For example, in 1985, 531 out of 720 housewives surveyed in
Sankei Living Newspaper reported that they did not want to be

Table 7.2: Preferred Burial Partners

Multiple Answers, N = 1,524, M = 713, F = 811

Spouse	70.1%
Children	41.1%
Ancestors of the *Ie*	25.7%
Parents	24.9%
Spouse's Parents	9.6%
Brothers and Sisters	3.5%
Alone	1.4%
Non-linears	0.8%
Close Friends	0.8%
No Preference	5.4%
Other	0.5%
I do not know	7.3%

Source: The 1998 National Survey, Ministry of Health and Welfare. Stratified
random sampling.

buried at their husbands' family graves.[20] Such a sentiment is comically portrayed by the following cartoon entitled "Rebellious Women Speaking of Independence after Death" published in a weekly magazine (*Shūkan Asahi,* July 2, 1992). In this cartoon, fed up with her husband's incessant demands such as "Hey you! Give me a cup of tea," "Where is my ash tray?," and "My mother is asking if you've already prepared dinner," an older female ghost is leaving her unpleasant conjugal grave. Frowned and with her eyes tightly closed, the chubby female ghost is carrying luggage wrapped in *furoshiki* (a wrapping cloth used for transportation of goods) and shaking in anger, as she floats away from her burial partners.

A female journalist Inoue (1990) also portrays voices of women contesting the family grave system. In her survey (1989–90), 36.4 percent of the female respondents: 1) wished to be buried with their own parents; 2) wished to be buried at their natal family graves; 3) refused to be buried with their husbands; 4) refused to be buried with their husband's parents; or 5) refused to be buried with their husband's family's ancestors. Therefore, these respondents either seek connections by tracing natal family ties or avoid making connections with linears of their husband's families. A woman can trace both natal family and conjugal family ties to seek coresidents after death; some of the respondents in this category reported that they wanted their ashes to be divided and a portion buried at their natal family graves. Therefore, not all of the 36.4 percent of the respondents in Inoue's survey "rejected" the idea of the conjugal *ie* or took a complete departure from the *ie* system. Nonetheless, when seeking connections after death, an inclination toward natal family ties is present.

Although the majority of respondents in the 1998 national survey seek connections with their kin after death, 1.4 percent reported that they want to be buried alone. The idea of an individual, independent grave, however, does not deny the idea of connection itself; to achieve ancestorhood, the deceased buried at an individual grave is likely to depend on the living for ritual care. Therefore, just because a person wants to be buried alone in an individual grave, he or she is not necessarily denying the idea of his or her connections to their family members.[21]

Finally, some people seek connections beyond kinship—with friends or others with similar ideas. Although only 0.8 percent reported that they wanted to be buried with close friends (*shitashii hito*; the 1998 national survey), the idea of being buried in the collective grave with non-kin (*gōshibaka*) is spreading.

Graves with Permanent Ritual Care

Eitai Kuyōbo, or a grave that is permanently cared for, has become a new option for those who have difficulty securing a grave successor. In this new system, instead of descendants, religious organizations provide ritual care for the dead, usually for thirty-three years after death. Therefore, even though a person cannot provide a grave successor, he or she will not become a homeless soul with the new system.

One of the earliest cemeteries with permanent ritual care appeared in Hieizan Enryakuji Grand Cemetery in 1985. A salesman told me that the idea of building such a cemetery came from a funeral organization in Tokyo, which frequently dealt with the dead without family—the dead whose ashes were not collected after cremation. The number of these cemeteries is spreading rapidly. The cost to be buried at these graves is much lower, between ¥100,000 (=$900) and ¥5,000,000 (=$45,500) per person. According to Inoue,[22] eight cemeteries with permanent ritual care were established between 1985 and 1989, forty-one cemeteries between 1990 and 1994, and fifty-two cemeteries between 1995 and 1997. *Eitai kuyōbo no hon* (2000), a recent guide describing cemeteries with permanent ritual care, lists 230 cemeteries. Based on these figures, the number of these cemeteries grew at least five times between 1990 and 2000.

Among 147 cemeteries identified by Inoue in 1997, a large number of cemeteries with permanent ritual care are located in Tokyo (31%) and its surrounding bedroom cities such as Kanagawa, Chiba, and Saitama (33%), wheras the rest are spread all over Japan (28%) with a small concentration in Osaka, Kyoto, and Hyōgo (6%). Although the presence of these cemeteries is not limited to urban areas, the Kansai area accommodates a significantly lower number of new cemeteries, indicating regional variations beyond simple urban/rural distinctions. Members of *eitai kuyōbo* tend to come from local areas where the cemeteries are located. For example, among 2,793 members of Moyai no kai in Tokyo, 92 percent of the members were the residents of Tokyo, Saitama, Chiba, and Kanagawa prefectures. At Annonbyō in rural northern Japan (Niigata), a pioneer in this field, 133 out of 232 members are the residents in Niigata, whereas fifty-nine members are the residents in Tokyo and Kanagawa (as of 1993). Therefore, although Tokyo and the surrounding areas provide the majority of *eitai kuyōbo* and their clients, we cannot ignore the needs for these cemeteries in other parts of Japan, including rural areas. Yet, this does not imply that the social factors that influence people's choice to use such graves are the same in various regions of Japan.

Cemeteries with permanent ritual care follow a membership system based on individual participation, rather than the conventional, family-based parishioner system (*danka*). They strategically incorporate the idea of connections beyond family (*kazoku*) and consanguinity (*ketsuen*). For example, Annonbyō, started in 1989, aims to provide graves for people without successors. Among 232 persons who became members of Annonbyō (March 1993), 24 percent were childless, 21 percent had only daughters, and 11 percent were unmarried women. Others had children but felt that they could not expect them to become successors or would not want to do so (10%). Annonbyō is also a home for women who contest the gender ideology behind the family grave system. In 1993, 11% of the 232 respondents reported that they do not want to be buried with their husbands or at their conjugal family graves. Unlike typical regulations for family graves, Annonbyō's regulations state that persons with different family names can be buried together—whether they are connected by blood, marriage, or friendship. The head priest Ogawa does not deny blood relations, but regrets that Buddhist temples have long focused on blood relations since the foundation of the family-based parishioner system. He proposes to shape a Buddhist temple where people can make connections beyond kinship (*kechien*) and encourage interactions among the members of Annonbyō. Since 1990, the Annon festival has been conducted for such a purpose. The 1994 festival consisted of lectures, discussions, communal meals, chatting, musical entertainment, and Buddhist rituals. There were lectures on family and health care in the aging society, and discussions were held on whether one can ask non-kin to be caregivers during dying and after death.

In 1990, a citizens' group, Moyai no kai, originally started their activities to venerate children who died during the Second World War. Moyai no kai stands against discriminatory practices that prevent people without successors from buying graves. The head priest of Moyai no kai told me, "Even gay and lesbian couples are welcome, although, so far, we have none." There are 2,930 members in Moyai no kai (May 1998), and cremated remains of 740 people have been placed under the group's monument. The words engraved on the Moyai no kai monument broaden the idea of connections (*en*). The inscription states: "Life begins with connections. All people live in the web of connections throughout their lives. . . . This monument symbolizes a place of *moyai* (which means to connect boats together; to do things together); people gathered here can talk with each other forever."

Shienbaka, literally meaning "a grave connecting persons with the same wishes," was completed in 1990. The movement to build such a grave has been led by a women's antiwar movement, Onna no hi no kai, or Supporters of the Women's Monument. The group currently has approximately 800 members, and its core members are women who stayed unmarried because the war deprived them of marriageable men in their generation. In 1979, they inscribed their antiwar sentiments on the monument: "A woman, living alone all by herself, rests here, and wishes for peace." The leader of this movement, Tani Kayoko, states, "We wanted the word, 'here' (*kokoni*), to express the idea that women with similar experiences rest together" (1982, 14). Although they had to live alone, they can be connected after death.

Architecturally, graves with permanent ritual care take various forms. At Hieizan Enryakuji Grand Cemetery, individual small graves can be used for an individual, a couple, or a family. Others are graves for group enshrinement (*gōshibaka*). The idea to rest with numerous strangers has a negative connotation. In the film mentioned earlier, when a female customer is recommended a collective grave for her deceased husband, she replies: "My husband is very shy and nervous. I do not think he can cope with so many strangers around him." Some graves have two structures that facilitate the transition from the newly dead to the aging dead. At Annonbyō, individual graves are built on the wall surrounding a central tomb. A person can choose to use one of the independent graves for the first seventeen years, and then the cremated remains are moved into a central tomb for collective enshrinement.

Although the idea of a collective grave is not completely new,[23] the emerging graves differ from the conventional grave for homeless souls (*muenbaka*). The dead who become "disconnected" are forced to be (re)buried at the latter as nameless souls. In contrast, the names of the dead are inscribed in some form at the new collective graves, which helps maintain the dead's individual identities.

Conclusions

Both positive and negative views of *eitai kuyōbo* exist among grave-providers and grave-users, and the future of this new burial system depends on the workings of intertwined social and economic factors. For commercially oriented grave providers, *eitai kuyōbo* opens

up a new market for the dead, those who were previously un-
wanted customers. In particular, a collective grave only requires a
small space and thus can be built easily within crowed urban temple
cemeteries. However, some of the gravestone providers I interviewed
are afraid that the popularity of collective graves may seriously
reduce the future demand for gravestones.

From grave users' perspectives, unlike the family grave that
continuously requires maintenance fee and labor, burial at graves
with permanent ritual care is much less expensive and carefree
(starting around $900 per person). Some people report that they
"do not want to become burden on their children" *(kodomo ni
meiwaku o kaketaku nai)* and choose these graves because they are
easily maintained. In spite of these positive aspects of the new
burial system, for some grave providers and users, *eitai kuyōbo*
remains a second-rate solution for "pitiable minorities" in Japanese
society: those who *cannot* get married or have children. A salesman
I interviewed pointed out: "A grave with permanent ritual care
takes a new form, but the idea behind it is old. Somebody has to
take care of the dead. The new system simply transfers the ritual
responsibility from the family to the temple." In other words, the
new system provides a substitute to meet the dead's dependence on
the living that still remains in present-day Japan. Such a perspective is not uncommon. According to the 1998 national survey, only
14.2 percent of the respondents reported that they are interested
in or value collective graves. The majority (57.7%) reported that it
is a solution in case of crisis, in other words, when there is no grave
successor. Fourteen point six percent of the respondents even reported that such graves are "inadequate" *(fusawashiku nai)*. Negative images associated with *eitai kuyōbo* sometimes become a source
of conflict between temple parishioners and a Buddhist temple that
provides *eitai kuyōbo*.

In addition to such negative images associated with *eitai
kuyōbo*, more practical issues were raised during the 1998 seminar on graves that are permanently cared for: the quality of
their management. What does *eitai kuyō* (permanent ritual care)
mean? Who serves as the quality controller—-to make sure
whether the dead actually receives the ceremonial care? If the
contract with religious organizations provides ceremonial care
for the dead, how permanent are religious organizations? Some
organizations may go bankrupt. Their policies may change when
a new priest becomes the head of the organization. Furthermore,
some graves for homeless souls *(muenbaka)* are falsely claimed
to be new graves that are permanently cared for. In short, there

are great variations among these new graves—their quality of service and management.

Despite all the ambiguities and problems surrounding the new burial practice, some people positively emphasize their sense of agency in choosing *eitai kuyōbo*. A 50-year-old single professional woman in Tokyo (*Asahi Shinbun*, September 17, 1996, pp. 16–17) chose *eitai kuyōbo* and reported, "I thought that I might as well keep my independence (*jiritsu*) after death, since I've lived my life on my own." Although she was not prevented from being buried at her natal family grave, which her brother inherits, making her own choice about burial signaled her financial and social independence. Unlike the family grave system, in which women often obtain their membership as wives, *eitai kuyōbo* provides a burial place regardless of a woman's marital status, which constitutes a gendered critique.

Similarly, the leaders of Annonbyō and Moyai no kai emphasize the positive aspects of new burial practices. Aiming to provide what is more than a second-rate solution to the present-day grave problems, these leaders stress the communal effort by non-kin to face the dead's dependence on the living. Monk Ogawa stated, "Annonbyō is not a grave for those 'poor people' without successors." For the followers of Annonbyō and Moyai no kai, new burial systems have positively redefined the notion of connections—so central in Japanese social life—by incorporating non-kin. These movements, both inclusive and creative, constitute a cultural critique. Therefore, graves with permanent ritual care have a great potential for forming common ground in a changing Japanese society.

Notes

1. An earlier version of this paper was presented at the Director's Seminar at the Center for the Study of World Religions at Harvard University in 1999. I am thankful for useful comments provided by Misty Bastian, Scott Littleton, Susan O. Long, and Lawrence Sullivan. I am also grateful for the comments provided by the editors and the anonymous reviewers of this volume.

2. According to a municipal survey conducted among residents of Tokyo (1987), 89.1 percent of the respondents reported that they either strongly or weakly believe that it is the descendents' duty to tend the ancestral grave to venerate ancestors.

3. According to Article 987, "The successor of the *ie* inherits the privileged ownership of the family pedigree, ritual utensils, and the grave."

4. Yet, according to recent lawsuits concerning the inheritance of family graves, "the custom" in Article 897 refers to "the new custom under the New Civil Code." (For example, see the verdict of the Osaka High Court in 1949, discussed in Takeuchi 1993, 109–10).

5. From "Succession rules for the users of municipal cemeteries in Tokyo," December 13, 1971, revised in April 1, 1981.

6. According to the Supreme Court, the disconnected grave is "a grave that lacks connected parties (*enkosha*) who are responsible for providing ritual care for the dead (September 30, 1963)" (Takeuchi 1993, 114).

7. There are other demographic contexts that cause difficulties in maintaining family graves. For example, the movement of young people from rural areas to large cities depopulates their home villages and towns. This makes it difficult for their aging parents to secure successors for their graves, since their children often live far away. The lack of successors for graves is not strictly an urban phenomenon, although the demographic contexts that influence the veneration systems for the dead differ according to urban/rural settings.

8. Fifty point three percent of the respondents reported that they have inherited or are going to inherit family graves. Seventeen point eight percent reported that their spouses have inherited their family graves. Thirteen point three percent reported that they have purchased graves on their own.

9. Buddhist temple graves as well as private cemeteries often specify that persons living alone are not qualified to purchase the right to use grave lots (Fujii 1991, 225).

10. Legal Regulations concerning Graves and Burials. July 13, 1948. Ministry of Health and Welfare, No. 24, Article 3.

11. Legally, Article 725 in the New Civil Code defines the potential successor to be within the sixth-grades of relatives by blood and the third-grades of relatives by marriage. In reality it is almost impossible to investigate all the possible successors according to the above article (Takeuchi 1993, 119)

12. According to a municipal survey conducted among residents of Tokyo (1987), a cemetery was defined to be a place for memorializing the dead (73.6%).

13. According to the 1998 national survey, 86.6 percent of the respondents reported that they pay visits to their family graves more than once a year.

14. According to a Tokyo municipal survey (1987), 41.9 percent of the respondents reported that a cemetery is a solemn place (*ogosokana tokoro*), whereas 24.2 percent reported that it is a bright, park-like place.

Only 7.4 percent reported that cemeteries are dark, creepy places (*kuraku bukimina tokoro*).

15. In *Be-Common*, September 1992, in *Publicity Collection* No. 3, 1992 (2), 13, published by a leading provider of gravestones, Ōnoya.

16. "New residents of Tokyo in Search of Graves [Shin tokyo-jin no ohaka sagashi], in *Be-Common*, September 1992, in *Publicity Collection* No. 3, 1992 (2), 13, published by a leading provider of gravestones, Ōnoya.

17. This is a product of history. It has been pointed out that the attitude of valuing the bodily remains of the dead was strongly supported by the Meiji state policies. The Meiji government legally defined the grave (*haka*) to be a place where the bodily remains of the dead are buried. This led to the standardization and centralization of burial practices across the nation (See, for example, Mori 1993 and Takeuchi 1993 for further discussions on this issue).

18. A report on the 1998 national survey on graves [Bochi ni kansuru ishiki chōsa, sokuhō-ban]. March 20, 1998. Ministry of Health and Welfare. Stratified random sampling. Question 7 (Multiple answers; N=1,524; M=713, F=811).

19. Adequate information is not available to examine the extent to which natal family ties are sought by married-out women in the report on the 1998 national survey on graves. Thirty-four point four percent of the male respondents reported that they want to be buried with their parents, whereas the figure was 16.5 percent for female respondents. Meanwhile, 4.8 percent of the male respondents reported that they want to be buried with their spouse's parents, whereas the figure was 13.8 percent for female respondents.

20. In Inoue (1990).

21. We should further distinguish the ideas of being buried alone, individualism, and individuality. Currently, a common choice is to custom design a grave (often called the "original" grave) to embody the dead's individuality. For example, a salesman told me, "These days, we can design graves to represent the deceased persons. For example, if your deceased father loved to play golf, it is a good idea to incorporate a golf ball into the design of his grave." By designing an original gravestone, the individuality of the deceased is permanently displayed in a material form. Such a practice is closely related to the present inclination toward memorialism (Smith 1974). Although expressions of individuality of the dead have been reported, for example, in the practice of offering favorite foods to the deceased, it is a relatively new phenomenon to permanently inscribe the dead's individuality on custom-made gravestones.

22. The list of graves with permanent ritual care (Appendix 2) was distributed at the *Eitai Kuyōbo* Seminar, held in Tokyo in May, 1998.

23. A group of religious followers, residents of a village, members of a *dōzoku* group, and the disconnected dead are reported to be buried at collective graves (Mori 1990, 115).

References

Asahi Shinbun. 1996. Ie no haka yori kyōdō nōkotsu de, jibun no haka motome, [Choosing collective graves rather than family graves: Looking for "one's own grave"], September 17.

Be-Common. 1992. Shin tōkyō-jin no ohaka sagashi [New residents in Tokyo in search of graves]. In *Publicity Collection* No. 3, (2): 13, published by a leading provider of graves, Ōnoya.

Butsuji Gaido Henshūbu, ed. 2000. *Eitai kuyōbo no hon*. Rev. ed. Tokyo: Seiunsha.

Caudill, William, and David W. Plath. 1966. Who sleeps by whom? Parent-child involvement in urban Japanese families. *Psychiatry*, 29:344–66.

Fujii, Masao. 1993. *Kazoku to haka* [Family and graves]. Edited by Fujii Masao, Yoshie Akio, and Kōmo Mitsugi. Tokyo: Waseda daigaku shuppanbu.

———. 1991. *Ohaka no subete ga wakaru hon* [Everything you want to know about graves]. Tokyo: Purejidentosha.

Hamabata, Matthews. 1990. *Crested Kimono: Power and love in the Japanese business family*. Ithaca, N.Y.: CornellUniversity Press.

Hana, Takahito. 1997. *Ohaka ga nai!* [I have no grave for myself!] Original story by Ōmori Sumio. 111 munites, color. Shōchiku movie production.

Inoue Haruyo. 1990. *Gendai ohaka jijyō* [Reports on graves today]. Osaka, Japan: Sōgensha.

Kondo, Dorinne K. 1990. *Crafting selves: Power, gender, and discourses of identity in a Japanese workplace*. Chicago: University of Chicago Press.

Lebra, Takie. 1976. *Japanese patterns of behavior*. Honolulu: University of Hawaii Press.

Ministry of Health and Welfare. 1998. A report on the 1998 national survey on graves. Kōsei kagaku tokubetsu kenkyū jigyō.

———. 1996. *Jinkō dōtai tōkei* [Vital statistics of Japan]. Volume 1. Tokyo: Ministry of Welfare.

Mori Kenji. 1990. *Haka to sōsō no shakaishi* [Social history of graves and funerals]. Tokyo: Kōdansha.

Ōkawa Seisuke. 1993. Rebellious Women Speaking of Independence after Death (Cartoon), in the article entitled "We do not want to be buried with our husbands." In *Asahi Weekly* (Shūkan Asahi), July 2, pp. 130–2.

Plath, David. 1964. Where the family of God is the family: The role of the dead in Japanese households. *American Anthropologist* 66: 300–17.

Sōmuchō Tōkeikyoku. [Statistics Bureau, Management and Coordination Agency]. 1996. *Nihon tōkei nenkan* [Japan statistical yearbook]. Tokyo: Statistics Bureau, Management and Coordination Agency.

Sōrifu. 1990. *Bochi ni kansuru yoron chōsa* [Survey on graves].

Smith, Robert J. 1983. *Japanese society: Tradition, self, and the social order*. Cambridge: Cambridge University Press.

————. 1974. *Ancestor worship in contemporary Japan*. Stanford: Stanford University Press.

Tani Kayoko. 1982. *Onna hitori ikiru*. Kyoto: Mineruva Shobō.

Takeuchi Yasuhiro. 1993. *Saishi keishō ni okeru haka to hōritsu mondai* [Legal issues associated with inheritance of graves]. In *Kazoku to haka* [Family and graves], edited by Fujii Masao, Yoshie Akio, and Kōmoto Mitsugi. Tokyo: Waseda daigaku shuppanbu. pp. 107–128.

Tokyō-to [City of Tokyo]. 1987. A survey on graves. Tokyo: City of Tokyo.

Demographic Change and Aging

In the previous section, the authors considered how people in Japan are coping with changes in demographic behavior. Problems associated with population aging affect not only older people themselves, but the families and caregivers with whom they interact on a regular basis. In Japan, where the vast majority of elder care is provided by women (estimated to be as much as 90%), care provision is a clearly gendered issue. Central to elder care is the issue of well-being, not only for elders themselves, but for those who provide care. It is not unusual in Japan for women to be hospitalized for exhaustion as a result of the extreme demands placed on them by caring for parents or parents-in-law, in addition to caring for their own conjugal families.

In the following chapters, the authors examine the issue of well-being as it relates to both the elderly and to the women who provide care. Toshiko Kaneda and James Raymo consider declining mortality and improved life expectancy that have occurred in Japan since the end of World War II. Although extended longevity is of course a desirable goal, the question remains as to the quality of life to be lived in later years. A number of salient questions arise in this context. To what extent do people need help with activities of daily living? What proportion of the elderly population is bedridden? How do governments provide care for people who live longer and need increased help?

145

Kaneda and Raymo point out that although the issue of well-being in old age has been well studied in Western societies, it has not been sufficiently explored in Japan. The authors explore current trends in the physical well-being of older Japanese in terms of specific physical problems and abilities (such as standing up for extended periods of time) that can arise in later life. Turning to the perspectives of care providers, both Brenda Robb Jenike and John Traphagan consider how attitudes towards care provision have been undergoing change and have been contested in contemporary Japan. Jenike, working in one of Japan's major metropolitan areas, examines the experiences of two daughters-in-law living in urban Japan to explore how intergenerational contracts have been shifting in relation to the growth of public forms of social support and care. She notes the pressures experienced by women arising from expectations of care provision to elders. Although public services are available, women do not necessarily find it easy to access those resources. Women are often hesitant to give up the caregiver role for a number of reasons, including family pressures and difficulties in dealing with the welfare bureaucracy.

Traphagan, whose research was conducted in a rural part of Japan, also employs case study data to consider women's decision making about residence with in-laws. He presents the experiences of three women, whose life courses were significantly influenced by decisions over coresidence and expectations and experiences of associated provision of elder care to in-laws. He finds that women (even living in more "traditional" parts of Japan) do not necessarily simply accept the coresident caregiver role, but contest co-residence with in-laws or negotiate the terms under which they are willing to coreside and, should the need arise, provide care to those in-laws.

The well-being of care providers is closely intertwined with the pressures they experience from family and that they put on themselves, as well as the extent to which they are able to control their situations. In these chapters we see that well-being for elders, too, is intertwined with the well-being of those who provide care. Furthermore, it is clear that although the stem family system has undergone change in contemporary Japan, it has by no means been discarded as the idiom through which people experience and express familial interrelationships. The family system is the object of negotiation, contestation, and improvisation on the part of men and women who generate new ways to solve old problems, such as provision of elder care, within the framework of that system.

8

Trends in the Quantity and Quality of Life at Older Ages in Japan

Toshiko Kaneda and James M. Raymo

At the end of World War II, Japanese life expectancy was among the lowest in developed countries. During the following decades, it increased rapidly to become the world's highest by the mid-1970s (Atoh 1995). Dramatic improvements in life expectancy during the early postwar years were primarily the result of large improvements in mortality at young ages, especially in infant mortality (Kobayashi et al. 1993). With little room for further reductions in mortality at younger ages, recent gains in life expectancy are largely attributable to rapid mortality decline at older ages (Ogawa 1986; Feeney 1990). This chapter has two objectives. The first is to examine the causes of these dramatic improvements in longevity. We approach this objective by recognizing that the mortality decline responsible for increasing life expectancy at older ages has not been uniform across different causes of death. We evaluate the importance of declining mortality for ten major causes of death at older ages by decomposing the large postwar change in life expectancy into the contributions made by changes in mortality for each cause of death.

Our second objective is to explore the implications of longer life for the physical well-being of older Japanese. Although there are a large number of studies examining trends in physical well-being at older ages in Western countries (especially the United States), there are very few related studies on Japan (see Liu et al. 1995; Tsuji et al. 1995). With older Japanese now enjoying longer lives than their predecessors as well as their contemporaries in other countries, it is important to better understand the implications of increasing longevity for physical well-being in later life. In the second half of the chapter, we explore trends in the physical

147

well-being of older Japanese and examine the relationship between individual sociodemographic characteristics and physical well-being in old age.

Life Expectancy of the Japanese Elderly

In the early postwar years, the major causes of death in Japan shifted from infectious diseases (e.g., tuberculosis, gastroenteritis, and pneumonia) to noninfectious, chronic degenerative diseases (e.g., malignant neoplasm, heart disease, and cerebrovascular disease) (Kobayashi 1967; Takahashi 1982). The introduction of modern medicine (i.e., antibiotics), improved sanitation, and the expansion of medical services (including vaccination) are important reasons for the large declines in mortality from infectious diseases. The reduction in mortality from these diseases was particularly apparent at younger ages where deaths from such causes were most prevalent. As the risk of death from infectious disease declined, increases in life expectancy due to mortality decline at younger ages approached a threshold level. At 4.3 deaths per 1,000 births in 1995, Japan now has the lowest infant mortality rate in the world (Ministry of Health and Welfare 1996), making it unlikely that future improvement in infant mortality will contribute substantially to increasing life expectancy.

As mortality from chronic degenerative diseases has come to account for a larger proportion of all deaths, recent improvements in life expectancy have been driven by mortality declines at older ages. The trends in life expectancy at various ages for the period 1955 to 1995 presented in Table 8.1 clearly show that recent increases in life expectancy have been concentrated at older ages. For example, the number of years that 65 year-old women can expect to live increased from 14.1 years in 1955 to 16.6 years in 1975, then jumped to 20.9 years in 1995. The corresponding figures for men are 11.8, 13.7, and 16.5 years. These changes are proportionally larger than recent mortality improvements for younger age groups.

With mortality now concentrated at older ages, the prospect for further improvements in life expectancy depends primarily on changes in death rates for various chronic degenerative diseases (Martin 1989). In this section, we first examine the leading causes of death at older ages, and then decompose changes in life expectancy at older ages into the contributions made by mortality changes for the ten major causes of death.

Table 8.1: Life Expectancy at Selected Ages for Japanese Males and Females, 1995–95

Age	0		20		40		65		75		85		90	
Year	Male	Female	Male	Female	Male	Female	Male	Female	Male	Female	Male	Female	Male	Female
1955	63.6	67.8	48.5	52.3	30.9	34.3	11.8	14.1	7.0	8.3	3.9	4.4	2.9	3.1
1965	67.7	72.9	50.2	54.9	31.7	35.9	11.9	14.6	6.6	8.1	3.5	4.2	2.6	3.0
1975	71.7	76.9	53.3	58.0	34.4	38.8	13.7	16.6	7.9	9.5	4.1	4.8	3.1	3.4
1985	74.8	80.5	55.7	61.2	36.6	41.7	15.5	18.9	8.9	11.2	4.6	5.6	3.3	3.8
1995	76.4	82.9	57.2	63.5	37.9	43.9	16.5	20.9	9.8	12.9	5.1	6.7	3.6	4.6

Source: Abridged Life Table, Ministry of Health and Welfare, Japan

Trends in Main Causes of Death at Older Ages

Table 8.2 describes trends in the leading causes of old age mortality for the period 1955 to 1995. Age-specific death rates and the percentage of total deaths for the three main causes of death are presented by sex and three age groups: ages 65–74, 75–84, and 85 and above. We refer to these three age groups as the young-old, the middle-old, and the old-old, respectively.

During the last four decades, the main causes of death at older ages have primarily been chronic degenerative diseases, in other words, cerebrovascular disease, heart disease, malignant neoplasms (hereafter referred to as cancer), and senility without mention of psychosis (hereafter referred to as senility). Although the death rate from cerebrovascular disease increased during earlier decades, it has declined sharply for the young-old and the middle-old since 1965 and for the old-old since 1975. At the same time, cancer has become an increasingly important cause of death, especially among the young-old and the middle-old. This is partly due to increases in the death rate from cancer, but is also largely due to decreases in death rates for other diseases. Senility, which was an important cause of death for the middle-old and the old-old in earlier decades, has declined in importance for all ages over the four decades.[1] The death rates for heart disease were relatively high until 1985, then declined rapidly during the 1990s. It is these changes in cause-specific mortality that have contributed to bring about the large increase in the life expectancy of older Japanese over the last four decades.

Factors Contributing to the Post-War Mortality Decline

In this section, we provide a theoretical underpinning for the subsequent analyses by considering several factors that are responsible for the large mortality declines at older ages in Japan. We first consider the relationship between rapid economic growth during the post-World War II period and commonly cited explanations for declining old-age mortality. These explanations focus on: (1) behavioral factors (e.g., changes in diet); (2) socioeconomic factors (e.g., improvements in housing conditions); and (3) technological factors (e.g., advances in medical technology) (Yanagishita and Guralnik 1988; Kōno and Takahashi 1989; Kobayashi, Matsukura, and Ogawa 1993; Atoh 1995).

Table 8.2: Age-Specific Death Rates (ASDR) for the Three Most Common Causes of Death in Old Age for Japanese Males and Females (per 100,000), 1955–95

Ages			1955			1965			1975			1985			1995		
			Cause of Death	ASDR^a	%^{b}	Cause of Death	ASDR	%	Cause of Death	ASDR	%	Cause of Death	ASDR	%	Cause of Death	ASDR	%
65–74	Male	1	CVD^c	3239.8	28.6	CVD	3612.9	33.9	CVD	2293.8	28.7	MN	2061.5	35.1	MN	2192.7	42.5
		2	MN^d	1761.9	15.6	MN	2013.5	18.9	MN	2061.5	25.8	HD	1026.4	17.5	HD	686.5	13.3
		3	HD^e	1194.5	10.5	HD	1264.8	11.9	HD	1126.1	14.1	CVD	974.5	16.6	CVD	644.6	12.5
	Female	1	CVD	2336.7	30.3	CVD	2325.9	35.4	CVD	1433.7	30.7	MN	955.0	30.8	MN	871.9	36.7
		2	MN	1063.9	13.8	MN	1131.4	17.2	MN	1061.5	22.8	HD	613.4	19.8	CVD	354.7	14.9
		3	HD	833.4	10.8	HD	821.1	12.5	HD	705.7	15.1	CVD	603.1	19.4	HD	350.8	14.8
75–84	Male	1	SEN^f	6958.6	27.1	CVD	8237.8	29.1	CVD	6840.9	31.5	MN	3775.4	21.7	MN	4146.1	27.7
		2	CVD	5678.6	22.1	HD	3844.0	13.6	HD	3585.0	16.5	CVD	3612.8	20.8	CVD	2559.2	17.1
		3	HD	2290.9	8.9	SEN	3821.2	13.5	MN	3004.4	13.8	HD	3558.1	20.5	HD	2289.2	15.3
	Female	1	SEN	6058.5	30.7	CVD	6253.7	29.6	CVD	5219.8	33.0	CVD	2730.0	24.7	MN	1791.3	21.7
		2	CVD	4404.9	22.3	SEN	3728.0	17.7	HD	2855.2	18.1	HD	2573.5	23.3	CVD	1709.8	20.7
		3	HD	1740.7	8.8	HD	2818.7	13.4	MN	1624.2	10.3	MN	1799.9	16.3	HD	1559.9	18.9
85+	Male	1	SEN	30613.6	53.1	SEN	18707.2	33.8	CVD	12304.8	23.9	HD	10384.7	23.8	CVD	7890.9	18.6
		2	CVD	6597.7	11.5	CVD	9706.1	17.6	HD	10391.9	20.2	CVD	8379.4	19.2	PNEU^g	7720.7	18.2
		3	HD	3323.1	5.8	HD	7173.1	13.0	SEN	10106.5	19.7	SEN	5948.4	13.7	HD	7079.1	16.7
	Female	1	SEN	26024.1	55.3	SEN	19124.6	39.6	SEN	11148.6	24.6	HD	8646.4	24.3	CVD	6496.7	21.9
		2	CVD	5224.9	11.1	CVD	8217.2	17.0	CVD	1757.5	23.7	CVD	7641.4	21.5	HD	5646.8	19.1
		3	HD	2551.6	5.4	HD	5924.9	12.3	HD	9054.0	20.0	SEN	6371.1	17.9	PNEU	4208.2	10.2

^{a}Age-Specific Death Rates
^{b}Percentage of Total Death
^{c}CVD = cerebrovascular diseases
^{d}MN=malignant neoplasms
^{e}HD=heart diseases
^{f}SEN=senility without mention of psychosis
^{g}PNEU=pneumonia

Source: Vital Statistics of Japan, Ministry of Health and Welfare, Japan

Rapid post-war economic growth has brought a drastic change in the Japanese diet (Tanaka et al. 1982; Martin 1989; Ohno 1985; Atoh 1995). The traditional diet in Japan, characterized by high salt and low animal protein intake, has been associated with a high incidence of cerebrovascular disease (Kōno and Takahashi 1989; Martin 1989). The traditionally high level of mortality from cerebrovascular disease saw a large decline over postwar period as the Japanese adopted a more Western diet that included less salt and more animal protein (Komachi 1971; Tanaka et al. 1982; Ohno 1985).

Postwar prosperity also led to improved housing conditions, including the introduction of refrigerators and modern heating systems. By reducing the need for salt as a food preservative, the widespread use of refrigerators has contributed to a reduction in salt intake (Takahashi 1993). By making it possible to heat all rooms (including bathrooms) and decreasing temperature differences inside the house, improved heating systems have helped reduce the risk of cerebral hemorrhage, a common cause of death at older ages in the past (Kobayashi, Matsukura, and Ogawa 1993; Takahashi 1993).

Postwar economic growth has also been accompanied by advances in medical technology. Medical advances enabling early diagnosis and more efficacious treatment have lowered mortality by slowing the progression of diseases. For example, improved control of hypertension has contributed to declines in mortality from cerebrovascular disease (Ohno 1985; Ueshima et al. 1987; Imaizumi 1991). Recent declines in mortality from heart disease are also largely attributable to advances in the treatment (Iso et al. 1999).

The impact of medical advances on mortality has been augmented by the implementation of a national health insurance system in the 1960s (Yanagishita and Guralnik 1988). Greater access to medical care has increased preventive care, especially among the elderly, and has facilitated early diagnosis and medical intervention. For example, the postwar declines in death rates for gastric cancer and uterine cancer are largely attributable to earlier diagnosis and intervention made possible by greater access to preventive care (Imaizumi 1991). Early diagnosis is particularly important as it enables individuals to make behavioral adaptations that influence the disease process (e.g., reduced smoking and alcohol consumption) (Verbrugge 1984).

Decomposition of Changes in Life Expectancy at Older Ages

Because we are interested specifically in life expectancy changes at older ages, we focus our decomposition analysis on the mortality experiences of men and women aged 65 and older.[2] Our analysis focuses on changes in life expectancy due to changes in mortality from the ten most common causes of death at these older ages for the period 1955 to 1995. These causes of death are diabetes, cancer, heart disease, hypertensive disease, cerebrovascular disease, liver disease, senility, pneumonia, accidents (including automobile accidents), and suicide. At age 65–69, these ten causes together account for nearly 75 percent of all deaths in 1955 and 85 percent of all deaths in 1995. Other causes of death are included in our analysis under "all other causes."[3]

We use multiple decrement life tables (MDLTs) to decompose the overall changes in life expectancy at older ages into the component contributions made by mortality changes from the ten causes of death. MDLTs are a valuable tool for analyzing the complex relationships between changes in life expectancy and changes in mortality rates for multiple causes of death. A change in the mortality rate for a given cause of death affects life expectancy both directly (i.e., by reducing deaths from that cause) and indirectly (i.e., by increasing exposure to other causes of death).[4] By accounting for both of these effects, MDLTs enable us to measure the contribution made by changes in mortality from each cause of death to the overall change in life expectancy.

The first step in the analysis is to construct MDLTs by sex and age (five-year age groups) at ten-year intervals for the period 1955 to 1995. These tables are constructed using age-specific death rates for the ten selected causes of death from the Vital Statistics of Japan (Ministry of Health and Welfare 1995). The next step is to construct hypothetical MDLTs in which the mortality rates for a given cause of death are substituted with the corresponding mortality rates from the previous period (i.e., the mortality rates that prevailed ten years earlier). This substitution procedure enables us to simulate what life expectancy would have been in a given year if no change in mortality had occurred over the preceding ten-year period. By taking the difference between this simulated life expectancy and the observed life expectancy, we can calculate the change in life expectancy attributable to change in mortality for a particular disease.[5]

The results of this decomposition procedure are presented in Tables 8.3a through 8.3d, each of which corresponds to a decade between 1955 and 1995. We present the contributions to change in life expectancy made by changes in mortality from each of the ten major causes of death, both in number of years and as a percentage of the absolute value of the total change in life expectancy. A positive number of years indicates that changes in mortality from a given cause contributed to an increase in life expectancy, whereas a negative number of years indicates that changes in mortality from a given cause contributed to a decrease in life expectancy, net of changes in mortality from all other causes. For example, in Table 8.3a, the figure of 0.08 in the first column for senility indicates that, between 1955 and 1965, changes in mortality from senility contributed 0.08 years to life expectancy for 65–69 year-old men, net of changes in mortality from other causes of death. As shown in the subsequent row, this contribution is equivalent to 7.8 percent of the absolute value of the total change in life expectancy for 65–69 year-old men. In the same column, the figure of –0.06 for diabetes indicates that changes in mortality from diabetes reduced life expectancy for 65–69 year-old men by 0.06 years, or 5.4 percent of the absolute value of the total change in life expectancy, net of changes in mortality from other causes of death.

The ten causes of death most common in old age together accounted for between 42 percent and 91 percent of all change in life expectancy at older ages for the period between 1955 and 1995. From 1955 to 1965 (Table 8.3a), increases in life expectancy for men and women at all ages is attributable primarily to declines in death rates for senility. This is particularly true at the oldest ages where over one-third of the increase in life expectancy can be explained by declines in mortality from senility. The large declines in death rates from senility are considered to reflect a change in diagnostic practices (i.e., a reduction in doctors' propensity to attribute death to senility). All other causes of death included in the analysis made negative or negligible contributions to life expectancy during this decade.

During the following decade, 1965–75 (Table 8.3b), declines in mortality from both senility and cerebrovascular disease contributed to life expectancy increases among the young-old. Changes in cerebrovascular disease were particularly important at younger ages (i.e., men up to age 74 and women up to age 69) where it replaced senility as the main contributor to the increase in life expectancy.

Between 1975 and 1985 (Table 8.3c), declining mortality from cerebrovascular disease emerged as the largest contributor to the increase in life expectancy for men and women at nearly all ages (i.e., up to age 90 for men and age 85 for women). The dramatic declines in mortality from cerebrovascular disease during this decade accounted for one-third and nearly one-half of the life expectancy increases for men and women aged 65–69, respectively. During the same period, declining death rates from senility continued to

Table 8.3: Contributions of the Ten Most Common Causes of Death to the Total Change in Life Expectancy at Older Ages for Japanese Males and Females, 1955–95

8.3a. 1955–65

Cause of Death	65–69 Male	65–69 Female	70–74 Male	70–74 Female	75–79 Male	75–79 Female	80–84 Male	80–84 Female	85–89 Male	85–89 Female	90+ Male	90+ Female
Diabetes Mellitus	-0.06 (5.4)	-0.14 (5.1)	0.06 (5.3)	-0.05 (5.0)	0.23 (5.3)	0.15 (4.9)	0.44 (5.4)	0.40 (5.1)	0.13 (5.1)	0.14 (4.9)	0.00 (0.3)	0.00 (0.0)
Malignant Neoplams	-0.05 (5.1)	-0.11 (4.1)	0.06 (4.9)	-0.04 (4.4)	0.22 (5.1)	0.14 (4.5)	0.41 (5.0)	0.36 (4.6)	0.12 (4.9)	0.13 (4.6)	-0.02 (1.3)	0.00 (0.9)
Heart Diseases	-0.05 (4.6)	-0.14 (5.1)	0.06 (5.0)	-0.05 (5.7)	0.24 (5.5)	0.19 (6.3)	0.48 (5.9)	0.51 (6.5)	0.16 (6.3)	0.19 (7.0)	-0.26 (16.8)	0.00 (21.2)
Hypertensive Diseases	-0.06 (5.4)	-0.15 (5.4)	0.06 (5.3)	-0.05 (5.3)	0.22 (5.2)	0.16 (5.2)	0.42 (5.1)	0.40 (5.1)	0.12 (4.8)	0.13 (4.8)	-0.02 (1.6)	0.00 (2.5)
Cerebrovascular Disease	-0.05 (4.9)	-0.12 (4.3)	0.06 (5.3)	-0.05 (5.5)	0.22 (5.2)	0.19 (6.2)	0.38 (4.6)	0.45 (5.7)	0.11 (4.4)	0.14 (5.1)	-0.12 (7.8)	0.00 (16.7)
Diseases of Liver	-0.04 (4.3)	-0.10 (3.8)	0.05 (4.6)	-0.04 (4.0)	0.21 (4.8)	0.14 (4.4)	0.42 (5.1)	0.38 (4.8)	0.12 (4.9)	0.13 (4.8)	0.00 (0.2)	0.00 (0.6)
Senility	0.08 (7.8)	0.36 (13.1)	-0.09 (7.7)	0.12 (12.4)	-0.30 (7.0)	-0.33 (10.7)	-0.53 (6.5)	-0.68 (8.7)	-0.25 (9.9)	-0.28 (10.0)	0.79 (51.5)	0.00 (37.2)
Pneumonia	-0.05 (5.3)	-0.14 (5.3)	0.06 (5.3)	-0.05 (5.3)	0.23 (5.3)	0.17 (5.5)	0.44 (5.4)	0.43 (5.5)	0.14 (5.4)	0.15 (5.4)	-0.08 (4.9)	0.00 (6.1)
Accidents	-0.06 (5.8)	-0.15 (5.5)	0.06 (5.5)	-0.05 (5.3)	0.23 (5.3)	0.16 (5.2)	0.44 (5.4)	0.42 (5.3)	0.13 (5.2)	0.14 (5.2)	-0.02 (1.3)	0.00 (1.9)
Suicide	-0.04 (4.3)	-0.11 (4.0)	0.05 (4.5)	-0.04 (4.2)	0.21 (4.8)	0.14 (4.5)	0.42 (5.1)	0.38 (4.8)	0.13 (5.0)	0.13 (5.2)	0.00 (0.3)	0.00 (0.3)
All Other Causes	0.48 (47.0)	1.20 (44.2)	-0.54 (46.6)	0.40 (42.9)	-1.99 (46.5)	-1.31 (42.5)	-3.82 (46.6)	-3.44 (43.8)	-1.11 (44.0)	-1.21 (43.6)	0.21 (14.0)	0.00 (12.6)
Total Change	0.10 (100.0)	0.40 (100.0)	-0.10 (100.0)	0.10 (100.0)	-0.30 (100.0)	-0.20 (100.0)	-0.50 (100.0)	-0.040 (100.0)	-0.20 (100.0)	-0.20 (100.0)	0.50 (100.0)	0.00 (100.0)

Note: Figures in parenthesis represent the percentage of the absolute value of the total change in life expectancy.

8.3b. 1965–75

Cause of Death	65–69 Male	65–69 Female	70–74 Male	70–74 Female	75–79 Male	75–79 Female	80–84 Male	80–84 Female	85–89 Male	85–89 Female	90+ Male	90+ Female
Diabetes Mellitus	-0.25 (6.1)	-0.20 (5.3)	-0.26 (6.1)	-0.20 (5.3)	-0.25 (6.0)	-0.19 (5.3)	-0.22 (5.4)	-0.18 (4.9)	-0.15 (4.4)	-0.14 (4.0)	-0.01 (0.1)	0.00 (0.0)
Malignant Neoplams	-0.14 (3.4)	-0.07 (1.8)	-0.18 (4.4)	-0.11 (2.8)	-0.19 (4.7)	-0.13 (3.7)	-0.19 (4.8)	-0.15 (4.1)	-0.14 (4.3)	-0.13 (3.7)	-0.06 (0.9)	0.00 (0.4)
Heart Diseases	0.01 (0.2)	-0.02 (0.6)	-0.03 (0.8)	-0.07 (1.9)	-0.08 (2.0)	-0.11 (3.0)	-0.14 (3.4)	-0.15 (4.3)	-0.16 (4.9)	-0.18 (5.3)	-0.45 (6.3)	0.00 (5.7)
Hypertensive Diseases	-0.08 (2.0)	-0.05 (1.4)	0.12 (2.8)	-0.08 (2.1)	-0.15 (3.7)	-0.11 (3.1)	-0.17 (4.3)	-0.14 (3.9)	-0.14 (4.1)	-0.14 (4.0)	-0.09 (1.2)	0.00 (1.3)
Cerebrovascular Disease	0.71 (16.9)	0.58 (15.4)	0.43 (10.3)	0.36 (9.5)	0.14 (3.3)	0.10 (2.7)	-0.09 (2.3)	-0.13 (3.6)	-0.24 (7.2)	-0.31 (9.0)	-1.32 (18.5)	-0.00 (16.2)
Diseases of Liver	-0.19 (4.6)	-0.14 (3.8)	-0.20 (4.7)	-0.16 (4.1)	-0.21 (5.0)	-0.15 (4.3)	-0.20 (4.9)	-0.16 (4.4)	-0.14 (4.3)	-0.13 (3.8)	-0.04 (0.5)	0.00 (0.4)
Senility	0.23 (5.4)	0.43 (11.3)	0.22 (5.3)	0.43 (11.3)	0.20 (4.9)	0.37 (10.3)	0.13 (3.1)	0.23 (6.4)	-0.03 (1.0)	-0.05 (1.5)	-1.50 (21.0)	0.00 (24.6)
Pneumonia	-0.14 (3.3)	-0.09 (2.5)	-0.14 (3.4)	-0.11 (2.8)	-0.15 (3.6)	-0.11 (3.2)	-0.15 (3.8)	-0.12 (3.4)	-0.12 (3.6)	-0.12 (3.4)	-0.07 (1.0)	0.00 (0.7)
Accidents	-0.17 (4.1)	-0.14 (3.7)	-0.19 (4.6)	-0.16 (4.1)	-0.21 (5.0)	-0.16 (4.5)	-0.20 (4.9)	-0.16 (4.4)	-0.15 (4.4)	-0.14 (4.1)	-0.07 (1.0)	0.00 (0.9)
Suicide	-0.21 (5.0)	-0.17 (4.4)	-0.22 (5.3)	-0.17 (4.5)	-0.22 (5.4)	-0.17 (4.7)	-0.21 (5.1)	-0.16 (4.5)	-0.14 (4.3)	-0.13 (3.9)	-0.10 (0.2)	0.00 (0.1)
All Other Causes	2.05 (49.1)	1.88 (49.7)	2.19 (52.2)	1.96 (51.6)	2.32 (56.3)	1.97 (55.1)	2.35 (58.0)	2.02 (56.1)	1.91 (57.6)	1.96 (57.3)	3.52 (49.3)	0.00 (49.7)
Total Change	1.80 (100.0)	2.00 (100.0)	1.50 (100.0)	1.70 (100.0)	1.20 (100.0)	1.30 (100.0)	0.90 (100.0)	0.90 (100.0)	0.50 (100.0)	0.50 (100.0)	-0.10 (100.0)	0.00 (100.0)

8.3c. 1975–85

Cause of Death	65–69 Male	65–69 Female	70–74 Male	70–74 Female	75–79 Male	75–79 Female	80–84 Male	80–84 Female	85–89 Male	85–89 Female	90+ Male	90+ Female
Diabetes Mellitus	-0.17 (4.6)	-0.11 (2.1)	-0.19 (5.1)	-0.13 (2.7)	-0.20 (5.5)	-0.17 (3.6)	-0.21 (5.8)	-0.19 (5.0)	-0.17 (5.8)	-0.15 (6.0)	0.00 (0.3)	-0.01 (0.3)
Malignant Neoplams	-0.19 (5.0)	-0.06 (1.1)	-0.23 (6.0)	-0.12 (2.4)	-0.25 (6.9)	-0.18 (3.9)	-0.24 (6.8)	-0.21 (5.7)	-0.20 (6.9)	-0.18 (7.4)	-0.13 (11.0)	0.08 (3.1)
Heart Diseases	0.05 (1.4)	0.20 (3.9)	0.02 (0.5)	0.18 (3.7)	-0.02 (0.5)	0.15 (3.2)	-0.04 (1.1)	0.11 (2.9)	-0.05 (1.6)	0.02 (1.0)	0.03 (2.4)	0.06 (2.4)
Hypertensive Diseases	0.02 (0.5)	0.18 (3.6)	0.00 (0.1)	0.17 (3.4)	-0.04 (1.1)	0.13 (2.8)	-0.08 (2.2)	0.06 (1.7)	-0.09 (3.0)	-0.01 (0.5)	0.08 (6.9)	0.08 (3.1)
Cerebrovascular Disease	1.28 (33.6)	2.38 (46.8)	1.05 (27.7)	2.21 (44.4)	0.70 (19.6)	1.85 (40.3)	0.43 (11.9)	1.32 (35.1)	0.18 (6.2)	0.62 (24.7)	0.28 (23.6)	0.41 (16.5)
Diseases of Liver	-0.14 (3.6)	0.01 (0.2)	-0.16 (4.2)	-0.01 (0.2)	-0.17 (4.7)	-0.04 (0.8)	-0.18 (5.1)	-0.06 (1.6)	-0.15 (5.3)	-0.06 (2.6)	0.00 (0.1)	0.02 (0.8)
Senility	0.09 (2.5)	1.02 (20.1)	0.10 (2.6)	1.08 (21.6)	0.09 (2.5)	1.12 (24.4)	0.09 (2.5)	1.14 (30.2)	0.09 (3.3)	0.88 (35.2)	0.41 (33.8)	1.13 (45.0)
Pneumonia	-0.19 (4.9)	-0.06 (1.2)	-0.20 (5.4)	-0.08 (1.6)	-0.21 (5.8)	-0.11 (2.4)	-0.21 (5.7)	-0.14 (3.7)	-0.17 (6.0)	-0.13 (5.4)	-0.12 (9.6)	-0.06 (2.5)
Accidents	-0.13 (3.4)	-0.11 (2.1)	-0.16 (4.2)	-0.11 (2.2)	-0.17 (4.8)	-0.11 (2.3)	-0.19 (5.3)	-0.10 (2.7)	-0.15 (5.3)	-0.08 (3.1)	0.01 (0.8)	0.00 (0.1)
Suicide	-0.18 (4.8)	-0.01 (0.2)	-0.19 (5.1)	-0.03 (0.6)	-0.19 (5.3)	-0.06 (1.2)	-0.20 (5.5)	-0.08 (2.2)	-0.16 (5.6)	-0.07 (3.0)	0.00 (0.1)	0.01 (0.2)
All Other Causes	1.36 (35.7)	-0.95 (18.7)	1.47 (39.0)	-0.86 (17.2)	1.55 (43.2)	-0.69 (15.1)	1.73 (48.1)	-0.35 (9.2)	1.46 (50.9)	0.28 (11.2)	0.14 (11.4)	-0.65 (26.0)
Total Change	1.80 (100.0)	2.50 (100.0)	1.50 (100.0)	2.30 (100.0)	1.10 (100.0)	1.90 (100.0)	0.90 (100.0)	1.50 (100.0)	0.60 (100.0)	1.10 (100.0)	0.70 (100.0)	0.90 (100.0)

8.3d. 1985–95

Cause of Death	65–69 Male	65–69 Female	70–74 Male	70–74 Female	75–79 Male	75–79 Female	80–84 Male	80–84 Female	85–89 Male	85–89 Female	90+ Male	90+ Female
Diabetes Mellitus	-0.15 (5.7)	-0.09 (2.9)	-0.15 (5.7)	-0.09 (3.2)	-0.16 (5.8)	-0.10 (3.5)	-0.14 (5.7)	-0.11 (3.5)	-0.10 (4.6)	-0.11 (2.7)	-0.02 (0.4)	-0.02 (0.3)
Malignant Neoplasms	-0.13 (5.0)	-0.02 (0.7)	-0.10 (3.8)	-0.01 (0.4)	-0.11 (4.0)	-0.06 (2.0)	-0.12 (5.1)	-0.12 (3.7)	-0.11 (5.1)	-0.14 (3.6)	-0.21 (5.5)	-0.14 (2.2)
Heart Diseases	0.45 (17.8)	0.86 (28.2)	0.42 (16.1)	0.78 (26.8)	0.36 (13.0)	0.70 (24.2)	0.21 (8.8)	0.57 (18.1)	0.11 (5.4)	0.44 (11.3)	0.23 (6.1)	0.44 (6.9)
Hypertensive Diseases	-0.05 (2.1)	0.10 (3.4)	-0.06 (2.3)	0.10 (3.3)	-0.07 (2.7)	0.09 (3.0)	-0.07 (3.0)	0.07 (2.2)	-0.05 (2.6)	0.05 (1.2)	0.05 (1.4)	0.12 (1.9)
Cerebrovascular Disease	0.25 (9.8)	0.27 (8.8)	0.21 (7.9)	0.19 (6.7)	0.12 (4.2)	0.08 (2.8)	-0.02 (0.9)	-0.13 (4.1)	-0.13 (6.3)	-0.47 (12.1)	-0.89 (23.2)	-1.48 (23.1)
Diseases of Liver	-0.08 (3.1)	-0.04 (1.3)	-0.09 (3.6)	-0.05 (1.8)	-0.12 (4.4)	-0.07 (2.4)	-0.12 (4.8)	-0.09 (2.7)	-0.09 (4.2)	-0.09 (2.4)	-0.02 (0.5)	-0.03 (0.4)
Senility	-0.05 (1.9)	-0.02 (0.8)	-0.05 (2.0)	-0.03 (0.9)	-0.06 (2.2)	-0.03 (1.2)	-0.06 (2.6)	-0.07 (2.3)	-0.08 (3.9)	-0.20 (5.2)	-0.41 (10.7)	-0.79 (12.3)
Pneumonia	-0.09 (3.5)	-0.12 (4.0)	-0.10 (3.8)	-0.12 (4.3)	-0.13 (4.7)	-0.14 (4.8)	-0.14 (5.8)	-0.17 (5.4)	-0.14 (6.4)	-0.20 (5.2)	-0.34 (8.9)	-0.27 (4.2)
Accidents	-0.17 (6.8)	-0.20 (6.6)	-0.18 (6.9)	-0.19 (6.4)	-0.19 (6.8)	-0.17 (5.9)	-0.16 (6.5)	-0.16 (5.1)	-0.12 (5.5)	-0.15 (3.8)	-0.12 (3.0)	-0.12 (1.8)
Suicide	-0.11 (4.3)	-0.05 (1.7)	-0.12 (4.6)	-0.06 (2.0)	-0.14 (5.0)	-0.07 (2.4)	-0.12 (5.2)	-0.09 (2.7)	-0.09 (4.3)	-0.09 (2.2)	-0.02 (0.4)	-0.01 (0.2)
All Other Causes	1.02 (40.1)	1.27 (41.7)	1.13 (43.2)	1.28 (44.2)	1.31 (47.3)	1.38 (47.9)	1.24 (51.6)	1.59 (50.2)	1.09 (51.7)	1.97 (50.2)	1.53 (39.9)	2.99 (46.6)
Total Change	0.90 (100.0)	2.00 (100.0)	0.90 (100.0)	1.80 (100.0)	0.80 (100.0)	1.60 (100.0)	0.50 (100.0)	1.30 (100.0)	0.30 (100.0)	1.00 (100.0)	-0.20 (100.0)	0.70 (100.0)

contribute to life expectancy increases at all ages, particularly among older women. Mortality declines from heart disease and hypertensive disease also contributed to the increase in life expectancy during this decade for men and women in most age groups.

In the most recent decade, 1985–95 (Table 8.3d), declining mortality from heart disease replaced cerebrovascular disease and senility as the main source of increasing life expectancy at all ages up to 90 for both men and women. During the same decade, continued decline in mortality from cerebrovascular disease contributed to further increases in life expectancy among the younger age groups but actually worked to reduce life expectancy at the oldest ages (i.e., ages 80 and older). The fact that declining mortality from cerebrovascular disease contributed to reduce life expectancy at older ages indicates that its indirect, negative effect on life expectancy was greater than its direct, positive effect. In other words, older men and women who would have died from cerebrovascular disease in the past, in fact, died at increased rates from other diseases.[6] For example, the increasing levels of mortality from pneumonia among the old-old reflect the fact that pneumonia often accompanies the last stages of chronic degenerative diseases among older adults (Manton 1982).

Tables 8.3b and 8.3c show clear age differences over the 20-year period, 1965–85, in the relationship between declining mortality from cerebrovascular disease and increasing life expectancy. More specifically, these figures show that the longevity benefits of declining mortality from cerebrovascular disease were larger at younger ages than at older ages. In 1975–85, for example, 33.6 percent (46.8%) of the absolute value of the total change in life expectancy for men (women) at ages 65–69 was due to reduced mortality from cerebrovascular disease. The corresponding percentages for men and women at older ages were much smaller: 6.2 percent (24.7%) at ages 85–89 and 23.6 percent (16.5%) at ages 90 and above.

The results from the decomposition analysis show that, over the past four decades, the main source of increasing life expectancy for older Japanese shifted from reductions in mortality from senility to cerebrovascular disease, and then to heart disease.[7] The particularly large contribution made by declines in mortality from cerebrovascular disease over the last three decades (1965–95) suggests that socioeconomic and behavioral factors, such as better housing and a more balanced diet, have played an important role in achieving the dramatic increases in postwar life expectancy at older ages, along with advances in medical treatment. The improved access to medical care through the national health care system has also contributed to reductions in mortality at older ages by providing greater access to medical treatment and preventive care (Yanagishita and Guralnik 1988). The large improvement in life expectancy due to mortality decline in heart disease during the most recent decade (1985–95) is consistent with the advancement in medical treatment discussed earlier (Iso et al. 1999).

Functional Status of the Japanese Elderly

Although changes in mortality from various diseases have contributed to dramatic gains in life expectancy over the postwar period, the effect of these changes on the quality of life at older ages is not well documented. One obvious reason for this lack of information is the inherent difficulty of measuring "quality of life." Though there is much debate on what constitutes quality of life in old age, there is a consensus that physical well-being is of primary importance (Hauser 1986; Maeda 1986).[8] In the second half of the chapter, we assess the physical well-being of the Japanese elderly by using measures of their functional status.

Measures of functional status are generally considered more informative in assessing the general well-being of older adults than are diagnostic measures referring to specific diseases (George 1996). Because older adults diagnosed with the same disease may differ greatly in their ability to perform various physical activities, to care for themselves, and to enjoy social activities, prevalence of disease alone provides little information about one's quality of life.

In the remainder of this chapter, we first document recent trends in the prevalence of limitations in performing activities of daily living (ADLs) (Katz and Akpom 1976) based on published survey data for 1989, 1992, and 1995. We then use standard statistical techniques to examine the sociodemographic correlates of functional limitations based on individual-level survey data.

Trends in ADL Limitations

The relationship between increasing life expectancy and physical well-being in the later years of life is a subject of considerable debate. Some scholars argue that today's elderly not only live longer, but also live more healthy years of life than did their predecessors (Fries 1980, 1983). In other words, the added years of life consist primarily of years free of disability, or "active life expectancy." Others argue that, although today's elderly live longer, they also spend a proportionately longer period of life in disabled states (Gruenberg 1977; Manton and Singer 1994; Manton, Stallard, and Corder 1997). In other words, the added years of life consist primarily of years with disability, and thus represent little increase in active life expectancy.

We use measures of difficulties in performing ADLs (a set of tasks necessary to function independently) included in *Kokumin Seikatsu Kiso Chōsa* (hereafter referred to as KSKC) to describe physical well-being at older ages in Japan. KSKC has been conducted annually by the Ministry of Health and Welfare since 1986 and includes a wide range of information including that on the health of approximately 800,000 individuals in 270,000 households. Data on limitations with ADLs have been collected every third year beginning in 1989, with the respondent asked to report whether or not each household member required any help performing selected ADLs during the three-day survey period. These activities consist of bathing, eating, dressing, toileting, changing position, walking, and washing face/brushing teeth. The prevalence of ADL limitations during the three-day survey period are fairly representative of their prevalence throughout the year, because limitations in the ability to perform these activities reflect chronic limitations rather than acute conditions.

Table 8.4 presents the number of elderly per 1,000 who required help in performing these ADLs in 1989, 1992, and 1995. Rates of limitation are presented by sex and three ten-year age groups, ages 60–69, 70–79, and 80 and older.[9] In each of the three survey years, the most commonly reported functional limitation at all ages is difficulty with bathing. Bathing is followed by walking outside (asked in 1989 only), walking (asked in 1992 and 1995), and dressing. Not surprisingly, ADL limitations are more prevalent at older ages for both sexes. A comparison of men and women shows that, while the prevalence of ADL limitations is higher for men than for women at ages 60–79, the opposite is true at ages 80 and above. This gender difference holds for all ADLs in all survey years.

The results over the three survey years show that the prevalence of functional limitations has declined over time for all the ADLs that were included in two or more survey years. The largest declines were observed for limitations with bathing, followed by dressing, and eating. Rates of all the limitations declined across all age groups, though the extent of the declines were somewhat greater among the youngest age group. Patterns of declines have been similar for men and women.

Table 8.4: Trends in the Prevalence of Disability as Measured by Selected Activities of Daily Living for Japanese Males and Females (per 1,000), 1989–95

ADL	Ages	Male			Female		
		1989	*1992*	*1995*	*1989*	*1992*	*1995*
Bathing	60–69	10.0	5.2	4.5	5.7	3.0	2.8
	70–79	32.6	17.0	15.2	23.4	11.7	10.3
	80+	81.4	50.0	45.0	102.3	64.5	61.4
Dressing	60–69	7.7	4.2	3.7	4.3	2.5	2.2
	70–79	25.5	15.3	12.7	16.8	9.1	7.6
	80+	61.9	43.6	35.2	80.7	53.8	48.7
Toileting	60–69	5.0	3.7	3.4	2.8	2.3	2.0
	70–79	18.7	14.0	11.7	13.7	8.9	7.6
	80+	53.6	40.9	36.0	68.4	53.3	49.1
Eating	60–69	5.4	3.2	2.9	2.8	1.9	1.7
	70–79	15.8	11.9	9.8	12.5	7.7	6.1
	80+	43.3	33.6	28.6	62.2	43.0	39.1
Washing Face/	60–69	n/a	3.6	3.1	n/a	1.9	1.8
Brushing Teeth	70–79		13.6	11.1		8.2	6.5
	80+		38.1	31.1		48.2	42.3
Walking	60–69	n/a	4.4	4.0	n/a	2.6	2.4
	70–79		15.3	13.3		10.3	9.4
	80+		43.6	39.3		56.4	55.0
Changing Position	60–69	3.5	n/a	n/a	1.9	n/a	n/a
	70–79	11.5			7.9		
	80+	27.8			38.2		
Walking Outside	60–69	8.4	n/a	n/a	5.7	n/a	n/a
	70–79	27.3			22.4		
	80+	67.0			93.7		
Moving Indoor	60–69	5.0	n/a	n/a	3.3	n/a	n/a
	70–79	18.3			13.2		
	80+	43.3			59.8		

Source: Kokumin Seikatsu Kiso Chōsa, 1989, 1992, and 1995, Ministry of Health and Welfare, Japan

Because the rates of ADL limitations in Table 8.4 are based on responses to questions regarding individual ADLs, they do not provide information on the number of coexisting limitations. In 1995, KSKC asked a household respondent to provide the number of coexisting ADL limitations experienced by each of the household member at the time of survey. We present these figures in Table 8.5. The first column ("1 or More") presents the number of elderly

Table 8.5: Prevalence of Disability as Measured by the Number of Limitations in Activities of Daily Living Among Japanese Males and Females (per 1,000) in 1995

# of Limitations / Ages	1 or More		1		2		3		4		5		6	
	Male	Female	Male	Female	Male	Female	Male	Female	Male	Female	Male	Female	Male	Female
60–69	15.0	9.8	4.2	2.7	1.7	1.3	1.4	1.0	0.9	0.7	1.1	0.7	5.4	3.4
70–74	40.8	30.8	11.7	8.1	3.5	4.1	3.2	2.4	2.5	2.0	2.2	1.7	17.4	12.4
80+	127.7	153.7	35.2	35.0	10.6	15.9	9.8	12.3	9.8	10.0	9.8	11.4	51.6	69.1

Source: Kokumin Seikatsu Kiso Chōsa, 1995, Ministry of Health and Welfare, Japan

per 1,000 who have difficulty with at least one of the six ADL limitations included in the 1995 survey. For both sexes, there is a large increase in the number of coexisting ADL limitations with age, particularly between the two oldest age groups (70–79 and 80 and older). ADL limitations are concentrated among a relatively small group of the elderly population.[10] Among the elderly who have at least one ADL limitation, the largest proportion of them reported having all six limitations, followed by those reported having one limitation, and those with two limitations. This pattern is observed for all age groups and both sexes.

Relationships between Functional Limitations and Sociodemographic Characteristics

The survey results from KSKC (presented in Tables 8.4 and 8.5) show that the prevalence of ADL limitations at older ages varies by age and sex. Previous studies have also shown that it varies by other sociodemographic characteristics (George 1996). Social status and social support, in particular, are considered to be important indicators of the social and structural contexts within which health is protected or put at risk. Social status is often measured with educational attainment, income, and assets. A strong positive relationship between social status and health is well established in modern societies, though its magnitude varies and the mechanisms underlying this relationship remain the subject of much debate. Social support is often measured along a structural dimension (i.e., social network properties) and a functional dimension (i.e., types and levels of assistance provided by the social network). Social support is considered to positively affect health because social relationships in which some degree of intimacy and commitment occurs (e.g., marriage and friendship) help protect against illness, enhance the ability to cope with stress and illness, and speed recovery from illness.

In the remainder of this chapter, we use data from the 1987 wave of the National Survey of Japanese Elderly (hereafter referred to as NSJE87) to examine how the functional status of older adults in Japan varies by measures of social status (i.e., home ownership, educational level) and social support (i.e., marital status). Developing an understanding of the relationship between physical well-being and sociodemographic characteristics is of particular importance given the projected changes in the sociodemographic composition of future cohorts of Japanese elderly (e.g., increases in the proportion of divorced or never married elderly, increases in the proportion of elderly with higher education).

The NSJE87, conducted jointly by the Institute of Gerontology at the University of Michigan and the Tokyo Metropolitan Institute of Gerontology, contains individual-level information for a nationally representative sample of 2,200 noninstitutionalized persons aged 60 and older in 1987. In addition to the information on sociodemographic characteristics, NSJE87 respondents provided detailed information on their functional status. In our analysis, we use information on the difficulties in performing the following seven activities:

1. standing for two hours
2. stooping, crouching, or kneeling
3. reaching hands above the head
4. using fingers to grasp or handle
5. lifting or carrying objects weighing twenty-five pounds
6. climbing two to three flights of stairs
7. walking 200 to 300 meters

The dependent variable in our analysis is the number of activities with which a respondent reported having difficulty. This limitation count, therefore, ranges from 0 to 7. We control for age and sex and we examine the relationship between the number of functional limitations one experiences and three key independent variables: marital status, educational attainment, and home ownership.

Marital status, included as a measure of the structural dimension of social support (Berkman and Syme 1979), takes two values: "currently married" and "not currently married" (i.e., never married, separated, divorced, or widowed). We expect a negative relationship between the limitation count and being currently married. The health advantage enjoyed by married people may be viewed as the result of marriage selection effects (i.e., married people are healthier because healthier people are more likely to marry in the first place) or, alternatively, as the result of the protective effect of marriage (i.e., marriage provides health protection through social support and social control) (Lillard and Panis 1996). Previous studies have suggested that the selection effect may play a greater role than the protection effect in the Japanese context because arranged marriages, in which health status was often an important spouse selection criterion, were very common in Japan until the recent past (Goldman 1990; Hu and Goldman 1990; Goldman, Takahashi, and Hu 1995).

Years of educational attainment and home ownership are included in our model as measures of social status. Educational attainment is generally regarded as a more reliable measure of social status than income which is heavily influenced by employment history and retirement status (especially for women and older adults). Home ownership is used as a proxy for assets beyond income that may be a particularly important resource in old age (Crystal 1995). We expect that educational attainment and home ownership (versus not owning a home) both have a negative effect on the number of functional limitations. Possible mechanisms linking social status and health include the financial ability to seek medical care and the access to information on health (including health-related behaviors, such as smoking and diet) and where to obtain care. Because previous studies suggest that the effect of education on health and mortality decreases with age (Elo and Preston 1996), we test this empirically by including a term for the interaction between age and educational attainment in our model. Descriptive statistics for all variables included in the model are presented in the first column of Table 8.6. Older adults in our sample have, on average, one ADL limitation (0.70 for men and 1.24 for women). They are 55 percent female, have a mean age of 69.2 and an average of 8.6 years of education. Sixty-three percent of them are currently married and 83 percent own their homes.

Because the dependent variable is a count variable, we estimate the model using negative binomial regression, an appropriate statistical method for predicting count outcomes (Long 1997). Parameter estimates for the model are presented in the second column of Table 8.6. The model chi-square is statistically significant at the 0.01 level, indicating that the variables in the model significantly contribute to the explanation of variation in the number of functional limitations. The signs of all variables in the model are in the expected direction and, except for the interaction between age and educational attainment, are all statistically significant at the 0.01 level. The parameter estimates for our control variables, age and sex, indicate that the number of functional limitations significantly increases with age and is significantly higher for women than for men, net of all other variables in the model.[11] Coefficients for the key independent variables indicate that being currently married, having more years of education, and owning a home are all associated with a significantly lower number of functional limitations among older Japanese. Although the interaction between age and education is not statistically significant at a conventional level, the sign is in the predicted direction, thus, hinting

Table 8.6: Descriptive Statistics and Coefficient Estimates from Negative Binomial Regression Model for the Number of Functional Limitations

Variable	Mean (s.d.)	Coefficient Estimate (s.e.)
Dependent Variable		
No. of Functional Limitations	1.00	n/a
	(1.70)	
—Male	0.70	
	(1.49)	
—Female	1.24	
	(1.81)	
Independent Variables		
Marital Status	0.63	−0.17 **
1=currently married	(0.48)	(0.09)
0=not currently married		
Home Ownership	0.83	−0.26 ***
1=own home	(0.38)	(0.10)
0=do not own home		
Education (in years)	8.63	−0.29 **
(range: 0–17)	(2.82)	(0.14)
Age*Education	n/a	0.00 *
		(0.00)
Sex	0.55	0.41 ***
1=female	(0.50)	(0.09)
0=male		
Age	69.16	0.05 ***
(range: 60–93)	(6.75)	(0.02)
Intercept	n/a	−3.10 ***
N	2200	2178
Model Chi-Squares	n/a	310.41 ***

Note: Standard deviations and standard errors are in parentheses.
***p<.01, **p<.05, *p<.10

at the possibility that the health protection associated with education declines at older ages. The findings from our negative binomial regression analysis are consistent with expectations derived from previous research.

Summary and Implications

As a result of large declines in mortality since World War II, Japanese men and women today enjoy the world's longest life expectancy.

With mortality at younger ages reaching very low levels during the early postwar decades, recent increases in life expectancy have been driven primarily by mortality improvements at older ages. In this paper, we described changes in the quantity and the quality (i.e., physical well-being) of later life in Japan by examining (1) the causes of increasing life expectancy at older ages and (2) temporal and sociodemographic variations in the functional status of the Japanese elderly.

In the first half of the chapter, we showed that declining mortality from senility, cerebrovascular disease, and heart disease, in order of chronological importance, have been the main contributors to the increase in life expectancy at older ages for the decades between 1955 to 1995. This suggests the importance of socioeconomic and behavioral changes in postwar Japan (e.g., dietary changes and better housing conditions) along with advances in medical technology in reducing mortality from these diseases.

In the second half of the chapter, we showed that the prevalence of functional limitations among older Japanese declined between 1989 and 1995. In our analysis of the sociodemographic correlates of functional limitation, we also showed that social status (as measured by educational attainment and home ownership) and social support (as measured by marital status) are significantly associated with physical well-being of older Japanese. It must be noted, however, that the data on functional limitations are currently available only for a short period of time; data over a longer period are needed to assess long-term trends in the prevalence of functional limitations among the Japanese elderly.

Several behavioral, socioeconomic, and technological changes currently underway have implications for the quantity and quality of life for older Japanese in the future. A Japan-Sweden comparison of death rates for various types of cancer has shown that there is much room for improvement in cancer mortality in Japan, especially from lung cancer (Yanagishita and Guralnik 1988). Recent statistics show that the percentage of male smokers aged 20 and older has declined in recent decades (Japan Tobacco Corporation 1990), suggesting that the incidence of lung cancer and associated death rates should decline in the future if this trend continues.[12] Given that death from cancer is now the main inhibitor of an increase in life expectancy at older ages in Japan (see Table 8.3d), any decline in cancer mortality will likely contribute to further increases in life expectancy.

Although the low cholesterol content of the traditional Japanese diet has contributed to low levels of mortality from heart

disease in the past, dietary changes in recent decades are characterized by an increase in animal fat intake and excessive caloric
intake. These dietary changes, in conjunction with other changes
in health-related behaviors, such as lower levels of physical activity, have contributed to increasing death rates for heart disease
and other chronic diseases, including diabetes and colon cancer
(Martin 1989; Imaizumi 1991). Despite recent advances in the treatment of these diseases, further increases in mortality associated
with a continued trend toward higher caloric and cholesterol intake
may limit further improvements in life expectancy.

It is also worth noting that, despite large postwar declines,
mortality from cerebrovascular disease in Japan remains at higher
levels than in many other developed countries (WHO 1996). Further improvements in Japanese life expectancy are clearly possible if the death rate from cerebrovascular disease approaches
the low levels observed in Western countries. It is also possible,
however, that death rates for cerebrovascular disease in Japan
may actually increase in the near future, as the cohorts of men
and women who experienced war-related deprivation during child-
hood enter old age. It has been suggested that, among those Japanese who grew up during and immediately following World War
II, severe malnutrition and a shortage of animal protein intake
may have resulted in weaker blood vessel tissue and, consequently,
an increased vulnerability to cerebral hemorrhage (Kōno and
Takahashi 1989).

Government policies related to health care provision for the
elderly are also likely to influence future trends in life expectancy.
Utilization of medical care by older Japanese grew rapidly over the
postwar period, particularly after 1973 when free medical services
for the elderly were legislated (Hatano 1994). The legislation of
free geriatric care was, however, revised in 1983 due to the drastic
increase in medical costs. The medical expenses that the elderly
must bear have increased and are expected to increase further as
the population ages, which may hinder older adults' access to medical
care and slow future improvements in longevity.

With respect to future trends in the physical well-being of older
Japanese, the relationship between sociodemographic characteristics
(e.g., educational attainment, marital status) and functional status
found in our analysis provides some insight. The average educational attainment of the Japanese elderly will increase substantially
as cohorts who benefited from large postwar improvements in educational attainment begin to enter old age. If the negative relationship between educational attainment and functional limitations in

old age persists, further improvements in physical well-being of the elderly are likely.

Couples can also expect to remain married into older ages, as a result of improved joint survival due to reductions in mortality (Raymo and Kaneda, chapter 2). This is particularly true for older women. If the negative relationship between being married and functional limitations in old age persists, the physical well-being of the elderly may see further improvements. However, recent changes in marriage behavior at younger ages (i.e., increases in the likelihood of divorcing or never marrying) may have negative implications for the physical well-being of future cohorts of elderly.

It is also possible, however, that changes in the sociodemographic composition of the elderly population, in conjunction with other social changes, may alter the relationships between sociodemographic characteristics and health outcomes in old age. For example, as the elderly population becomes increasingly better educated, the health advantages conferred by higher education may decline in importance. The health benefits associated with marriage may also decline in response to the decrease in arranged marriages. Large projected increases in the proportion of Japanese men and women who never marry are also likely to reduce the positive selection effects on health that have characterized marriage in the past.

Understanding trends in the quantity and quality of life at older ages is increasingly important, given that older adults comprise a growing proportion of the population in Japan. Japan's population is aging at an unprecedentedly rapid pace, with the proportion of the population aged 65 and older projected to increase from 12.6 percent in 1991 to 25.8 percent by 2025 (Atoh 1995). Recent projections of Japanese life expectancies for men and women show increases from 76.4 and 82.9 in 1995 to 78.8 and 85.8 in 2025, then to 79.4 and 86.5 in 2050, respectively (National Institute of Population and Social Security Research 1997). The extent to which these projections are realized, and the extent to which the years added to life are healthy years will be largely determined by further changes in behavioral, socioeconomic, and technological factors.

Notes

1. It has been suggested that the high death rates associated with senility, traditionally considered a natural and ideal way to die in Japan, are overstated. It is likely that the large decline in senility as a cause of

death for older Japanese reflects alterations in the way that doctors report causes of death (Yanagishita and Guralnik 1988).

2. Most previous analyses have only examined changes in life expectancy at birth (e.g., Kōno and Takahashi 1989). Other studies examining changes in life expectancy at various age groups do not include the oldest age groups (e.g., Yanagishita and Guralnik 1988).

3. All other causes of death consist of various diseases, including infectious diseases and diseases of respiratory system, digestive system, and circulatory system, such as tuberculosis, chronic bronchitis, gastric and duodenal ulcer, enteritis, nephritis, and intestinal obstruction. For a complete list of causes of death included in the Vital Statistics of Japan, see *Jinkō Dōtai Tōkei* (Vital Statistics) published annually by the Ministry of Health, Labor and Welfare, formerly known as the Ministry of Health and Welfare in Japan.

4. For example, a decline in the death rate from heart disease will have a positive direct effect on life expectancy (reflecting the reduced likelihood of death from heart disease). The indirect effect, however, will be negative, reflecting increased exposure to death from other diseases. In other words, those who survive as a result of the reduced risk of death from heart disease face the increased risk of dying from other diseases.

5. For example, to determine the extent to which changes in death rates for heart disease contributed to the increase in life expectancy between 1955 and 1965, we first substitute the age-specific probabilities of dying from heart disease in the 1965 MDLT with the corresponding probabilities from the 1955 MDLT. After reconstructing the 1965 MDLT using these substituted death rates, we subtract the "simulated" life expectancy from the corresponding life expectancy in the original 1965 MDLT. The difference between these two figures is the contribution to the increase in life expectancy between 1955 and 1965 made by changes in mortality from heart disease. In a similar manner, we can calculate the contribution to the overall increase in life expectancy made by each cause of death included in the analysis. More detailed discussions on multiple decrement life tables and decomposition of changes in life expectancy can be found in Shryock and Siegel (1971), Pollard, Yusuf, and Pollard (1974), and Arriaga (1984).

6. Gender differences in the pattern of cause-specific contributions to changes in life expectancy are also noteworthy. Compared to men, women enjoyed much greater longevity benefits during all decades from the mortality decline in senility and during the last two decades from declines in cerebrovascular disease and heart disease. Also, changes in mortality from hypertensive disease in recent decades has increased life expectancy for women while decreasing it for men.

7. If, as suggested above, deaths due to senility were overreported in earlier years, the large decline in mortality from senility may partly reflect

a decline in mortality from cerebrovascular (and perhaps other) diseases. The decline in death rates for cerebrovascular disease may, therefore, have been even greater than suggested by our analysis.

8. Other important components include socioeconomic status, self-esteem, and life satisfaction (Hauser 1986; Maeda 1986).

9. Note that the ADLs included in the survey are not identical across different waves.

10. It is important to note that the figures presented in Tables 8.4 and 8.5 represent only the noninstitutionalized elderly, or the elderly living in the community. If rates of functional limitation are higher among the institutionalized elderly, the figures from KSKC will understate the prevalence of functional limitations among the entire elderly population.

11. It should be noted, however, that because our analysis is based on cross-sectional data, the observed effect of age may be confounded with the effect of cohort. In other words, the estimated effect of age in our model may either underestimate or overestimate the pure effect of age on functional limitations depending on the level of improvements made in the health of the elderly over time. If longitudinal data on the Japanese elderly become available in the future, it will be possible to isolate the effect of age, as well as the cumulative effects of various socioeconomic factors across the life course.

12. The corresponding rates for women have changed little during the same period, but are much lower than the rates for men.

References

Arriaga, E. E. 1984. Measuring and explaining the change in life expectancies. *Demography* 21: 83–96.

Atoh, M. 1995. *Population dynamics: Its social and economic impact and policy responses in Japan.* Reprint Series, No. 22. Tokyo: Institute of Population Problems.

Berkman L., and L. Syme. 1979. Social networks, host resistance, and mortality: A nine-year follow-up study of Almeda County residents. *American Journal of Epidemiology* 109: 186–204.

Crystal, S. 1995. Economic status of the elderly. In *Handbook of aging and the social sciences,* edited by R. H. Binstock and L. K. George. San Diego, Calif.: Academic Press.

Elo, I. T., and S. H. Preston. 1996. Educational differences in mortality: United States 1979–1985. *Social Science and Medicine* 42: 47–57.

Feeney, G. 1990. The demography of aging in Japan: 1950–2025. NUPRI Research Paper Series No. 55. Tokyo: Nihon University Population Research Institute.

Fries, J. F. 1980. Aging, natural death and the compression of morbidity. *New England Journal of Medicine* 303: 130–35.

————. 1983. The compression of morbidity. *Milbank Memorial Fund Quarterly* 61: 397–419.

George, L. K. 1996. Social factors and illness. In *Handbook of aging and the social sciences,* 4th ed. San Diego: Academic Press.

Goldman, N. 1990. The perils of single life in contemporary Japan. *Journal of Marriage and the Family* 55: 194–204.

Goldman, N., S. Takahashi, and Y. Hu. 1995. Mortality among Japanese singles: A re-investigation. *Population Studies* 49: 227–39.

Gruenberg, E. M. 1977. The failures of success. *Milbank Memorial Fund Quarterly* 55: 3–24.

Hatano, S. 1994. Medical services for the elderly in Japan. In *Ageing in Japan and Singapore.* Department of Japanese Studies, National University of Singapore.

Hauser, P. M. 1986. Life-satisfaction and quality of life. Paper presented at Japan-United States Conference on Aging: Quality of Life in Aging Societies, September 15–18, 1986, Tokyo.

Hu, Y., and N. Goldman. 1990. Mortality differentials by marital status: An international comparison. *Demography* 27: 233–50.

Imaizumi, Y. 1991. *Wagakuni ni okeru chūkōnen no shibōbunseki* [Mortality in the elderly population aged over 40 in Japan, 1947–1988]. *Jinkō Mondai Kenkyū* [Journal of Population Problems] 47: 40–57.

Institute of Population Problems. 1997. *Nihon no Shōrai Suikei Jinkō* [Japanese Population Projections]. Tokyo: Ministry of Health and Welfare.

Iso, H, T. Shimamoto, A. Kitamura, M. Iida, and Y. Komachi. 1999. Trends of cardiovascular risk factors and diseases in Japan: Implications for primordial prevention. *Preventive Medicine* 29: S102–S105.

Japan Tobacco Corporation. 1990. *Heisei Ninendo Zenkoku Tabako Kitsuensharitsu Chōsa* [1990 National Survey on Cigarette Smoking]. Tokyo: Author.

Katz, S., and C. A. Akpom. 1976. A measure of primary sociobiological functions. *International Journal of Health Services* 6: 493–508.

Kobayashi, K. 1967. Mortality. *Jinkō Mondai Kenkyū* [Journal of Population Problems] 100: 82–114.

Kobayashi, K., R. Matsukura, and N. Ogawa. 1993. Demographic transition in postwar Japan: A time-series analysis. Research Paper Series No. 62. Tokyo: Nihon University Population Research Institute.

Komachi, Y. 1971. Geographic and occupational comparisons of risk factors in cardiovascular diseases in Japan. *Japan Circulatory Journal* 35: 189–207.

Kōno, S., and S. Takahashi. 1989. Mortality trends in Japan: Why has the Japanese life expectancy kept on increasing. Working Paper Series, No.1. Tokyo: Institute of Population Problems.

Lillard, L. A., and C. W. A. Panis. 1996. Marital status and mortality: The role of health. *Demography* 33: 313–28.

Liang, Jersey, and Daisaku Maeda. 1997. National survey of the Japanese elderly, 1987 (computer file). ICPSR version. Tokyo: Tokyo Metropolitan Institute of Gerontology. Ann Arbor, MI: Inter-University Consortium for Political and Social Research.

Liu, X., J. Liang, N. Muramatsu, and K. Sugisawa. 1995. Transitions in functional status and active life expectancy among older people in Japan. *Journal of Gerontology: Social Sciences* 50B: S383–S394.

Long, J. S. 1997. Regression models for categorical and limited dependent variables. Thousand Oaks, Calif.: Sage Publications.

Maeda, D. 1986. Subjective well-being in old age: An aspect of the quality of life. Paper presented at Japan-United States Conference on Aging: Quality of Life in Aging Societies, September 15–18, 1986, Tokyo.

Manton, K. G. 1982. Changing concept of morbidity and mortality in the elderly population. *Milbank Memorial Fund Quarterly* 60: 183–244.

Manton, K. G., and B. Singer. 1994. What's the fuss about compression of mortality. *Chance* 7: 21–30.

Manton, K. G., E. Stallard, and L. Corder. 1997. Changes in the age dependence of mortality and disability: Cohort and other determinants. *Demography* 34: 135–58.

Martin, L. G. 1989. The graying of Japan. *Population Bulletin* 44: 1–42.

Ministry of Health and Welfare. 1995. Japan. *Jinkō Dōtai Tōkei* [Vital statistics]. Tokyo: Ministry of Health and Welfare.

———. 1996. Japan. *Jinkō Dōtai Tōkei* [Vital statistics]. Tokyo: Ministry of Health and Welfare.

National Institute of Population and Social Security Research. 1997. *Annual Report.* Tokyo: National Institute of Population and Social Security Research.

Ogawa, N. 1986. Consequences of mortality change on aging. In *Consequences of mortality trends and differentials*. Population Studies No. 95. New York: United Nations.

Ohno, Y. 1985. Health development in Japan: Determinants, implication and perspectives. *World Health Statistics Quarterly* 38: 176–92.

Pollard, A. H., F. Yusuf, G. N. Pollard. 1974. *Demographic techniques*. Sydney: Pergamon Press.

Shryock, H. S., Jr., and J. S. Siegel. 1971. Methods and materials of demography. Washington, D.C.: Government Printing Office.

Takahashi, S. 1982. Cause of death and age pattern of mortality in Japan since 1950. *Jinkō Mondai Kenkyū* [Journal of Population Problems] 165: 43–53.

————. 1993. Health and mortality differentials among the elderly in Japan: A regional analysis with special emphasis on Okinawa. Working Paper Series, No. 17. Tokyo: Institute of Population Problems.

Tanaka, H., Y. Tanaka, Y. Hayashi, Y. Ueda, C. Date, T. Baba, and H. Shōji. 1982. Secular trends in mortality for cerebrovascular diseases in Japan, 1960 to 1979. *Stroke* 13: 574–81.

Tsuji, I., Y. Minami, A. Fukao, S. Hisamichi, H. Asano, and M. Satō. 1995. Active life expectancy among elderly Japanese. *Journal of Gerontology* 50A: M173–M176.

Ueshima, H., K. Tatara, S. Asakura, and M. Okamoto. 1987. Declining trends in blood pressure level and the prevalence of hypertension and changes in related factors in Japan, 1956–1980. *Journal of Chronic Diseases* 40: 137–47.

Verbrugge, L. M. 1984. Longer life but worsening health? Trends in health and mortality of middle-aged and older persons. *Milbank Memorial Fund Quarterly* 62: 475–519.

World Health Organization. 1996. *World Health Statistics Annual* 1996 Edition. Geneva: World Health Organization.

Yanagishita, M., and J. M. Guralnik. 1988. Changing mortality patterns that led life expectancy in Japan to surpass Sweden's: 1972–1982. *Demography* 25: 611–62.

9

Parent Care and Shifting Family Obligations in Urban Japan[1]

Brenda Robb Jenike

In the end, it is the yome *[daughter-in-law] who has to caregive. In the past we would have to take care of all aspects of the home. We had that mentality. The twenty-first century will be an era when there aren't enough people to do the caring [for elderly parents]. The community outside the home has to do the caring. One person is just not able to do it. This is how my outlook has completely changed.*

—Daughter-in-law caregiver in
Itabashi, Tokyo, who had just begun using
adult day care for her mother-in-law

About halfway through a two-hour support group meeting for family caregivers in northern Tokyo, a thin woman in her fifties hesitantly entered the room. The look of utter desperation on her face—the intense stress and exhaustion—was striking. After the woman had finished consulting with a representative from the ward's social services department, Mrs. Suzuki, a former family caregiver herself and organizer of this local support group, invited her to our table to talk with us. Speaking softly, the woman told us that this was her first visit to a support group. She was a *yome*, caring for her elderly mother-in-law who suffers from chronic depression (*utsu*). Her forehead was creased with worry, and her face flushed, perhaps because it was the first time she was attempting to share her family trouble with outsiders. Suddenly she blurted out the question, "How long can an elderly person with mental illness live?" When Mrs. Suzuki replied that mental illness alone wasn't fatal, that a person with otherwise good physical health might live twenty years or more, the woman looked as if she might collapse. "I can't handle living much longer like this," she said quietly. With empathy, Mrs. Suzuki proceeded to introduce the distraught woman to day care and nursing home options in their district.

Drawing from extended ethnographic fieldwork in Itabashi Ward,[2] a primarily blue-collar district of northwestern Tokyo, this chapter presents an experiential account of how set intergenerational contracts within the urban Japanese family are shifting in response to the growing availability of public care services for the frail elderly. My residence in Itabashi, from early 1996 through May 1997, coincided with a period of intense public debate in Japan over the sharing of responsibility between the private and public sectors for the care of the frail elderly. It was in June 1997 when the Diet finally passed plans for a controversial national long-term care insurance program for the elderly. During my fieldwork, I sought to explore changing perceptions of elder care obligations and expectations at both the private and public levels, and from the viewpoints of both family caregivers and elderly care recipients. I participated in an eight-week training course for family caregivers in my neighborhood, volunteered weekly for nine months as a caregiver at a local nursing home and an adult day care center, and was an active member of both local and national caregiver support groups. Throughout the year of my stay, I was able to extensively interact with and interview thirty-two family caregivers and twenty-eight elderly care recipients. Out of these caregivers, I formally interviewed ten daughters-in-law, six daughters, and two sons in a series of in-depth, life history interviews. This chapter draws primarily from my life history interviews with daughters-in-law caring for cognitively impaired parents-in-law.

The transition from exclusively private, family care for the elderly to the increased use of public, professional care services during the 1990s appears, at the societal level, to be a smooth process. At the *individual level*, however, a caregiver's attempt to relinquish her obligation of total care for her parents-in-law to outsiders is often a traumatic process. By presenting an "experience-near" account (Hollan and Wellenkamp 1994; Hollan 2001; cf. Kohut 1971) of the caregiving relationship in Japan, one that draws from the salient, subjective experiences of two daughter-in-law caregivers in Itabashi, I hope to convey both the ambivalence and tensions hidden within the private realm of the Japanese family as caregivers and elderly parents alike make the transition from private to public care.

Based on my interviews with caregivers, I address the following broad questions: How do middle-aged and upper-middle-aged

Japanese women who have been socialized to provide *total* care for their parents and parents-in-law themselves relinquish that duty to others? How do family caregivers conceptualize this change in the intergenerational contract—a contract built upon a lifetime of reciprocal behavior between the two generations and the amassing of social capital by the older generation? And, what is the impact of turning to public care for caregivers? It is my conviction that through the voices of the caregivers, themselves, situated within specific social and cultural context, we can better understand the interpersonal and emotional aspects involved in current transitions in elder care practices in urban Japan.

The Responsibility of the *Yome*

What has always intrigued me about parent care practices in Japan is the tradition of assigning the total responsibility of care for a frail elderly parent to one family member, even when there are other members who could share the care burden. In Japan, it has been and still is the wife of the eldest son, known as the *yome* or junior wife, who is responsible for the total care of her husband's parents (Harris and Long 1993; Higuchi 1992; Jenike 1997; Lebra 1984; Lock 1993a; Plath 1980; Sodei 1995). If there is no son, or the son remains unmarried, the responsibility falls to a daughter. According to a nationwide survey in 1992 by the Ministry of Health and Welfare of Japan, 85.9 percent of family caregivers to the bedridden elderly at home were women. Daughters-in-law comprised 33.4 percent, and 20.6 percent were daughters, with the remaining being elderly wives (*Ministry of Health and Welfare* 1996). This structural obligation of the *yome* (Hashimoto 1996) is a holdover from the *ie* system, the patrilineal, patriarchal and virilocal stem family system prevalent in prewar Japan. Following preferences for the right of primogeniture in the *ie* system, a retiring patriarch handed over his estate in its entirety to his eldest son, who was then responsible for continuing the family line. In exchange for this inheritance, the eldest son's wife, the *yome*, would be responsible for looking after the senior couple until their deaths.

The primary domestic relationship in this family system is that between the daughter-in-law (*yome*) and her mother-in-law (*shūtome*). The majority of my respondents who are *yome* of an eldest son have resided with their parents-in-law since marriage, a residence pattern typical for women of their generation (aged 50–70). A long-term relationship between a *yome* and her coresident

mother-in-law that is based on reciprocity over the life course
(Akiyama, Antonucci, and Campbell 1997) can be mutually
beneficial. The greatest benefit of living in an extended family
household for the *yome* is assistance with childcare as a young
mother. A *shūtome* often takes on much of the responsibility for
care of her grandchildren, especially if the *yome* works outside
the home. In addition, *shūtome* may help with housework, such as
laundry, grocery shopping, and meal preparation. Through these
acts a *shūtome* secures the devotion of her *yome* for her later
years. As the senior wife of the household, a *shūtome* is also
responsible for proper care of the family Buddhist altar (*butsudan*)
and the observance of religious rituals. In the most ideal sce-
narios reported to me, the *yome* and *shūtome* shared an intimate
bond built from decades of companionship and mutual support.
Yet, coresiding with one's parents-in-law may also be undesirable
for the *yome*. Negative aspects of the *yome-shūtome* relationship
for the *yome* include having to bow to the *shūtome's* domestic
authority, a lack of privacy and freedom, and the burden of caring
for the *shūtome* in old age.

Until about two decades ago, becoming a *yome* typically meant
a period of perhaps ten to twenty years of servitude as a junior wife
before progressing to the role of senior wife, and the main power
of the household. The period of nursing the mother-in-law or father-in-law before their deaths was usually under one year in
duration. Today, due to increased longevity, a woman may remain
a *yome* past the age of sixty, and in some cases seventy, with the
period of long-term care for her aged parents-in-law measured by
years and even decades rather than months. According to the
Ministry of Health and Welfare of Japan, half of all caregivers to
the disabled elderly are aged sixty and over (*Ministry of Health
and Welfare* 1996, 118). Out of my pool of respondents, the ages of
caregiving daughters-in-law ranged from 45 to 77 years, with the
period of caregiving spanning from three to twelve years (and counting). Although the caring demands required of a *yome* have increased dramatically, she is still bound to this traditional obligation
by the former inheritance system, by her acceptance of these structural obligations upon her entrance into her family of marriage,
and by her lifelong socialization into the role. These *yome*, now in
their late forties, fifties, and sixties are essentially caught in the
middle of Japan's social welfare transition. While they sacrifice to
fulfill an intergenerational contract set decades ago, a yet unknown
contract is being scripted for them for when they, in turn, progress
into old age dependency.

Transitioning to Community Care

Social Welfare Resources for Elder Care

Over the past decade local social welfare departments throughout Japan have greatly expanded public services for dependent and frail senior citizens in their districts. This increase is in accordance with goals laid out in the 1994 New Gold Plan. A revised and expanded version of the 1989 ten-year strategic social welfare plan for the elderly known as the Gold Plan, the New Gold Plan promoted home care support services over long-term institutionalization. This evolution of social welfare programs in Japan during the 1990s resulted in the nationwide availability of community-based home care services for the elderly by the year 2000. These care services include home helpers, visiting nurses, day care (regular and dementia special care), meal delivery, bathing service, physical therapy ("rehabilitation"), and short-stay service at local public nursing homes. With public services heavily subsidized under the Gold Plan, residents paid only minimal fees, usually on a sliding scale according to family income. Care centers also offer free classes on caregiving techniques to family caregivers in their community, a service known as "caregiver classroom" (kaigosha kyōshitsu).

On April 1, 2000, the state implemented a national long-term care insurance system (kaigo hoken) that replaced the New Gold Plan. Unlike the previous Gold Plan public welfare programs provided by municipalities, the national insurance system is an entitlement program that allows elderly Japanese to choose from public or private-sector care service providers. All Japanese citizens aged 40 and over must now pay a mandatory monthly premium for this long-term care insurance. If deemed eligible by their assigned district case managers, disabled Japanese aged 65 and over can receive care services, with 90 percent of the cost covered by the plan (Uranaka 2000). Persons between the ages of 40 and 65 can also receive care services if they become disabled by an "age-related" condition such as early-onset Alzheimer's Disease or stroke. As with the Gold Plan, municipal governments remain in charge of running the new program for local residents.

For long-term residential care, not yet covered under the insurance plan, there is an increasing number of large-scale nursing homes throughout Japan, as well as various types of group homes and assisted living complexes such as Tokyo's "silver peer" housing program (shirubā piā). In addition to public housing programs for seniors, there has been a boom in the building of private, large-scale assisted living retirement complexes in rural and seaside areas. The seaside resort of Atami located 100 kilometers southwest of Tokyo on the Izu Peninsula brims with sparkling high-rise retirement complexes for those who can afford them. This private side of senior care is referred to as the silver business. It is seen by Japanese economists and entrepreneurs as an area of continuing exponential growth in the years to come.

Although all public services are theoretically available nationwide, actual availability of services in Tokyo in 1997 varied by district depending upon both the tax resources of the area and the foresight of local social welfare administrators. Demand for the most popular resources such as home helpers, day care, and nursing home beds, has always been higher than supply. In every district, the age of the caregiver, health status of the care recipient as judged by the social welfare office, and household structure (the family unit being the object of evaluation rather than the individual senior citizen) were taken into account during the cumbersome application process in order to ration these scarce resources. In practice, an elderly person living alone or with an elderly spouse had the first priority for all public services. Elderly taken care of by a single working child, whether a son or daughter, came next. Those cared for by a married daughter or daughter-in-law wound up last. Married women caregivers thus were often rebuffed by the local social welfare clerk upon applying for services for their elderly parent-in-law or parent. In Mitaka City, a western suburb of Tokyo where I also conducted interviews, the social welfare program lagged so far behind that of Itabashi Ward that many of the caregivers there were simply unaware of the existence of services they qualified for in their district.

Even if accepted into the social welfare program, there are one-year waiting lists for day care, and two- to four-year waits for nursing homes within Tokyo wards and cities. By contrast, placement in nursing homes in neighboring rural prefectures such as Saitama is immediate. In Tokyo, the impediments to building new nursing homes are both the scarcity of available land and the exorbitant cost. Add to this Tokyo's extremely high population density, and nursing home beds become precious commodities. In more sparsely populated regions with land to spare, beautiful new nursing homes, built with federal subsidies, abound. Unfortunately, many families in Tokyo who plan to visit their elderly parent at least weekly do not wish to take advantage of open bed space in a nursing home that would require a long commute. Instead they wait and wait for space to open up in their local nursing home.

The Public Promotion of Community Care

During the mid-1990s, there was a noticeable shift in the public culture regarding filial obligations and care of elderly parents that coincided with this vast makeover in senior social welfare resources for the frail elderly. Public discourse on elder care in Japan during the late 1980s and early 1990s carried an overt moral message, emphasizing the need for adult children to fulfill their filial obligations (Jenike 1997; Lock 1993b). By 1996, the public message had changed from this moralizing discourse to one that privileged the merits of professional, institutional care over those of informal home care.

A brief examination of social welfare publications, print and television media illustrates this significant shift in tone. The 1993 cover of the senior services brochure in the city of Kawasaki, for example, was a cartoon depiction of an adult son and wife literally supporting two elderly parents in a palanquin "home" on their shoulders. The cartoon *yome* is denoted as a caregiver by her white apron and white kerchief on her head. By 1996, this visual moral message had disappeared. Instead, social welfare pamphlets and brochures showed either neutral photographs of seniors in care facilities or had plain color covers. Likewise, a Ministry of Health and Welfare ad to promote volunteerism at senior centers that appeared in the *Yomiuri Shinbun* in 1996 shows male and female high school students looking on as two elderly women make crafts at a table. Additional small photos show smiling young men assisting wheelchair-bound seniors. The large caption reads "I have fun with seniors." Only a few years earlier this call for volunteerism had been reserved largely for middle-aged housewives (Jenike 1997).

During the same time period, the tone, volume, and content of reporting on elder care changed in the print and television media. Articles on elder care in the three major national newspapers (*Asahi, Yomiuri,* and *Mainichi Shinbun*) not only greatly increased in number in the mid-1990s, but also began to primarily present medical and social welfare information, make academic international comparisons, and include celebratory accounts of healthy and independent seniors. The prominent themes of newspaper columns on elder care before this time were concern over the demise of the extended family and advice on how to continue home care. During my stay in Itabashi, I could also learn about elder care from two weekly television shows, aired during prime evening viewing hours on state-sponsored NHK's educational channel: *Healthy Senior Caregiving (Sukoyaka Shirubā Kaigo)* and *Welfare for Tomorrow (Kyō ni Ikiru Ashita)*. In addition, numerous documentaries on national and international elder care issues aired on the major Japanese commercial television networks. Even television dramas had changed their tune regarding parent care in particular. For example, unlike the filial piety genre of dramas I viewed during 1992–93 (*Son's Return Home, Blessed with Grandma, Double Kitchen*), the 1996 TBS drama *In My World Only Demons* (*Wataru Seken wa Oni Bakari*) included the overly dramatic depiction of a distraught young couple caring for a 62-year-old mother-in-law with early-onset Alzheimer's. The advice given to the fictional *yome* was to seek professional care for her mother-in-law.

As use of elder care services continues to be actively promoted in the media, and service availability expands, utilizing public care resources will continue to become more socially acceptable for Japanese families. National records on the use of home-care support services (day services, home helpers, short-stays) under the Gold Plan social welfare program do indeed show a doubling in usage from 1991 to 1994, and a doubling again from 1994 to 1997, the latest year statistics are available. For the year 1997, the Ministry of Health and Welfare reported a national cumulative total of over 35 million uses of day services (day care, rehabilitation, and bathing services); home helper services were utilized over 29 million times for the same year (*Ministry of Health and Welfare* 2000, 126). This shift in public acceptance of support services is being further fueled by the state's move away from the "welfare" of the Gold Plan (with welfare still stigmatized as something for the impoverished or for those without family support) to the entitlement of the new national long-term care insurance program (with all who pay premiums entitled to services).

As stated above, despite societal trends of increased service usage, at the individual level, the transition from total home care to some use of community care is not necessarily a smooth or easy process for either caregiving families or the elderly care recipients. Rather, a daughter-in-law's attempts to relinquish her obligation of total care for her parents-in-law to outsiders can be a highly traumatic process. This is primarily because, despite the more progressive, neutral tone of senior welfare service promotions, Japanese women in middle and upper-middle age still firmly believe that the home is the best place for the elderly. They know that the current generation of elderly parents still expects and desires care at home. This belief is coupled with a moral commitment to persevere. For women in these age groups and older, the ability to place other's needs first, especially those of family members, and endure hardship (*gaman*) is synonymous with being a woman and a proper *yome* (Kondo 1990; Lebra 1984; Lock 1993a; Tamanoi 1998).

The major obstacles a *yome* encounters, then, when seeking help from the public sector are three-fold: her own misgivings over not continuing her effort to fulfill her familial obligation; the objections of her husband, in-laws, and elderly parent-in-law; and the prohibitory bureaucratic process which serves to ration care. The two case studies I present clearly illustrate the tensions that arise between a caregiving daughter-in-law and her in-laws when faced with the extremely difficult care of an elderly parent with advanced dementia. It is these tensions over perceived lack of cooperation and understanding from in-laws that have led caregiving daughters-in-law to deeply question the logic of an intergenerational contract that heaps the burdens of parent care so heavily on to their shoulders alone.

Caregiver Experiences: Two Success Stories from Itabashi

I now turn to the personal experiences of Mrs. Shimura and Mrs. Inami,[3] two *yome* living in Itabashi Ward, Tokyo, whom I met in the ward's caregiver classroom course. Both women are caring for parents-in-law with advanced dementia. After years of being engulfed by family obligations, these two *yome* have successfully turned to public services to help alleviate their burdens of twenty-four-hour caregiving.

Why is Grannie Just My Responsibility?

Small and slight to the point of fragility, quiet and timid in manner, Mrs. Shimura surprised me when we sat down to talk privately by her immediate outpouring of frustrations and concerns regarding her mother-in-law and her life as a *yome* in one rapid, verbal tidal wave. A 54-year-old housewife, Mrs. Shimura lives with her husband, her adult son (28) and daughter (26), and *obaachan* ("grannie")—her 92-year-old mother-in-law Toki. Her husband is the eldest son from a family of five children. They are a middle-class family, owning their own home in one of the nicer neighborhoods in Itabashi. Mr. Shimura is a retired civil servant who now runs his own store. Both children work, and plan to live at home until marriage, the typical and socially acceptable pattern in Tokyo where housing costs are high.

Mrs. Shimura agreed to live with and look after her husband's parents when she married into his family. "I came to live in a house/family [*ie*] with parents, so that's how it is [*shō ga nai*]." Her father-in-law passed away in 1980 without needing prolonged care. What she was not prepared for, however, was for her sharp-minded mother-in-law to suffer from severe dementia in her later years. Like most Japanese in their fifties and older, Mrs. Shimura had never encountered a person with dementia, and did not initially recognize the symptoms in her mother-in-law. She assumed that Toki's increasing forgetfulness was "normal aging." "In the past, people died before they became senile," she explained. Both her own parents and her grandparents had died younger than Toki is now, without any signs of cognitive decline.

Unfortunately, Toki's dementia has resulted in her being verbally abusive to her daughter-in-law. Toki is now also afraid to bathe, and is unwilling to change her clothes. Mobile but fragile, Toki is unable to perform most daily activities without assistance. Mrs. Shimura must be vigilant to prevent her from wandering and becoming lost in the neighborhood, which she has done many times. Neighbors now stay on the lookout for Toki, and will bring her back to the Shimura home if they see her out walking aimlessly. Mrs. Shimura comments, "We don't hide *obaachan*'s senility. The neighbors all know about it anyway. They can help me out, warn me if they see her wandering. The community [*chiiki*] needs to do this. It's good to have this village mentality, taking care of each other."

Mrs. Shimura made the decision to quit her own part-time job and care for Toki in 1995, two years prior to interview, when her mother-in-law was hospitalized for an illness. "Even though I enjoyed work, I couldn't continue it. I thought that to continue working would be selfish [*wagamama*] of me." Mrs. Shimura related her present life to me in this way:

"I have *obaachan* to care for now. I'm not working, so I have some free time, but if I try to do something on my own, *obaachan* comes in to talk with me. She'll say strange things. She'll interrupt. I have to stop right in the midst of what I'm doing, so I can't have time to myself. I came to realize that it's no use. She'll just keep on talking. There's nothing to be done about it.

"She used to be a housewife, right. That former role seems to have come back to her. She will obsess about the time—just stare at the clock. When it's about two o'clock in the afternoon, she'll say 'You have to prepare dinner.' 'It's still okay, *obaachan*,' I'll say. 'It's still just two. It's fine to wait until around four.' But she doesn't accept this. She stands in the kitchen, staring at the stove. I go and get her and say, 'It's okay.' Then, five minutes later, she goes back in the kitchen. She does this all year long. It gets so tiring! I think, I can't do anything about this. I'm always getting up, then sitting back down, and getting up again. I guess it's just what happens when you have to look after someone with dementia. I finally get her to understand, then in another five minutes she has forgotten all about it and it happens all over again."

Mrs. Shimura says she can stand the physical tasks of caring for her mother-in-law, including cleaning up toileting accidents and other unpleasant chores, but that emotionally, Toki's angry outbursts, vicious verbal attacks, and complete lack of gratitude discourage and depress her. "It is hard to keep my confidence up, to keep an outward kindness to her. I got so mad the other day. It wells up in my heart and sometimes I just want to yell. If someone [a caregiver] says they don't have such harsh feelings, they're lying. It's the biggest problem, to keep showing kindness, even when I get mad. You understand don't you? Trying to keep up a good face in front of strangers?" This is especially true since her mother-in-law will act graciously to strangers like her professional caregivers. When I met Toki at day care, she had been freshly bathed, and simply sat and laughed. She told me that she couldn't remember what she did today, and allowed me to help her with her coat—a sweet grandma for the outside world. "I think of Kin-*san* and Gin-*san*," says Mrs. Shimura, referring to the celebrated centenarian twin women who were graying Japan's celebrities until their deaths in 2000 and 2001 at ages 107 and 108, respectively. "I thought she'd grow old like them. But she's not like them at all. She's frightening—when she gets angry." Mrs. Shimura reports that she and Toki had a good relationship before the dementia. "She wouldn't criticize me. I don't understand why she acts this way to me now."

When I first met Mrs. Shimura in my local nursing home's caregiver training course in early October of 1996, she was wan and thin, anxious, exhausted, sullen, and somewhat disheveled in her appearance. Her mother-in-law had just begun special dementia day care at the nursing home that week. This meant that Mrs. Shimura would finally be getting two days of respite on a weekly basis from her twenty-four-hour, seven-day week of caregiving. When I sat down with her six months later to formally interview her, her appearance had dramatically improved. The tiredness and anxiety in her eyes and face had lessened. She had gained a bit of weight.

Her hair was styled, and the gray was gone. She laughed freely, something she had not done in the caregiver course.

Mrs. Shimura turned to public services gradually. Her sister-in-law (wife of her husband's younger brother) had completed the first level of home helper training, and urged Mrs. Shimura to call Itabashi Ward's Senior Welfare Center for advice on getting Toki to bathe. After a visit from a social worker, Mrs. Shimura applied for a home helper to come to the house two mornings each week to change Toki's clothes. The same sister-in-law had tried to bathe Toki herself, with success until the third try, when Toki again refused to be bathed. Luckily, the home helper has been successful in bathing Toki. "I think that's because she can distinguish those who are strangers to her," explains Mrs. Shimura. "I wish she would act the same towards me as she does with the helper."

Mrs. Shimura next applied for special dementia day care at the local nursing home, and after a year wait, Toki was accepted. She spends the time Toki is away cleaning Toki's room and doing her laundry, but also occasionally shops or meets with friends. Mrs. Shimura has used short-stay service only once so that she could go mountain climbing, a previous frequent pastime. She immensely enjoyed her three days of respite, but because Toki told her off so ferociously when she returned, she says that she probably will not do this again for some time.

Mrs. Shimura and her husband have no intention to institutionalize her mother-in-law, and, at this point, truthfully, Toki's condition is too advanced to be admitted to one of the ward's nursing homes. Mrs. Shimura says she will continue to look after Toki "until the upper limits." Only as a last resort, if Mrs. Shimura herself were to fall seriously ill, would the family consider placing Toki in a hospital. When things get really rough, Mrs. Shimura says to Toki, *"Osaki ni shitsurei shimasu"* (Pardon me for going before you), by which she means that she can envision herself dying from exhaustion before her mother-in-law passes on. "I'm always worried about what would happen if I were to collapse. A *yome* has to be strong and healthy. She can't fall ill. Japanese *yome* have to be in good health or it will all fall apart. My children are not yet married. I think when they get married [and move out] it will become much easier. Now I am taking care of everyone, because none of them do anything."

Mrs. Shimura is grateful for the respite she now receives from public day care, and the assistance of the home helper which helps to avoid struggles over hygiene. She continues to rely on the Senior Center's telephone consultation service for advice. She also credits the caregiver course with giving her confidence in her ability to care properly. Along with learning care techniques, she enjoyed the support of the group, relieved to see how many other women were faced with her similar situation. Mrs. Shimura now attends seminars on caring for elderly with dementia and says that the information has helped her understand what is happening with her mother-in-law.

What Mrs. Shimura truly desires, however, is not more public services, but more cooperation from her in-laws, specifically her husband's sisters. She explains:

"In Japan it is just expected [tōzen] that the person living with the parent should look after them. This is how my in-laws think, and I have agreed to this. But, looking after a senile person is incredibly difficult. There needs to be someone who can come and trade places with the caregiver once in a while. Not a facility, but a family member from outside the household—a daughter. There should be that sort of cooperation. It is regrettable that society has not developed this system yet. If my sisters-in-law had the initiative, they could say, 'It's obviously rough for you, so I'll come take your place for a while.' But they don't think this way, and I can't force them. I can't order them to come in and care for their own mother. If they offered, I would be delighted. But so far they haven't offered. That's my current situation."

Mrs. Shimura harbors the most resentment for her husband's eldest sister, a childless widow, who lives close by but has refused Mrs. Shimura's requests to come over to care for her mother. She will only come to visit when Mrs. Shimura is there to do the caring. Mrs. Shimura wonders why a woman with no family or work obligations is not willing to help. "None of his sisters have lived with their parents-in-law. So they don't understand what it's like for me. Even if I tell them about it, they don't understand. I'd like to tell them to come over and try it themselves, so they know what it's really like. If they don't experience it firsthand, they'll never understand my point of view. . . . When a person has dementia, it would be nice to be able to take care of them with great kindness. But when you have to do it for years on end, neither person [yome nor parent-in-law] can keep that up. We're together the whole year through. She gets tired of me."

Although neither her in-laws nor her husband have criticized her use of day care (an inexpensive, subsidized service), Mrs. Shimura resents that she had to look for outside help when there were family members who could have stepped in. She is hurt and frustrated by the lack of understanding of and appreciation for her

efforts by her mother-in-law's own children, whom she characterizes as cold-hearted (*tsumetai*).

To Mrs. Shimura, then, it is this continuing lack of appreciation for and understanding of her daily life as a caregiver that was
foremost on her mind. Despite devoting the past three years of her
life to the constant care of Toki, her mother-in-law is not able to
comprehend her efforts, and instead lashes out at her continually.
Mrs. Shimura is not able to deal well emotionally with her mother-
in-law's change in personality, and is frustrated by the symptoms
of her dementia. The respite received from the city ward has had
a noticeable positive physical and emotional impact, and Mrs.
Shimura acknowledges that women who had to caregive without
any public assistance in the preceding decade had it much tougher
than she has it now. She is, however, distraught over the continued
lack of cooperation from her in-laws. As a *yome* of an eldest son,
who still has the responsibility to care for her own adult children
and husband, she feels overly burdened. Yet, she remains firmly
committed to her duty to care for her mother-in-law at home. I now
turn to Mrs. Inami, whose experience illustrates what this care
commitment can become when the long-term caregiver is not the
wife of the eldest son, but the wife of a younger son who resigns
herself to the care of her mother-in-law when other family members refuse to do so.

Accommodating an "Old-Fashioned" Husband

In the northern part of Itabashi, away from the older neighborhood
of single-family homes where the Shimura family lives, we find
Mrs. Inami living in the midst of a massive, high-rise condominium
complex that houses 30,000 people in three square blocks. Mrs.
Inami, at 66, is a decade older than Mrs. Shimura. She has an
amiable personality—outgoing and confident. She lives with her
71-year-old husband, and the youngest of her three children, a
daughter who is 28 and single. Her older daughter and son are
both married and live in neighboring cities. Mrs. Inami's 96-year-
old mother-in-law has been residing in a public nursing home in
Itabashi for one year, and was hospitalized in various geriatric
hospitals for the prior three years.

Unlike Mrs. Shimura, the wife of an eldest son, Mrs. Inami is
not obligated through kinship to care for her mother-in-law. Her
husband is a third-born son. However, since age 19, when he made
a deathbed promise to his dying father, her husband has been

committed to providing and caring for his widowed mother, much to his wife's chagrin. His eldest brother was in the military and stationed abroad at the time his father died, and the second son was working in Manchuria. According to Mrs. Inami, neither has ever upheld his duties as an elder son. As for the husband's younger two sisters, both are married into other families and do not feel responsible for the care of their own mother.

Despite advancing age, both Mrs. Inami and her husband continue to work in the barbershop they have owned for over thirty years. Mrs. Inami proudly labels herself as *shitamachi* (downtown, working-class), and highly values her long work history and ability to earn money. Her education was abruptly halted by the war when she was only in the sixth grade. From that time on, Mrs. Inami has had to work, first in her family's farm in Saitama, then until marriage as a young hairdresser in Tokyo, and ever since as an assistant at her husband's barbershop. She and her husband have supported his mother since their marriage, with no help from any of her husband's siblings.

Mrs. Inami was the sole caregiver to her husband's mother at home for three years until her mother-in-law, who suffers from stroke-induced dementia, broke her leg and needed hospitalization. The two generations had not lived together prior to caregiving, but had lived down the street from each other. Mrs. Inami had always been responsible for looking after her mother-in-law, cooking her meals and doing her laundry and cleaning. She characterizes her mother-in-law, who in the past refused to assist Mrs. Inami with childcare or even simple housework, as argumentative and self-centered. The following story, which Mrs. Inami repeated twice without prompting during the interview, reveals the lasting hurt of this unhappy relationship:

"In spite of my just having given birth to a baby, she would come over at eleven in the morning and I would have to make lunch and serve her. She would go back home at two. I asked her to please come to the house earlier, to hang up the laundry to dry. There were so many diapers to launder. She got so angry when I suggested this. She cut off our relationship. She said since we weren't mother and daughter, we would no longer interact. I said that was fine with me. Of course, my husband didn't want his wife speaking like this. He said it was important for the children to have a grandmother. So I went to apologize. I told my husband I didn't want to apologize. My husband said to apologize for his sake. It's how it had to be I guess [*shō ga nai ka na*]. It would have been better for her to have had to come and apologize to me. The most important thing to my husband is his mother. After her come the children and me. That's wrong. I told him so. But my husband is a stubborn person."

Since this early rift, Mrs. Inami says that she has tried to maintain a civil relationship with her mother-in-law for the sake of her husband and her children. Unfortunately, the onset of dementia only enhanced her mother-in-law's quarrelsome disposition, adding the dimension of a mistrust of strangers and delusions that people are stealing from her.

Before being admitted to the public nursing home, Mrs. Inami's mother-in-law was hospitalized for almost three years in three different hospitals for the elderly. Her habit of wandering at night led to her being asked to leave facility after facility. Although medical insurance covered "medical treatment," additional fees for all services rendered added up to a bill of ¥100,000 to ¥300,000 ($800—$2,400) per month for Mrs. Inami and her husband to pay. The high costs, plus the constant pressure to bring her mother-in-law back home after the maximum three-month stay led Mrs. Inami to fight to admit her mother-in-law into one of the ward's public nursing homes. She credits her good fortune at only having to wait two years for a place in a nursing home, rather than the typical four years, to her own tenacity at the city office. Rebuffed by the caseworkers, she returned repeatedly to plead her case directly to the head of the social welfare office.

When finally offered a space in a public nursing home, her mother-in-law objected to the move, and her husband insisted that they bring his mother back home. Mrs. Inami absolutely refused to do this, and even had the head of the social welfare office convince her husband that his mother needed the higher quality care that only the nursing home could provide. She describes this time, until her mother-in-law adjusted to her new surroundings in the nursing home, as the most difficult period of all.

As she is not the eldest son's *yome*, Mrs. Inami views her obligation to care for her mother-in-law as something she does "for my husband," rather than an unquestioned duty. She has constantly reassessed her caregiving situation against her own needs, and views the care her mother-in-law receives as "professional" and far superior to any care she could provide at home. Throughout the process of institutionalizing her mother-in-law, Mrs. Inami was not shy about demanding help from her in-laws. Despite this, her in-laws acted much the same as those of Mrs. Shimura. And, like Mrs. Shimura, Mrs. Inami harbors great resentment toward them. She explains:

"Truthfully it's not my responsibility [*sekinin*] to care for *obaasan*.⁴ But it's the difference in attitudes between my husband and his elder brothers. My husband and I have always worked hard to make a living, and support his mother as his father asked him to. We agreed to look after my husband's mother on our own, the best we could. We had an old-fashioned way of thinking. . . . None of them helped to pay [her hospital bills]. They don't even visit her. Just my husband does. We ask them to visit her. 'Please come and see her,' we say, but none of her children will come. I would tell them, 'It's not only for us to do.' I was direct with them. They understood, but wouldn't give any money. When I'd ask, they'd say no [*iya da*]. . . . They assume we are wealthy because my husband runs his own barbershop. . . . So we paid by ourselves because my husband is an old-fashioned person [*furui ningen*]. I argue with him all the time about his siblings."

It was her husband who went to talk to each of his siblings to explain why their mother was now in a nursing home. When asked the current status of her relationship with her in-laws, she replied, "We don't interact at all." Fighting over care of the mother-in-law and the burdensome bills has completely severed the relationships.

Mrs. Inami attributes her current health problems to the stress of this one-sided parent care despite the presence of a large family that could feasibly have supported the caregiving burden. She suffers from adult-onset diabetes, and heart disease. Her husband has suffered two heart attacks, and has high blood pressure. Mrs. Inami views her life remaining as short, and wants to enjoy it while she can. She considers the care she now provides for her mother-in-law—weekly visits to check on her clothing and well-being—extremely easy compared to that of the previous six years. She says that her husband, although still emotionally uncomfortable with his mother living in a nursing home, is now also more at ease. Mrs. Shimura, as well, reports unusually high cholesterol and a difficult menopause, which she attributes to her troubled *kokoro* (mental state) from the stress of caregiving.

It should be noted that neither Mrs. Inami nor Mrs. Shimura have received or plan to receive any inheritance from their parents-in-law. There was never any inheritance to receive. In fact, Mrs. Inami and her husband have paid for all of her mother-in-law's living expenses for forty years. Today in Japan the obligations tied to the inheritance system of the past persist even when the monetary gain upon which the contract was built ceases to exist. When questioned whether they received any help with care tasks from their husbands, they laughed and replied that their husbands were *Shōwa hitoketa* (born in the single-digit Shōwa years). This means that they are of the prewar generation, a generation of men who "do not help out in the home in any manner, period."

What was most important to Mrs. Inami was the high cost of caregiving in financial and health terms that she and her husband have weathered. She does not particularly like her mother-in-law. An important factor in their lifelong relationship is that Mrs. Inami feels that, rather than benefiting from the expected reciprocal relationship, she has been forced into a unilateral relationship in which only she has helped her mother-in-law for all these years. She therefore feels in no way obligated to continue to care for her, and has only done so to this point for her husband's sake. Without personal affection, the structural obligation of kinship, or an inheritance, Mrs. Inami does not have the motivation necessary for committing to and persevering through the years of arduous care required to look after an elderly parent with dementia.

Perceived Generational Differences among Women

Daughters-in-law now coresiding with, and caring for elderly parents-in-law know that they are the last generation willing to take on this extended burden. They do not expect their children, in particular, their own daughters-in-law, to do this for them when they in turn need assistance. Mrs. Shimura reasons this way:

"I don't really want to live together with my son and his wife. It's important to intertwine our lives, but I think it would be difficult for his wife. She will have been brought up differently than I was. I don't think it would work out so smoothly for us to live together. We won't make them do that. It will be my husband and I who will have to exercise self-control [*gaman*]. It seems that today's young people do not *gaman*, but are more selfish [*wagamama*]. Well, I'm selfish, too, but compared to women in their fifties like me, women in their twenties think much more broadly, with bigger expectations. It's impossible for them to settle for the same things and reach the same conclusions that we women in our fifties have. Well, maybe towards the end I will decide that I want to be cared for by my *yome* and son, but right now I strongly feel that I don't want to live with them in the future."

Always having lived within a family, however, Mrs. Shimura confides that she cannot imagine living alone in old age. She would not want to be sick or have an accident with no one around to help her.

This desire for an independent old age—at least the desire that a similar fate of endless home caregiving not fall upon their own daughters and sons—was without question expressed by all women caregivers I spoke with. Mrs. Kanno, already an experienced caregiver for both of her parents-in-law at age 45, confided:

"I don't want my daughter to care for me. I don't want to burden her with that heavy thought. I tell her often, when you get married, you don't need to worry about your parents. I tell her that father and I will be just fine living by ourselves. I really want to make it easy for my daughter. I can't allow it to become like this for her. . . . My feeling is that I don't want my daughter to marry an eldest son. . . . Like me, I'm not distressed with my present life. [Repeats.] But, I can't take much time for myself, and I can't do things I'd like to. So I don't want my daughter to have this sort of life. I want her to do what she wants to do, and lead an enjoyable life."

Further, drawing from firsthand experience with their parents-in-law, caregivers are well aware of the consequences of increasing dependency in old age, and desire a more secure future than one that relies on the good will of a present or future daughter-in-law. Family caregivers of elderly parents with dementia may especially fear becoming senile (*boke*) themselves. Even though a daughter-in-law can console herself with the fact that she is not a blood relation of her mother-in-law, simply observing how a formerly sharp-minded, clever woman can now not even remember how to get dressed in the morning is frightening. Daughters-in-law also worry that their husbands may follow in their parents' footsteps, envisioning an old age taking care of a fully dependent husband. Although most Japanese I spoke with during my fieldwork were more favorably inclined toward home support services and assisted living complexes than they were toward institutionalization in a nursing home, Mrs. Inami stated that if she were to become senile, she would want to immediately enter a nursing home where she is convinced she could be taken care of better than she would be at home.

The Shifting Contract

The women I interviewed who were coresiding with and caring for their impaired parents-in-law had been socialized into a kinship system in which they agreed, upon marriage, to care for their husband's parents until their deaths. Today they still uphold this lifelong duty to care for the older generation, but have begun to question the traditional role of the *yome* in the face of the extremely difficult, long-term care required for elders with severe dementia. As Mrs. Shimura related to me, she had not ever imagined her mother-in-law becoming senile. That was not part of the bargain. Although this type of strenuous and difficult care can force even the most loyal *yome* to seek out city support services, the *yome* whom I met wanted to first receive help from their in-laws, namely, their mother-in-law's own daughters. The current cohort of caregivers and their husbands are from a generation brought up in large families. A caregiving *yome* reasons that, with so many children, why is she the only one to provide the physical and emotional care for her mother-in-law? Where are her real daughters? Along with this need for respite is a desire for appreciation, understanding, and gratitude for years of effort. Like my respondents, daughter-in-law caregivers in the support groups I attended commiserated at length with each other over hurtful criticism from their sisters-in-law, the lack of help freely offered, and the dismal state of their relationships with their in-laws.

What I have presented here is admittedly a highly qualitative study of perceived family relationships from the subjective viewpoints of a small number of Japanese family caregivers. As stated, my aim is to provide personal context for national statistics that simply report Japanese families are turning to community care services for the care of their elders, or that daughters are becoming the preferred caregivers (preferred, not actual). Of course, broader questions arise that can be better addressed by population level analyses than by qualitative ethnographic accounts. For example, how representative are the experiences of caregivers in Itabashi? Is the rate of service usage by caregivers proportionate to the functional loss (cognitive and/or physical) of the care recipients (i.e., greater service usage by those caring for severely disabled elderly), or are other variables more significant (age cohort of caregiver, socioeconomic status)? Do in-laws (daughters-in-law) turn to services at the same rates as adult children (daughters)?

Based upon my wider ethnographic inquiries, I could perceive that, although the current cohort of family caregivers in Japan, no matter the age, is still firmly committed to home care for their frail aged parents, the intergenerational contract upon which these women and men have been raised is indeed becoming a hollow system. At least in urban Tokyo, the foundations upon which the obligations of the *yome* were built have, in many cases, ceased to exist. Junior and senior couples no longer desire or practice lifelong coresidence, but instead may move in together for the senior couple's last years. Inheritance, meant to continue the family line, is now taxed away, nonexistent, or divided equally among offspring. The reward for a loyal *yome*, the symbolic or actual succession to *shūtome* (senior wife) is delayed too far into old age. Further, the former formidable authority of the *shūtome* has greatly eroded compared to even a decade ago. Finally, the *yome*, no matter how loyal and self-sacrificing, does not have the guarantee of receiving like care from her own *yome* in old age.

According to the Ministry of Health and Welfare of Japan, an estimated 2.8 million elderly Japanese out of a senior population of 21.8 million are currently in need of care (Uranaka 2000). Now included as part of the long-term care insurance entitlement program, elder care services provide Japanese citizens with a choice in how to care for their elderly family members. Although the stigma of welfare has been removed, a highly complex application process still unfortunately hampers the process of turning to community care. When the new insurance system replaced the Gold Plan welfare program in April 2000, all disabled seniors in Japan had to be newly assessed by appointed case managers to determine what home care support services they qualified for under the new plan's guidelines. To receive any of these services, elderly applicants also had to submit a "care service plan" compiled for them by an appointed "care plan manager" (Sakata 2000). Thus, some seniors already participating in day services under the Gold Plan were denied these services under the new insurance program, whereas other seniors not yet using services were introduced to available care options. Luckily, assessment for residential care in nursing homes is set to begin in the year 2005, so those family caregivers with aged parents already in nursing homes have a few more years without having to undergo reassessment and another challenging application process.

In budgeting for the insurance plan, the federal government assumed that filial obligations were strong enough to keep demand for services low in the initial years of the program. Once people are more familiar with the program, and have paid premiums that entitle them to services as policyholders, this may no longer be the case (Campbell and Ikegami 2000). At least initially, the lengthy application process and shortage of qualified staff at administering municipalities has caused a huge backlog in the system. Only half of the 2.2 million applicants were assessed by February 2000, and by the April 1 start date, care plans had not been processed for 27 percent of those who had been assessed (Uranaka 2000). As more and more people apply for services, there is a realistic fear of future ballooning, unmanageable costs for elder care, especially as the Japanese population continues to age and the economy sinks deeper into recession.

Based upon my caregiver respondents' positive experiences with community care and the growing demand nationwide in Japan for public services under the new insurance program, the logical conclusion regarding the future performance of parent care is that the former intergenerational contract, in which the *yome* or one designated adult child provides total care for aged parents, is collapsing in favor of community care. Yet, truly significant changes in parent care obligations, expectations, and practices in Japan will only come about with the succession of generations of caregivers and care recipients. Unlike my caregiver respondents in their mid-fifties, sixties, and seventies, women caregivers in their forties whom I interviewed eagerly applied for and fully utilized city senior services. These women, born and educated after the end of World War II (hence, not having undergone the Confucian moral education of the prewar and wartime periods), expect support, view it as superior "professional" care, and have fewer moral dilemmas relinquishing care to outsiders. For these younger caregivers as well, personal affection and gratitude towards their parents-in-law seemed to be crucial components in securing years of devoted care (Jenike 2002).

In the upcoming two decades, more women and men born in and socialized during the postwar era will become caregivers, and the current generation of caregivers will in turn become the older generation needing care. It is likely that the desires and expectations for independence prevalent among the future middle, young-old, and oldest generations will mean that parent care, once an unquestioned duty, will become a matter of personal choice. Add to this change in expectations a significantly decreased average family size and a socially acceptable means of providing alternative long-term care in the form of the national long-term care insurance program, and it is not hard to predict that the old system of family care for aged parents in Japan will continue to shift to a system of community-based and institutional care for the elderly. Optimistically speaking, as Japan turns to this socialized system of elder care, the situation of endless forced years of care for incapacitated elderly parents by overburdened *yome* or adult children—dismal for caregivers and elderly care recipients alike—can fade into history.

Notes

1. This chapter is based on excerpts from chapters 3 and 5 of my doctoral dissertation *From the Family to the Community: Renegotiating Responsibility for the Care of the Elderly in Japan,* Department of Anthropology, University of California, Los Angeles, 2002. I wish to thank the Japan Foundation for funding my research in Japan, and John Traphagan and John Knight for the opportunity to present and publish this work. I am grateful to Mayumi Sakai and Kazue Yamamoto for facilitating my research in Itabashi; to Yukiko (Morishima) Matsuo for advice and translation assistance with my interview materials; and to Mariko Tamanoi, Takako Sodei, Douglas Hollan, Francesca Bray, Emily Abel, and Anna Simons for their support and guidance. Most importantly, I thank my research participants for their generosity and cooperation.

2. Itabashi Ward is representative of a densely populated urban district with progressive social welfare programs. The ward provides a wide range of elder care services and established, high-quality care facilities, but demand is high and waiting lists are long. Itabashi Ward has a population of 500,000 residents, with 12.95 percent (over 64,000 persons) aged 65 and over (Itabashi-Kuritsu Otoshiyori Hoken Fukushi Sentā 1996). This is below the 1998 national average of 16.2 percent, and comparable with the majority of Tokyo's 22 other wards (*Asahi Shinbun* 1998; Takahashi et al. 1994). Itabashi has six public nursing homes, and thirteen home care service support centers, most of which provide adult day care services.

3. All personal names have been changed to protect privacy. All translations of transcribed interviews are my own.

4. Mrs. Inami uses the formal term for grandmother rather than the more intimate *obaachan* (grannie), an indicator of coldness in the relationship.

References

Akiyama, Hiroko, Toni C. Antonucci, and Ruth Campbell. 1997. Exchange and reciprocity among two generations of Japanese and American Women. In *The cultural context of aging: Worldwide perspectives,* 2nd ed., edited by Jay Sokolovsky. Westport, Conn.: Bergin and Garvey.

Asahi Shinbun. 1998. 65sai ijō 2000 mannin jidai totsunyū [Rushing headlong into the era of 65 and over population at 20 million persons], September 15. (Newspaper article) no author. *Ashahi Shinbun,* Sept. 15, 1998: p. 1.

Campbell, John Creighton, and Naoki Ikegami. 2000 . Long-term care insurance comes to Japan. *Health Affairs* 19(3): 26–39.

Harris, Phyllis B., and Susan O. Long. 1993. Daughter-in-law's burden: An exploratory study of caregiving in Japan. *Journal of Cross-Cultural Gerontology* 8: 97–118.

Hashimoto, Akiko. 1996 The gift of generations: Japanese and American perspectives on aging and the social contract. Cambridge: Cambridge University Press.

Higuchi, Keiko. 1992 Rōjin kea o dō suru ka—ronten [What to do about elder care—A discussion]. In *Nihon no Ronten* [Debates of Japan], compiled by Bungeishunju. Tokyo: Bungeishunju Co., Ltd.

Hollan, Douglas. 2001. Developments in person-centered ethnography. In *The psychology of cultural experience,* edited by Carmella Moore and Holly Mathews. Cambridge: Cambridge University Press.

Hollan, Douglas W., and Jane C. Wellenkamp. 1994. *Contentment and suffering: Culture and experience in Toraja.* New York: Columbia University Press.

———. 2002. From the family to the community: Renegotiating responsibility for the care of the elderly in Japan. Ph.D. diss., University of California, Los Angeles.

Itabashi-kuritsu Otoshiyori Hoken Fukushi Sentā [Itabashi Ward Elder Health and Welfare Center]. 1996 *Tōtaru Kea Itabashi II: Kōreisha no Zaitaku Kea ni Kakaru Katsudō Jōkyō Hōkoku* [Total care Itabashi II: Report on current home care activities for senior citizens]. Tokyo: Author.

Jenike, Brenda Robb. 1997. Gender and duty in Japan's aged society: The experience of family caregivers. In *The cultural context of aging: Worldwide perspectives,* 2nd ed., edited by Jay Sokolovsky. Westport, Conn.: Greenwood.

Kohut, Heinz. 1971 The analysis of the self. *New York: International Universities Press.*

Kondo, Dorinne K. 1990. *Crafting selves: Power, gender, and discourses of identity in a Japanese workplace.* Chicago: University of Chicago Press.

Lebra, Takie S. 1984. *Japanese women: Constraint and fulfillment.* Honolulu: University of Hawaii Press.

Lock, Margaret. 1993a. *Encounters with aging: Mythologies of menopause in Japan and North America.* Berkeley: University of California Press.

———. 1993b. Ideology, female midlife, and the greying of Japan. *Journal of Japanese Studies* 19: 43–78.

Ministry of Health and Welfare. 1996. *Kōsei Hakusho, Heisei 8 nen han* [White paper on public welfare, 1996 edition]. Tokyo: Author.

———. 2000. *Kōsei Hakusho, Heisei 12 nen han* [White paper on public welfare, 2000 ed.]. Tokyo: Author.

Plath, David. 1980. *Long engagements: Maturity in modern Japan*. Stanford, Calif.: Stanford University Press.

Sakata, Shūichi. 2000. *Kaigo Hoken no Shikumi to Riyōhō ga Wakaru Hon* [Book for understanding the structure and regulations of care insurance]. Tokyo: Seibido Shuppan.

Sodei, Takako. 1995. Care of the elderly: A women's issue. In *Japanese women: New feminist perspectives on the past, present, and future*, edited by Kumiko Fujimura-Faneslow and Atsuko Kameda. New York: Feminist Press.

Takahashi, Kōichi, Tōkyō no Fukushi Kenkyūkai, and Tōkyō Jichi Mondai Kenkyūkai, eds. 1994. *Zusetsu: Tōkyō no Fukushi Jittai, 1995 nen han*. [Explanatory diagrams: Actual conditions of welfare in Tokyo, 1995 ed.]. Tokyo: Hōbunsha.

Tamanoi, Mariko A. 1998. Under the shadow of nationalism: Politics and poetics of rural Japanese women. Honolulu: University of Hawaii Press.

Uranaka, Taiga. 2000 . Nursing-care system debuts with applicant backlog. *Japan Times,* April 1 (page 1).

10

Contesting Coresidence: Women, In-laws, and Health Care in Rural Japan

John W. Traphagan

My wife and I are the eldest in our households and my wife has no brothers. We have been very worried about how to manage care of our parents. My father thinks we will come to live with them, but my wife doesn't want to do this. I have already fought with my father about this once and I expect it to be more trouble in the future.

—34-year-old Japanese man

Expectations for care in old age among Japanese have traditionally centered on the provision of support by a daughter-in-law within the context of multigeneration households. Two trends in rural Japanese society have had a significant influence on the availability of coresident support to the elderly. First, out-migration of young people from rural areas to urban centers for education and work has lead to an increase in the number of households where there is no coresident daughter-in-law to provide support. Second, many women who do live in rural areas are unwilling to provide social support to nonconsanguineal relatives and are unwilling to coreside with in-laws. When faced with a decision about providing health care and other forms of social support to in-laws, many women contest their expected role by refusing to provide such support.

The aim of this chapter is to focus on the second of these trends. I will consider perceptions about coresidence among four women who either are coresiding with in-laws, have done so in the past, or have indicated an unwillingness to do so in the future. In chapter 2, James Raymo and Toshiko Kaneda use demographic analysis to show that frailty or failing health do not appear to be important correlates to coresidence, and suggest cultural variables

203

that play a role in coresidence. Here I will suggest that *resistance* to coresidence is connected to unwillingness to provide care to nonconsanguineal relatives and to conceptualizations of a generationally defined gap in values about autonomy and control within the family unit (Traphagan 2000, 1998b). From the narratives presented below, it will become clear that for some younger women, coresidence symbolizes familial conflict and loss of autonomy.

The data presented here also have broader theoretical implications related to the study of residence patterns, whether from macro- or micro-level perspectives. The compound-oriented pattern of coresidence, as with other variations in coresidence that are common in Japan, makes analysis of macro-level demographic data related to coresidence difficult (see chapter 3). Although people may reside on the same parcel of land, or in a two-family house in which older and younger generations of the same family have completely separate living spaces, they may not appear in population registers as being coresident. This presents problems for analyzing change in coresidence over time, although, as Raymo and Kaneda point out, there has clearly been a trend away from coresidence. More intriguing from an ethnological perspective is that the narratives discussed below suggest that coresidence is not an objectively observable state, but is culturally constructed. Depending upon the perspective of individuals, members of a compound may or may not be viewed as coresident members of the same household (*ie*).

The chapter begins by offering a brief discussion of demographic trends concerning out-migration and Japanese social norms related to coresidence and in-home provision of health care to the elderly. Following this, the cases of four women who either contested coresidence with in-laws or negotiated terms based upon which coresidence would occur will be discussed. Research for this chapter was conducted over six months during the summer and autumn of 1998.[1] Fieldwork was conducted in the City of Mizusawa and Town of Kanegasaki, both in Iwate Prefecture at the northern end of Japan's main island of Honshū. Data were collected via interviews with members of several families and three focus groups that were formed to discuss a variety of issues related to elder care.

Out-Migration and the Family in Rural Japan

In postwar rural areas of Japan, massive out-migration to cities has been an important part of the social landscape (Jussaume 1991; Knight 1994). Historically, out-migration for work among commoners and rural/urban movement among elites has long been a part of Japanese patterns of population movement (Liaw 1992; Fukurai 1991). In recent years, the outflow of younger people has been problematized by local and national governmental officials and a variety of programs have been instituted to retain population in rural areas (see chapters 5 and 6). Many cities and towns in rural prefectures like Iwate have attempted to entice companies and businesses to locate factories and stores within their boundaries to provide jobs and, thus, stem out-migration of young people. For example, in the early and mid-1980s the town of Kanegasaki, which borders on Mizusawa, used tax and other incentives to bring large corporations like Fujitsu and Toyota to town. As a result of constructing an industrial park, the town has experienced in-migration and there have been periods in the last ten years in which the town has actually shown a net gain in population as a result (see Figure 10.1). The town also built a sports and recreation center for townspeople in hopes of providing facilities that are attractive to younger people.

However, many young people continue to depart after high school graduation. This is evident, for example, by looking at population distributions for villages, towns, and cities in Iwate (see Figures 10.2 and 10.3). The capital of the prefecture, Morioka, shows more 20–24 year-olds than 15–19 year olds. Mizusawa, the fifth largest city in the prefecture, shows a decrease in the number of people in the 20–24 age group, and as one looks at smaller and more rural locales (areas in the mountains), there is a precipitous decline of people in the 20–24 age group. Some people, of course, return after attaining an education, but many remain in more urban areas and do not return until retirement, if at all. Interestingly, in the town of Kanegasaki, the average number of out-migrants from 1960 to 1994 (796) is virtually identical to the number of out-migrants in 1960 alone (792), indicating that the number of out-migrants has remained fairly constant (see Figure 10.1). Although in-migration has also increased, those who move to Kanegasaki are usually middle-aged managers who come for a few years and then move on to another location.

In order to understand the significance of out-migration for provision of social support to the elderly, it is necessary to consider its relationship to Japanese kinship ideals and the moral implications of the parent-child bond. Unlike the United States, in which descent and residence rules can largely be represented as bilateral and neolocal, thus emphasizing the conjugal bond and nuclear family, in Japan no single system of descent or residence characterizes family organization. In general, Japanese kin relations can be characterized

Figure 10.1 Migration for Kanegasaki, 1960–94

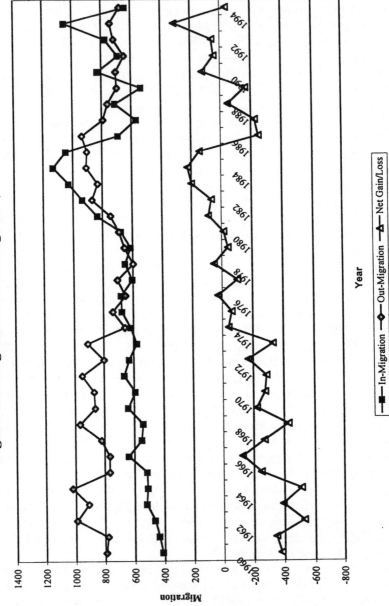

Year

In-Migration ■ Out-Migration ◇ Net Gain/Loss △

(Source: Kanegasaki Town Hall)

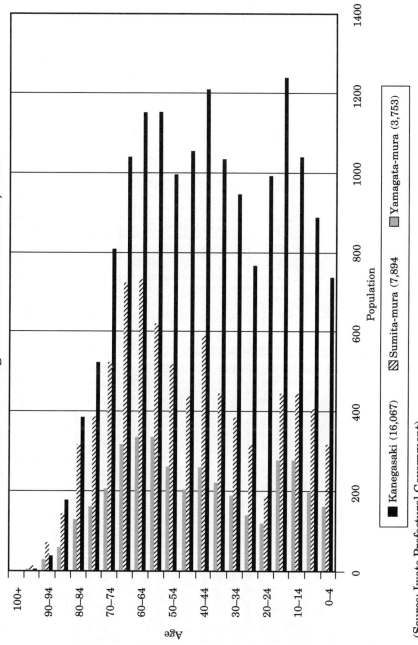

Figure 10.2 Population distributions for some towns and villages in Iwate Prefecture, 1998

■ Kanegasaki (16,067) ▨ Sumita-mura (7,894) ▦ Yamagata-mura (3,753)

(Source: Iwate Prefectural Government)

John W. Traphagan

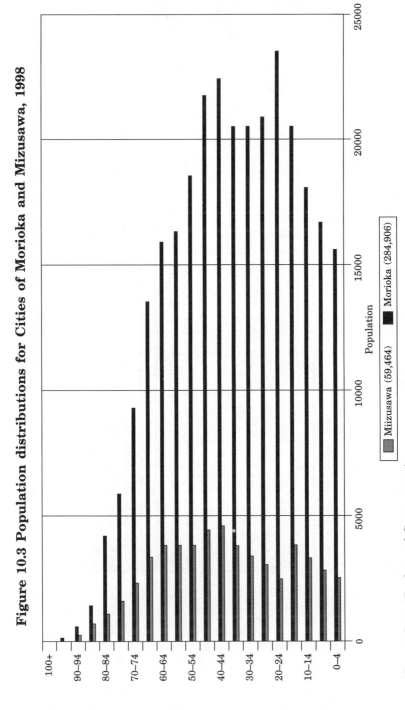

Figure 10.3 Population distributions for Cities of Morioka and Mizusawa, 1998

Miizusawa (59,464)   Morioka (284,906)

(Source: Iwate Prefectural Government)

through two different ways of reckoning kinship. On the one hand, Japanese refer to the "family" using the term *kazoku*. This term places emphasis on the conjugal bond and, thus, implies the nuclear family (*kaku kazoku*) as it is understood in the Euro-American context (Long, 1987, 7). In contemporary Japan, this nuclear family is identified administratively through the establishment of a *koseki* or family register (Brown 1980, 4). In addition to the term *kazoku*, another kinship term that is frequently used in reference to one's family or household is *ie*.

The term *ie* can be understood in two ways. As a kinship term in common usage, *ie* refers to both a house and its residents, hence it is normally translated into English as "household." When an individual speaks of her *ie*, the reference may be to either her house, those relatives who live with her in the same house, or inclusive of both. As an academic concept, *ie* is understood as "a multigenerational property-owning corporate group which continues through time" (Long 1987, 3). It is organized not on the basis of nuclear family structure, but on stem family structure consisting of multiple generations in which there is only one married couple from each adult generation who live together with their unmarried children. Continuity expressed in terms of time-depth is fundamental to the structure of the *ie*. As Aruga points out, the living and the dead are linked together by the idea that family genealogy is not simply relationships based on blood inheritance and succession, but that genealogical bonds are connected to the maintenance and continuation of the family as an institution (Aruga 1954, 362).

Historically, a central feature of maintaining this continuity has been the notion that the household forms what Nakane refers to as "a distinctive enterprise with insurance for old members" (Nakane 1967, 5). This insurance is a function of the obligation successors have to feed and care for their predecessors in old age (Traphagan 1998a). This obligation is reciprocal in that it is usually tied to the idea that the child destined to provide support will inherit most or all of his/her parents' property and the headship of the household-qua-enterprise.[2] Typically, the child who takes or is given the role of insurance provider is the eldest son or an eldest daughter in the event that there is no available male child to succeed to the headship of the household and assume the associated responsibilities of parental care and household management.

This obligation is not merely a transaction related to inheritance and succession, but also has moral content. A child who carries out his or her responsibility to care for parents, particularly through coresidence, is viewed as being a good child (the phrase used is *oya kōkō* which translates as filial piety). And parents are seen as having a legitimate claim to depend upon children for social support based on the notion that children have a moral responsibility to care for their parents (Hashimoto 1896; Traphagan 1998a). The moral overtones of the parent-child relationship are evident in the Japanese Law for the Welfare of the Aged. This law stipulates that older people are to be "loved and respected as those who have for many years contributed toward the development of society" (in Hashimoto 1996, 35). There is a sense that the young have a moral responsibility to care for their elders, based upon the idea that they should have gratitude for that which their elders have given to society, and more directly for that which they have received personally in terms of upbringing, earlier in life.

Caring for the Elderly

In the above quotation from Nakane's *Kinship and Economic Organization in Rural Japan*, the author was writing about rural Japan in the early 1960s, but the basic pattern of household-centered social insurance for the elderly remains central in provision of care to frail or disabled elderly today. More precisely, should an elderly family member become bedridden or otherwise incapacitated, the responsibility for daily health care or assistance with activities of daily living (ADL) typically falls upon the daughter-in-law or another related female. As Sodei indicates, there is some regional variation in determining which female family member is most likely to provide support. In nonmetropolitan areas like Kanegasaki and Mizusawa, the woman most likely to provide assistance with ADL or nursing care is a daughter-in-law—the wife of the eldest son or the coresident son who has been deemed the successor. In the event that a household has received an adoptive husband, the responsibility will fall on the daughter. In urban areas like Tokyo, this responsibility has been increasingly falling on a blood-related female family member such as a daughter. Nonetheless, regardless of location, throughout Japan approximately 90 percent of those providing in-home care to the elderly are women (Sodei 1998).

The demographic transition to low fertility in Japan has intensified the potential stresses related to the care of elderly parents. Sixty years ago, when people living in rural areas often had seven or eight children, were encouraged by the government to have as many children as possible, and were in marriages arranged by their parents, the likelihood of both members of a married couple having responsibility for caring for their own parents was relatively low. However, today low fertility and the consequent preponderance of families with only one or two children has meant that the likelihood of both members of a conjugal pair having shared or full responsibility for parental care is much higher than it was in the past.

Contesting Coresidence and the Care-giver Role

Although coresident, child- and female-based provision of social support is part of the prevailing discourse on aging, women often, and sometimes rather cynically, view the obligation as being little more than a transaction related to inheritance. As one coresident 33 year-old woman who is an only child, charged with the responsibility of caring for her parents as they grow older, stated:

> There are a lot of parents who feel that they are going to give the house over to one child, so they can expect to be cared for by that child. It seems like a condition (*jyōken*). There are people who feel that if they are going to be put into a home, they don't want to give over their property to their children. They want to leave something to the children or grandchildren, but in return they want to be able to live in the house and be cared for as needed. It really seems that in terms of giving over one's property (*zaisan*), there is a sense that the care is given in return for that.

To better understand the experience of those charged with coresidence and providing health care if needed, it will be helpful to consider the narratives of four women who are either coresiding with in-laws or have refused to do so. The four cases are narratives about the negotiation process concerning decisions to coreside or not coreside with in-laws or parents. Two of the cases involve women who are married to eldest sons, one case deals with an eldest daughter who married an eldest son, and one involves a third son who has taken the responsibility for coresidence because his elder brothers would not. All of the women in the following cases contested coresidence with their in-laws and their associated role as care giver to sick in-laws. In two cases, this contesting behavior was accompanied by support from the husband and in the other two it was a source of serious conjugal conflict.

Case 1. The Selfish Mother-in-Law

Shizuka is a woman in her early thirties and had been married for about one year at the time of our conversation. Her brother lives near her widowed mother in Osaka, thus Shizuka, although regularly consulting with her brother about their mother's situation, does not perceive of having a responsibility to live near her mother and provide care should the need arise. She and her brother have agreed that this responsibility largely will be his, although she indicates a desire to help in any way possible. Shizuka described an experience, prior to her marriage, in which her future mother-in-law expressed the expectation that Shizuka would care for her should the need arise in the future:

> Shizuka: When I went to visit my mother-in-law for the first time with my then future husband, I had a 'big shock' [spoken in English], because she stated that when we moved to Mizusawa for my husband's work, she would buy us land on which to build a house. She is currently 55 and is in fairly good physical condition. She understands that her son cannot move home because there is no work for him in the part of Tōhoku where she lives. Therefore, she decided that she would buy the property so that we could build a house and she would come to live with us in the event that she becomes ill or unable to handle the activities of daily life.
>
> This was a major shock and I cried a great deal as a result of the situation. Fortunately, my husband opposed his mother and stated that we do not know if we will permanently live in Mizusawa and that we cannot do what she asked. We want to live in an apartment and save money for our dream, which is to move to Hokkaido. My mother-in-law is very selfish [*wagamama*]; she only was thinking of herself and gave absolutely no thought to the needs, dreams, future, etc. of the two of us. Eventually, she agreed that she would not do this and that we would not build the house. In the end, my husband also encouraged her to use the money that she would have used to buy the land to pay for services like home helpers should she need them in the future. I think that if my husband had not pushed back against his mother on this, I would not have been able to marry him.

JWT: How do you think you would respond, should your husband decide he wants to coreside with his mother?

Shizuka: I suppose that if he did, I would have to consider divorcing him. The stress of living with my mother-in-law is more than I think I can tolerate.

Case 2. When Worlds Collide

Mariko is 39 and lives with her parents and her three children in her natal house. She has been divorced for approximately four years and describes the situation of her divorce as being directly related to her position as the eldest daughter in a family of three daughters. She spent approximately ten years living in Tokyo after high school, but was forced to return when her parents demanded she fulfill a promise, she made when she initially went to Tokyo, to return immediately after college.

> In Japan it is said that I am *"ie musume"* or *"atotori musume"* [household or successor daughter], therefore in truth it is not possible to leave my household. That is the situation for someone like me and it normally would be expected that I would stay in the household and receive an adoptive husband. I thought I would have no choice but to take an adoptive husband, but I met someone I fell in love with and decided to marry him.

> But there were problems, because I am the eldest daughter and he is the eldest son at a farm house. Originally, even though we were both eldest, we intended to live apart from either set of parents. We had our own place, but, not surprisingly, there were various things from his household. His grandmother became ill and we were forced to go and live with them. From their perspective, there was a sense that I had married into his household and was no longer directly connected to my natal household [the word used to describe this is *yome*, or daughter-in-law]. So I should be there to help in taking care of the needs of that household, particularly when his grandmother was sick. However, this was in conflict with my sense of responsibilities as the eldest daughter in this [natal] household.

There were other problems, too. I didn't fit in well at his household because we had different values about what is important in life. I married late, in my early thirties. The problem is that by that age, the only ones remaining are eldest sons and eldest daughters, because nobody wants to marry an eldest. They have a very difficult time getting married. This is unlike being a second son or second daughter. They have a smooth path to marriage because they don't have the responsibilities of the eldest. I guess I am rather envious of my younger sisters, who went off to Tokyo and married. If I had been the second daughter, I probably wouldn't have returned to Mizusawa from Tokyo and I'd probably still be married.

Case 3. It's Not Fair

Yoko is in her mid-forties. She has two sons, the younger of whom is 9 and the older 13. She lives in a largely agricultural part of Mizusawa, in a compound with two separate houses. The house in the rear of the compound belongs to her mother-in-law and is the natal house of her husband. Yoko's house is much newer than her mother-in-law's house and is a stark contrast to the other houses in the area. It looks as though it has been transported from a U.S. housing development, with wooden clapboard siding, a front porch with a swing, and a white picket fence around a front lawn. For Yoko the house appears to symbolize modernity in an environment she finds overly traditional. Yoko's husband does not live with them, but lives in Yokohama where he works for a large electronics company.

Yoko has long-term experience with caring for a sick in-law. She provided in-home care to her father-in-law when he became ill, and also much of the hospital care such as bringing food and diaper changing (activities usually done by family members rather than hospital staff, see Jenike 1997). While her father-in-law was hospitalized, she would spend the days with him and return home to cook for her family in the evening, a pattern that went on for about two years. She described herself as fortunate in that she was able to share some of the care responsibilities with other relatives.

> Yoko: Japanese think that being cared for by their children or daughter-in-law is natural and the idea that you have your own life until the end is rare [*jibun de saigo made,*

jibun no jinsei wa, jibun de mendo miru to iu kimochi wa sukunai].

JWT: When you married did you know that your husband would become the successor [*atatori*]?

Yoko: No, I had no idea [laughs]. My husband is the third son, but his elder brothers married and moved to Tokyo. Both of them married to women who are the only children in their families, so there is no chance for them to return, nor do they want to return. This has left it on my husband to be the successor. If I knew that he was going to become the *atotori* and we would have to live with his parents, I don't think I would have married him.

I went to college in Tokyo and worked there for a while, but my father wanted me to return so he kept asking me to come back. I returned home for about three or four years, but when I married I moved to Yokohama and lived there for eight years. We moved back because my parents kept demanding us to return [*shujin no ryōshin ga kaite koi to iimashita*]. They were getting old, but were not sick, but they had been bugging us to come back all along, constantly asking when we would come back and telling us to come back. They were very annoying [*urusai*]. Whenever we got a telephone call from my father-in-law, he would say, "when are you coming home?" or something like that. It was constant.

When my husband decided to return, I couldn't understand. We liked living there and he found his work in Yokohama very interesting. So I just couldn't understand why he felt we had to return. I asked why he decided to return, and he said, "my parents are getting old and I want to do *oya kōkō* (filial piety) one time before they die." He got himself transferred to the local office of his company plant and we moved back and I wound up caring for his father when he became ill.

What was really bad was that as soon as my father-in-law died, my husband got himself transferred back to Yokohama to work. I thought this was very unfair [*zurui*]. He went back and left us here to take care of his mother. My husband does not intend to return to Mizusawa. He has said that he will remain in Yokohama until retirement.

JWT: Why didn't the whole family go?

Yoko: Well, my husband's mother is living alone, so I was left to take care her. We asked her to move to Yokohama, but she is unwilling to do so. She said, "I will not move. I want to live here to the end."

We fought a great deal when my husband left for Yokohama, just as we did about returning to live with his parents in the first place. I told my husband, "you are being more concerned about the lives of your parents than you are of your own family." I thought about not coming back at all and about divorcing him at the time.

All of the old people around this area have the attitude that they raised their children and will give over the family fortune [zaisan] to the eldest son or successor, so he has the responsibility to take care of them. It is a transaction. People have the attitude that they save money for their child's college, intend to give the child the property, so it is natural that the parents should expect to be cared for by their children in the future. It's like they are buying their health care for the future.

But coresidence is extremely difficult. There is conflict between mother-in-law and daughter-in-law. A lot of old people say many negative things about their daughter-in-law [yome]. The farm households are very different in their way of thinking and the idea is that the young people work. Thus, the grandmothers want the daughter-in-law to go out and do some sort of work at a job while the grandmother takes care of the children. If the daughter-in-law doesn't want to do this, then there is conflict because the grandmother thinks she should be bringing in income. They think that younger generations lack good moral values. Thus, the grandmother is trying to take control over the grandchildren in order to raise them to behave and think in a way that they consider to be oya kōkō. It is a power struggle over the raising of the children and to some extent the grandmother has the upper hand because it is her household and the yome is essentially an outsider. All of the younger yome around here want to raise their own children, but the grandmother is strong on trying to get the yome to go out and leave the children to her. This creates a lot of stress between the yome and grandmother. The grandmothers don't like the *yome*'s ways of raising the children. They want to get the *yome* out of the way because they won't do things the way the *yome* did in the past and by getting *yome* out of the way, the grandmother can raise the grandchildren in a way she thinks right. They often say we did it this way, so we should keep doing it this way and the *yome* should go out and work like I did.

It feels as though the grandmothers are taking the children away from their mothers [*obaachan ga torechau kanji suru*]. Younger mothers around here say that they might as well go off and get their own apartment because they have no role in raising their children. And the husband won't say anything if the *yome* complains, he just defends the *ie* and his parents. If you live in the same house, it is very difficult because the grandmother says mean things.

JWT: Why did you build this separate house when the one behind is so large?

Yoko: One of the conditions of moving back was the building of a separate house. I told my husband that I would not return unless we built a separate house to live in. Fortunately, my in-laws did not oppose this. They understood that their grandchildren would not return unless the separate house was built.

JWT: What do you think will happen in your future?

Yoko: I intend to move back to Yokohama when my children go off on their own. I will not stay living with my in-laws. If my mother-in-law is still living, this will be a big problem. My mother-in-law believes that my husband will return from Yokohama in the near future. He has lied to her about the fact that he has no intention of returning. I am unwilling to provide care to her, as I did to my father-in-law.

Case 4. I Hate My Father-In-Law

Hitoshi and Miyuki live in a farming community known as Isawa that neighbors Mizusawa. They live amidst rice fields in a compound on a large lot where Hitoshi's *ie* has been for generations. Like Yoko, they live in a new house separate from that of the grandparents, which is about twenty meters away from their house. The narrative here is from an interview with both Miyuki and her husband Hitoshi. They are in their early forties and have a son (age 1) and a daughter (age 5). Hitoshi's parents and grandfather live in the other house in the compound.

Hitoshi is the eldest son and was born and grew up in Isawa. He went to a university in Sendai (160km to the south) and took a job with a construction company after graduation. His work brought him to many different parts of Japan, including Morioka, Chiba (where he and Miyuki met), and Kyūshū, where he worked at a construction company. The couple married when they were around thirty and they have been back in Mizusawa for the past five years. Hitoshi had great aspirations when he was younger to see the world and do well in business. By the time he had reached his position in Kitakyūshū, he had attained some of his goals and, he said, was on track to reach vice-president level in his company. Miyuki is from Chiba and went to college in Tokyo, where she received a degree from Meiji University. She had never lived in a rural area and had a difficult time in adjusting to her new life in Isawa.

> Hitoshi: At the time we returned, my grandmother had been bed-ridden for about fifteen years. She died not long after. We didn't return for the purpose of caring for my grandmother, but instead to help out my mother, who had been taking care of her for those fifteen years. She had become very tired and was having difficulties doing everything, so I decided it was time to return.
>
> We didn't initially directly return to live here. First, we moved to Sendai, where we started a clothing store. Because my wife grew up in a large city, I didn't think she would easily adjust to life in *inaka* [the rural countryside], so I thought that it would take some time to adjust. Therefore, we thought it would be good to start in a city.
>
> We consulted about this and agreed that a gradual return was needed. We also decided that for Miyuki to come to understand the thinking and lifestyle of my parents and a farm family, she would need time and also for my parents to come to understand her, they would need time. We also decided that when we did eventually return, it would be necessary to build a house of our own. My father opposed this. He wanted everyone to live in the same house and

thought that with such a big house (198 square meters) it was a total waste to build another house right next to theirs. But I felt that there was no chance that our family's lifestyle would work with my parents' lifestyle.

Miyuki: We first moved to Mizusawa after Sendai and my in-laws could not understand why we wanted to live there rather than just with them. Eventually, they came to understand that this was going to be the way it would be. If we were to return home, we would have to live separately. I also told them that the children would need their own space for studying. My in-laws agreed, but wanted to have supper and the evening bath together. I opposed this, so we live basically separately.

The thing that is most difficult is that the way of thinking is totally opposite between the older generation and us. Now, I don't have much problem with my mother-in-law or grandfather-in-law because they seem to have relaxed around me. But I really hate [daikirai] my father-in-law! There were several things that infuriated me about his behavior. For example, we received a planter as a gift from friends. My father-in-law thinks that the entire compound is under his control, so he does whatever he wants. When I was away, he came and saw the planter and thought it was useless, so he burned it as garbage. I was very angry and thought it was wrong for him to do that. So I told Hitoshi that I wanted an apology, and also that I wanted my father-in-law to buy the same thing to replace it because it was a gift and if our friends come to visit we want to have it here. So my husband told that to his father, but we never got anything—no apology, nothing.

Another thing was that my in-laws used to have a cow and he put a little stick in the ground to chain the cow right outside of my kitchen. I said, I don't want this right outside of my kitchen but he didn't listen to me. Either he didn't think that was a problem for us or he knew it was a problem and did it intentionally—I wasn't sure. Also, we have been collecting cans to put in the recycling machine for which you get a coupon to buy books. I put the bag of cans outside of my kitchen and we were doing this as an incentive with my kids to collect them so that they can go and buy books. A fun thing for kids. Father-in-law came and just took it and threw it away. I told him why I was collecting the cans, but he did it again after that.

So much of what he does infuriates me! He tries to control our lives! He feels that he is number one and has the power and right to control our lives. He doesn't have any sense that we have to have our own lives, and he doesn't see any value in having fun time as a family, or having rest. He has been working and doesn't rest—he always works. He feels that we should be doing the same. If he sees us inside the house, he thinks we are lazy. So if there is some work around his house or rice paddies, he will bang on the window and tell Hitoshi to come out to help him. I hated being here so much that I got a job, and now I go out to work three hours a day simply to get away from the house. It's not for money but to get away from my father-in-law.

Hitoshi: I don't like my father, either. We have had many fights, some of which have been physical fights in the rice paddies in the mud. That was some time ago, and we don't do that sort of thing now.

Discussion

From these cases, we can see several themes emerging. First, even if it is expected, coresidence with in-laws is by no means willingly embarked upon by these women, and in all cases, it was the daughter-in-law who represented the focal point of resistance and negotiation. In each case, coresidence was either outright rejected by the daughter-in-law or came only after negotiation among her, her husband, and in-laws. Furthermore, when coresidence did occur for an extended period, it was within a compound, but not within the confines of the same building. For both Miyuki and Yoko, the building of a separate house was a prerequisite to living with in-laws. This pattern of coresidence is by no means recent in Japan, having been reported by Dore in the 1970s and Bernstein in the 1980s (Dore 1978; Bernstein 1983), but the cases of these women indicates the degree to which women may be involved in the negotiation process related to building a separate house and some of the reasons behind the desire to live separately. In the case of Mariko, the potential problems with coresidence are clear, and coresidence within the same building resulted in divorce (although that was, as noted, not the only reason).

The discussion of compound-oriented coresidence is ethnologically interesting because it points out the difficulties in analyzing macro-level demographic data related to coresidence and the problems of understanding what, exactly, coresidence means in a given cultural context. In both of the coresidence cases discussed here, although living on the same parcel of land, members of the younger families do not wish to present themselves as part of a single *ie* with the elder generation. In both cases, the younger and older generations have separate *koseki* or household registers. These are a form of population register used in Japan that focus on the household, rather than the individual. Although these families occupy the same compound, in terms of government collected demographic data, these families are not coresiding with the older generations and are not part of the same households. This rasies a question: Can a simple focus on macro-level data that indicate whether or not multiple generations are living in the same abode obfuscate the cultural construction of coresidence? From the conversations with these women, coresidence cannot be taken alone as an objective variable.

In fact, coresidence is variously constructed by the generations or even within the same household. Yoko indicated that while she does not see herself and her children as living within the confines of the *ie* of her husband and mother-in-law, "outsiders in the neighborhood looking at us would undoubtedly assume that we are part of one *ie* and likely registered on one *koseki*." Furthermore, both her husband and mother-in-law see Yoko and her children as belonging to one household. Miyuki's situation is similar, although her husband agrees with her that they are a separate family, even if they inhabit the same property with his parents. In short, the cultural construction of coresidence in Japan is ambiguous and in some cases contested.

The reasons behind resisting coresidence, too, are multifaceted. All four of the women indicate an unwillingness to provide health care to their in-laws. From Shizuka's perspective, for example, her mother-in-law's attempt to buy them property in Mizusawa on which to build a house was, in fact, an attempt to buy insurance in the event that she needed health care or assistance with activities of daily living in the future. This would oblige them to provide living space and guarantee that she would have assistance provided by her son's wife in the future should she need it. Interestingly, and perhaps not surprisingly, these actions had the opposite effect. Shizuka indicated that because she dislikes her mother-in-law (in large part as a result of this situation) she thinks she would find it very difficult to provide daily nursing care for her in the future.

For the two women who accepted coresidence, the willingness to do so came with the condition that coresidence would mean separate living quarters and not the entire extended family living under one roof. Although perhaps reducing tensions, this did not alleviate them entirely. For Yoko, the whole situation surrounding coresidence with her husband's parents is associated with conflict. She sees her husband as being unfair, particularly in his willingness to dump care on her, while he returned to life in the city, which she, too, prefers. Miyuki indicates a deep hatred for her father-in-law and great tensions in her relationship with him. Although Hitoshi made efforts to smooth the process of transition from city life to rural life, conflicts remain. The lack of any affective bonds between Miyuki and her father-in-law make provision of health care for him seem virtually impossible to her (cf. Jenike 1997).

Beyond these potential conflicts associated with coresidence, as the quotation at the beginning of this chapter indicates, in situations where both members of the conjugal pair are expected or expect to provide for their parents, confusion and conflict may arise within families, due to problems of resource allocation (in terms of human labor) and preferences concerning living arrangements. In the case of Mariko, this tension ultimately resulted in divorce and her return to her natal home without, she states, the expectation that she will ever remarry. From her perspective, the conflict which resulted in her divorce was predominately a conflict of responsibility between respective successor children and their natal households. In the end, the natal households won out over the marriage.

Throughout all of these narratives, a theme that a generational gap causing differing values was at the root of why coresidence was impossible. The term *kachikan* (values) was repeated over and over during the conversations that generated these narratives. From the perspectives of these women, attitudes towards what these differences are can be summed up in a list recited by Miyuki:

- The old people do not have any sense of enjoyment in their lives. They only work and view any form of leisure or recreation as a waste of time. They do not do things like enjoying eating nice food. They just eat to live. And they just work and sleep, but do not do anything else.
- They have a different conceptualization of waste. Building a new house on the same land or living in Mizusawa is a waste

of money, so we should not do it. There is no concept of the need for separate living space or privacy.

- Parents think that children are always children and are, therefore, always under the control of the parents. There is no concept that, having become an adult, you have independence and have departed from the situation of being under your parents' control.

Lebra reports similar expressions of differing values concerning recreation and work by her informants, but also states that for some, at least, the work-centered characteristic was seen as admirable or outstanding (*rippa*), if difficult to live with (Lebra 1984, 142). She goes on to note that although frugality and hard work may be admired, for many women coresidence means being dominated by a mother-in-law and a loss of autonomous decision-making power (Lebra 1984, 143). For the women discussed here, there was little indication of admiration in their reflections upon their mothers-in-law or fathers-in-law. Instead, the focus of conversations invariably turned on the hardships and conflicts and lack of autonomy caused by the coresident situation.

A final theme that is important here is the emphasis on blood in terms of providing health care. The three daughters-in-law (Shizuka, Yoko, and Miyuki) all have limits on their willingness to provide care to their in-laws or are unwilling to do it altogether. Lacking affective bonds with their in-laws, and in the cases of Miyuki and Shizuka actually disliking in-laws, means that provision of health care is highly problematic. As noted above, the vast majority of those who care for the elderly at home are women and Japanese cultural norms emphasize care giving as being the role of women. Although none of the women interviewed here stated this directly, it is reasonable to suggest that for many coresidence implies the likelihood of eventually having to care for a bed-ridden or possibly demented in-laws. This image is reinforced by the numerous fictional or fictionalized accounts about the difficulties women face in caring for frail in-laws that occur in the Japanese press and in literature (Ariyoshi 1984; Sae 1995).

Shizuka indicated that she wanted to do whatever possible to care for her mother should the need arise, although she is aware that her distance from her mother will limit her ability to do so. Other women whose narratives are not included here also indicated a desire to care for their own parents, or had actually provided such care even while living apart at their husband's natal household. The most striking case described here is that of Mariko, whose concern about caring for her own parents and difficulties coresiding with her in-laws resulted in divorce and a return to her natal household. Similar to what Jenike points out in her research in Yokohama, in Iwate, without the affective bonds that one can expect between parents and children, women are often unwilling to provide care and are willing to resist to the point of seriously considering divorce should such a situation arise (Jenike 1997).

The data discussed in this chapter indicate the complexities involved with both analysis of demographic data and discerning the meanings associated with coresidence in Japan. For the women here, coresidence implies loss of autonomy, personal conflict, and emotional strain. As Raymo and Kaneda argue in chapter 2, declining coresidence correlates to a complex of social, economic, and cultural issues. Moreover, the concept of coresidence as a variable in research cannot be treated as simply a category of analysis to determine living situations, but carries emically charged cultural constructions that generate variegated meanings and interpretations by those living in a given cultural context.

Notes

1. Research for this chapter was supported by grants from the Wenner-Gren Foundation for Anthropological Research, the Michigan Exploratory Center for the Demography of Aging, and the Northeast Asia Council of the Association for Asian Studies.

2. Or the de jure headship in some cases where a daughter brings in an adoptive husband or *mukoyōshi* and the (consanguineal) daughter remains de facto head of household. See Hamabata 1990.

References

Ariyoshi, Sawako. 1984. *The twilight years*. Translated by Mildred Tahara. Kodansha International.

Aruga, Kizaemon. 1954. The family in Japan. *Marriage and Family* Living 16: 362–68.

Bernstein, Gail Lee. 1983. *Haruko's world: A Japanese farm woman and her community*. Stanford, Calif. Stanford University Press.

Brown, L. Keith. 1980. The family in Japan. World Conference on Records, Salt Lake City, August 12–15.

Brown, Naomi C. 1998. Housing the elderly: The effects of current and projected demographic movements on the composition of private family homes in contemporary Japan. Paper presented at the 97th annual meeting of the American Anthropological Association, Philadelphia.

Dore, Ronald P. 1978. *Shinohata: A portrait of a Japanese village.* New York: Pantheon Books.

Fukurai, Hiroshi. 1991. Japanese Migration in Contemporary Japan: Economic Sementation and Interprefectural Migration. *Social Biology* 38(1–2): 28–50.

Hamabata, Matthews Masayuki. 1990. *Crested kimono: Power and love in the Japanese business family.* Ithaca: Cornell University Press.

Hashinoto, Akiko. 1996. *The gift of generations: Japanese and American perspectives on aging and the social contract.* Cambridge: Cambridge University Press.

Jenike, Brenda Robb. 1997. Gender and duty in Japan's aged society: The experience of family caregivers in *The cultural context of aging: Worldwide perspectives,* 2nd ed., edited by Jay Sokolovsky. Westport, Conn.: Bergin and Garvey.

Jussaume, Raymond Adelard. 1991. *Japanese part-time farming: Evolution and impacts.* Ames: Iowa State University Press.

Knight, John. 1994. Rural revitalization in Japan: Spirit of the village and taste of the country. *Asian Survey* 34: 634–46.

Lebra, Takie Sugiyama. 1984. *Japanese women: Constraint and fulfillment.* Honolulu: University of Hawaii Press.

Liaw, Kao-Lee. 1992. Interprefectural Migration and its Effects on Prefectural Populations in Japan: An Analysis Based on the 1980 Census. *The Canadian Geographer* 36(4): 320–335.

Long, Susan O. 1987. *Family change and the life course in Japan.* Ithaca, NY: East Asia Program, Cornell University.

Nakane, Chie. 1967. *Kinship and economic organization in rural Japan.* New York: Humanities Press.

Raymo, James M., and Toshiko Kaneda. 1999. Changes in the living arrangements of Japanese elderly: The role of demographic factors. Presented at the 1999 Annual meeting Association for Asian Studies, Boston.

Sae, Shūichi. 1995. *Kōraku.* Tokyo: Shichōsha.

Sodei, Takako. 1998. Role of the family in long-term care. *Keio Journal of Medicine* 47(2): A16–A17.

Traphagan, John W. 1998a. Contesting the transition to old age in Japan. *Ethnology* 37(4): 333–50.

———. 1998b. Reasons for gateball participation among older Japanese. *Journal of Cross-Cultural Gerontology* 13(2): 150–75.

———. 2000. *Taming oblivion: Aging bodies and the fear of senility in Japan.* Albany: State University of New York Press.

Epilogue

11

Demographic and Family Change: Problems and Solutions

Susan O. Long and C. Scott Littleton

Problematizing the Demographic Transition

The chapters in this volume have described the demographic changes that have occurred in Japan in the twentieth century and discussed their impact on the family: the decline in mortality, decreased fertility, increased life expectancy, the achievement of a low-growth stable population, urbanization, decreased household size, and the nuclearization of the family. Japan has clearly completed the demographic transition and has kept going. In modernization theory, popular in the 1960s and 1970s in the social sciences, these trends were seen as positive social indicators. They signified that a country had become "modern," promising economic prosperity; the liberation of the young and women from the domination of senior men; democracy; and respect for individuals.

Indeed, these trends have continued in Japan, so that it now has the highest life expectancy in the world—and by 2025, will be among the few countries whose elderly comprise more than a quarter of its total population. It has one of the lowest fertility rates in the world, with decreasing rates of marriage and increasing rates of divorce—and a resulting concern with where the next generation of laborers will come from to fuel Japan's huge economy and support its social services such as education, health care, and old age pensions. Japan's mean household size has shrunk dramatically not only because of lowered fertility, but also because of nuclearization of the family. These statistical changes are correlated with changes in gender roles, in familial relationships regarding household and workplace responsibilities that have resulted in increased age segregation in daily activities and in suburbanization as young families search for affordable housing. Increased respect for the individual as the basic unit of society has resulted in demands for new forms of housing for the living and of burial for the dead.

Yet in the past several decades, the demographic promises of "modernity" have come to be redefined as "problems" in Japanese discourse. The chapters of this book have adopted the assumptions of Japanese bureaucrats, social critics, and ordinary citizens that the continuation of the trends of the demographic transition constitute "problems" for contemporary Japanese society. The problems identified in this volume fall under three themes.

The first theme is that of assuring a work force for the future. This concern, described statistically by John Raymo and Toshiko Kaneda in chapter 2, is national. Yet the chapters by Christopher Thompson and John Knight show that it is perhaps even more salient at the local level, with Tōwa-chō and Hongū-chō struggling for their very survival as they experience continued depopulation. The problem for such towns is not only that of remaining autonomous political units, but of redefining their economic and social roles in the larger Japanese society in order to create jobs which will offer the hope of maintaining or increasing the town's population.

The second theme is the question of who will do the work of reproduction and caring? This is related to the previous theme in that rural depopulation has primarily meant the departure of young adults in their childbearing years. Moreover, if young women such as those described by John Traphagan refuse to compromise their lifestyles to guarantee family care for elderly in-laws, there will be increased need for communities such as Hongū to serve as centers for institutional elder care. Whereas Kaneda challenges assumptions about the relationship between longevity and health at a collective level, the chapters by Leng Leng Thang, Brenda Robb Jenike, and Traphagan remind us that those who do need care can no longer assume, for a variety of reasons, that it will be provided by family members. Even care for deceased relatives' spirits and graves must now, as Satsuki Kawano explains, be consciously planned ahead.

The final theme of these chapters is the association of the demographic trends with moral or behavioral change, which is in turn seen as both cause and effect of the breakdown of social connectedness. If on the "modern" side, there is increased respect in Japan for individual autonomy, there is also a decreased sense of communalism in rural villages, in urban neighborhoods, and in families across generations. All of the chapters to some degree reflect concern rather than celebrate these changes.

Although these chapters reflect the view that demographic trends constitute social problems, they are also descriptions of how people attempt to solve them. The authors describe a number of approaches. Problems represent challenges for individuals and organizations who respond by introducing new innovative ideas such as the *jisaku shuen jigyō* described by Thompson, the designers of prefabricated two-family houses who can alter plans for son- or daughter-coresidence we hear about from Naomi Brown, Kawano's permanent ritual care, or the new long-term care insurance for the ill or frail elderly.

Other approaches to the challenges presented by demographic change involve the reinvention of tradition. Thompson's bureaucrats are accused of doing what isolated Tohoku villages have always done; prefabricated *nisetai jūtaku* became widespread because companies were able to successfully play on fears about the loss of three–generation families "under one roof;" communal graves for the disconnected dead are renovated; the use of the *daikazoku* metaphor forms the basis for the organization of the intergenerational welfare facility studied by Thang.

The Utilization of Tradition and the Localization of the "Modern"

Taken together, these chapters suggest that the reason these demographic changes are viewed as "problems" is that they create situations that disrupt consensus or social connectedness. Changes introduce new alternatives to old beliefs and behaviors. The range of options grows, among which is the use of "tradition." But in the context of choice, the old options take on new meanings, as when families decide to coreside or women stay home to take care of children or elderly in-laws, or when people seek connectedness in death.

Thus, the chapters not only explore the "problems" created by the demographic transition, but also problematize the tradition-modern dichotomy. The *use* of tradition does not *equal* tradition precisely because there is an awareness of alternatives. The intergenerational welfare institution attempts to create a new organization of and meaning for its services through the use of the "big family" metaphor, but it does not recreate the extended family as it was known historically. Coresidence may not indicate a rejection of formal elder care services; it might mean two separate kitchens rather than three-generational living, or living with a daughter rather than a son. Similarly, "modern" solutions take on a Japanese cast as they are given multiple interpretations in their local settings, such as neolocal residence on the family compound or the clever marketing of the "four Towas" in Tokyo or "hometown produce" in Osaka.

Furthermore, solutions that are presented as continuities may also represent real change. Anthropologist Keith Brown has described the purple-haired, body-pierced young people he met in rural northeastern Japan who, nonetheless, participated in family and ancestor-related activities. Likewise, for Littleton, the costumed Bōsōzoku ("Wild Driving Tribe") and Takenokozoku ("Bamboo Shoot Tribe") teenagers he studied who were the principal tourist attractions in Tokyo's Yoyogi Park on Sunday afternoons are "thoroughly Japanese." So was the lavender-haired senior citizen Long met on a train in suburban Osaka. Continuities underlie new forms and images, whereas new practices may form the basis of what are defined as traditions. But some skepticism seems also to be in order: do Buddhist temples offering burials based on voluntary associations benefit financially by offering "tradition" in new forms? Or as Naomi Brown asks, do manufacturers of prefabricated housing reflect demand for *nisetai jūtaku*, or do they create it? Do intergenerational activities in day care or graves based on voluntary association rather than blood relations represent continuity or change?

What then *is* change? This volume attests to the active involvement of people in culture change through decisions (for example, not to take care of an elderly relative) and through creating new options like the *bakamono* among Tōwa-chō's local bureaucrats. These decisions are shaped by the demographic circumstances in which people find themselves, but they also contribute to the statistics the demographers will report in the next round of surveys, as illustrated by Traphagan who finds the cause of change in living arrangements in out-migration of young people from the area and in the unwillingness of daughters-in-law to exchange caregiving for an inheritance if the price is loss of their own dreams and their control over their children. He implicitly notes a shift from obligatory caregiving to caregiving based on emotional ties, and describes a *process* of interpersonal negotiation leading to each family's decision about living arrangements.

Building Interdisciplinary Bridges

The editors of this volume state in their introduction that they intend not only to bring together chapters by demographers and chapters by anthropologists to contribute to the study of the family in Japan, but also to explore potential for synthesizing the two approaches. But is synthesis possible, or even desirable? Despite the juxtaposition of disciplinary approaches in this volume, there remains an obvious difference in level of analysis: aggregate versus individual, macro versus micro.

An alternative conception would be to recognize that very different methodologies and levels of analysis require different disciplinary homes, but that bridges that open traffic between the two will benefit both sides. These benefits are suggested in the organization of the volume, which points to the interdependence of demographic and anthropological approaches to cultural change. It shows clearly that population questions—births, deaths, and household size and composition—cannot be understood out of context of everyday life decisions and social interaction. Perhaps to demographers, the door-to-door counting of people, the analysis of relationships and changes over time historically done by anthropologists represents some sort of "primitive demography." The analysis of a complex society, however, requires utilization of population statistics generated by demographers' methods without making the "real people" data take a back seat. This collection of essays has shown the value of juxtaposing these: we see how industry leaders negotiating with the Ministry of Construction, babysitting grandpas, or divorced women caring for their parents or buying perpetual care graves create a new social order.

Raymo and Kaneda acknowledge limits to what they can explain with aggregate demographic data: there are social, economic, and cultural factors that their data do not reflect. The ethnographic chapters consider demographic changes as causative (if background) factors to the dilemmas experienced by the people they describe. We thus see in these chapters some tentative first steps toward bridge-building between the anthropology and the demography of Japan.

What then are the materials and tools needed to continue construction of the bridge they have begun? First, clearing the path requires some additional removal of roadblocks to ease communication. Jargon needs to be minimized: "decompose" and "deconstruct" are not words for building bridges. Terms such as "counterfactual question" and "decomposing" as used in demography are not obvious to those outside of the discipline. Neither are the meanings of "experiential account" and "emically charged cultural constructions" clear to non-anthropologists. These examples are obvious ones, but the more subtle problem in communication is that sometimes the same words are used to mean different things: "net of," "explain," "significance," "individual level," and "culture" carry different meanings depending on the author.

Second, to build the bridge, each side needs to take inventory of their materials and check to see if the other side has what it is lacking. For example, Raymo and Kaneda note that conditional coresidence has largely replaced obligatory or assumed forms—in particular, when an elderly parent is widowed or becomes ill, coresidence will begin. Yet their own data failed to show statistically significant results for health status. If they are building bridges, they might turn to Traphagan and Robb Jenike for help, but this first requires a willingness to question their data. Perhaps the sample is too weighted toward healthy people to show the differences. Perhaps it has to do with the 5-6 percent of elderly who are institutionalized, though that small a percentage seems unlikely to have much effect on the statistics. The responses are suggested in their chapters: Traphagan questions the category itself—coresidence is not an absolute "fact" but a culturally constructed reality given various meanings by each family and each participant. Robb Jenike suggests that coresidence doesn't solve the problems of elder care anyway. Both of the daughters-in-law she describes had in fact been coresiding for at least some period of time before the decision to institutionalize their relatives. Interdisciplinary discussion and collaboration can help to think through why the Raymo-Kaneda results are so counterintuitive.

On the other hand, those of us who "know" that in Japan people adjust their living arrangements when an elderly parent or in-law needs help with daily activities, could use some help in putting that knowledge into the broader context. How typical are these daughters-in-law that Traphagan and Robb Jenike describe? Are they different in perceptions or values from daughters-in-law who do not resist? If the micro-level studies acknowledge limits to their data and express what is missing, the demographers on the other side of the gap might just be able to toss over some steel beams. To the extent that scholars from each discipline can recognize their limits and explicate their needs, bridge construction will be speeded greatly. These chapters have begun to challenge other approaches to widen their view and to pose questions that the other may be able to help answer.

What might be the benefits? We should not envision that many individuals will actually do both sorts of research. But the micro-level researchers will benefit from broader understandings and from inclusion of their results in material that will reach a wider audience. Those working at the aggregate level will benefit from better questions and more nuanced interpretations. In bringing together papers from both approaches, this volume contributes to a more comprehensive understanding of complex issues such as coresidence, and serves as a first determined step in building a bridge between the anthropology and the demography of contemporary Japan.

The Tale of Two Disciplines

This book has offered us statistical analyses and personal narratives of the relation between demographic and family change in Japan. These chapters focus primarily on migration and the aging of the population, but in doing so, they point to the complexity of the relationship among all of the measures of the demographic transition. They also challenge modernization theory's assumption that these trends are positive ones by examining the creation of a sense of demographic crisis on the part of the Japanese government and its citizens.

The authors also implicitly challenge the modernist assumption of the objective nature of these changes. Once defined as "problems," the circumstances call out for solutions, and the solutions described here all involve some degree of cultural reinterpretation and manipulation. The bridge between demographic and ethnographic approaches is the recognition that both the utilization of tradition and the localization of change depend on the larger social environment *and* on individual agency negotiated in that environment.

The potential benefits to building bridges are not exclusively academic. Because the demographic trends that are the focus of this book are perceived as problems in Japan, they are the target of political debate and public policy. A collaborative, but not synthesized, effort by anthropologists and demographers can inform public discourse and policy debates by refusing to allow the focus to long remain on either the micro or the macro level, but to insist that both are needed to understand social phenomena. It is important to keep the "ordinary people" who are the subjects of anthropological study *and* the targets of public policy in the forefront of the debate, but such qualitative data must be supported by the larger picture that demographers can draw from their own discipline. Working together has greater potential to reformulate issues and envision new alternatives, as the population of Japan, and indeed the world, continues into the little known realm of mass longevity.

Contributors

Naomi Brown most recently held a position as assistant professor at the National University of Singapore, Department of Japanese Studies. Her doctoral studies were conducted at the Institute of Social and Cultural Anthropology (ISCA) and the Nissan Institute, University of Oxford and at the Department of Cultural Anthropology, University of Tokyo as a Monbushō (Ministry of Education, Japan) Research Scholar. Her doctoral fieldwork was conducted between 1992–94 as a researcher at Asahi Chemical Company Ltd., Tokyo and Misawa Engineering, Misawa Home Company Ltd., Tokyo with intermittent research continued from 1985 to 2000 in Japan. Her dissertation is titled *The Nisetai Jūtaku Phenomenon: The Prefabricated Housing Industry and Changing Family Patterns in Contemporary Japan* (to be published by Macmillan Press Ltd.) and her most recent publication is *Corporate Capitalism in Japan* by Hiroshi Okumura, translated by Douglas Anthony and Naomi Brown, Macmillan Press Ltd., 2000.

Brenda Robb Jenike is Lecturer in the Department of Anthropology and the Asian Studies Program at Pomona College. She conducted her doctoral studies at the University of California, Los Angeles, and at Ochanomizu University in Tokyo as a Japan Foundation research fellow. Her research interests include the cultural context of aging, intergenerational relations, gender ideology, transitions in social welfare, person-centered ethnography, and contemporary Japan.

Toshiko Kaneda is a doctoral candidate in sociology and a predoctoral fellow at the Carolina Population Center, University of North Carolina at Chapel Hill. Her main research interests are on population aging and its effect on family and intergenerational relationships in East and Southeast Asia. She is currently working on her doctoral dissertation that examines how caregiving responsibilities to elderly family members affect work behaviors in China.

Satsuki Kawano is assistant professor in the Department of Anthropology at the University of Notre Dame. She studies how changing moral systems in Japanese society are apparent in ritual life and, more recently, in how descendants fulfill obligations to care for the nation's elderly. Her current research focuses on challenges and creative solutions among Japanese migrant in the U.S. to care for their aging parents in Japan.

John Knight is lecturer at the School of Anthropological Studies, Queen's University Belfast. He has carried out field research in Japanese mountain villages and has written on a variety of topics to do with rural Japan. He is the editor of *Natural Enemies: People-Wildlife Conflicts in Anthropological Perspective* (Routledge, 2000) and the author of *Waiting for Wolves in Japan: An Anthropological Study of People-Wildlife Relations* (Oxford University Press, in press).

C. Scott Littleton is professor of anthropology, emeritus, at Occidental College. He specializes in Japanese culture, and has done extensive ethnographic fieldwork in a Tokyo neighborhood, with emphasis on the local *matsuri,* or Shinto shrine festival. He has also studied the costumed teenage dancers who, until recently, performed on Sunday afternoons in Tokyo's Yoyogi Park (see p. 232); this research is discussed in his article "Rituals of Rebellion among Contemporary Japanese Youth: The Outdoor Disco at Tokyo's Yoyogi Park," *Religion* 17:119–131 (1987). He is also the author of *Shinto* (Oxford University Press, 2002), and the editor of *The Sacred East: An Illustrated Guide to Buddhism, Hinduism, Confucianism, Taoism and Shinto* (Ulysses Press, 1999), to which he contributed the chapter on Shinto. Littleton has lectured at Waseda University and the University of Tokyo under the auspices of the Fulbright program.

Susan Orpett Long is professor of anthropology at John Carroll University, where she served as founding coordinator of the university's East Asian Studies program. She has published articles on end-of-life decisions, elder care, and women and family issues in Japan and has edited *Lives in Motion: Composing Circles of Self and Community in Japan* (Cornell East Asia Series, 1999) and *Caring for the Elderly in Japan and the U.S.: Policies and Practices* (Routledge, 2000)

James M. Raymo is assistant professor of sociology at the University of Wisconsin-Madison. His primary research interests are population aging and family change in Japan. His current work focuses on the relationships between economic resources, intergenerational relations, and the marriage timing of men and women in Japan. He is also engaged in research examining the relationships between family relations and labor supply in middle and later life.

Leng Leng Thang is assistant professor in the Department of Japanese Studies and Assistant Dean at the Faculty of Arts and Social Sciences, National University of Singapore. Her main areas of research interest are aging in Japan and Asia, the Japanese community in Singapore, and gender issues. She is the author of *Generations in Touch: Linking the Old and Young in a Tokyo Neighborhood* (Cornell University Press 2001).

Christopher Thompson is assistant professor of Japanese language and culture in the Department of Linguistics at Ohio University. He is also Director of Ohio University's study abroad program at Chubu University in Nagoya, Japan. Trained in both cultural anthropology and Japanese language pedagogy, his recent publications include, "Japanese in the Neighborhood" and "Let's Eat at the Hard Rock Cafe Tokyo," proficiency oriented teaching materials designed for intermediate level students of Japanese which appear in the January and September 2000 issues of the *Japanese Language Teacher's Quarterly*.

John W. Traphagan is assistant professor in the Department of Asian Studies, Research Associate of the Population Research Center, and Research Affiliate of the Institute of Gerontology at the University of Texas at Austin. He is also Editor-in-Chief of the *Journal of Cross-Cultural Gerontology*. Traphagan is the author of *Taming Oblivion: Aging Bodies and the Fear of Senility in Japan* (SUNY Press, 2000). His research interests include the anthropology of the body, the cultural construction of senility, migration, and the relationship between religious activity and aging.

Name Index

Subject Index

activities of daily living, 15, 48n.
  12, 160–67, 172n. 9, 210
afterlife. *See* death
ageism, 81
agency, 4, 235
age segregation, 82
aging problem, 120
aging society, 16, 57, 78
  and business, 57
agricultural reform, 93
Alzheimer's disease, 181, 184
ancestors
  conceptualization of, 126
ancestor veneration, 9, 75, 125
anthropology
  and demography, 3, 233–36
  economic, 6
  synthesis with demography,
    3–6
  symbolic, 4

bride drought or shortage, 11,
  110–11
bride searches, 113
Buddhism, 9–10, 110
burial practices, 9–10
  and partner preference, *134*,
    142n. 21
butsudan (domestic altar), 127, 180

care facilities, 77–86
  age-integrated, 79–86
care migrants, 17, 119
cemetery regulations, 127
census (Japanese national), 32
childbirth awards, 113–14

childcare, 81
childlessness, 32
community care, 183–85
conflict
  intergenerational, 25
  daughter-in-law/father-in-law,
    217–20
  with mother-in-law, 212–13
with spouse, 214–17
Confucianism, 14
convergence thesis, 6–7
coresidence, 18, 146, 179–80
  attitudes toward, 30, 40, 203
  and compounds, 220–21
  contestation of, 211–23, 221–23
  determination of, 204
  reasons for decline of, 28–31
coresident life expectancy, 32
culture and demography, 3–6

daughter-in-law, 177
  and conflict with mother-in-
    law, 179–80, 212–13
dead
  concept of, 126
  disconnected. *See muenbotoke*
death
  and afterlife, 133–35
  causes, 148, 150, *151*, 154,
    155–58, 170n. 1 and 3
demographic balance, 120–21
demography
  and anthropology. *See* anthro-
    pology
  and culture, 3–4
  "folk", 13

---

*Pages with tables and figures are indicated by italics.